Just War Thinking

Just War Thinking

Morality and Pragmatism in the Struggle Against Contemporary Threats

ERIC PATTERSON

LEXINGTON BOOKS

A division of
ROWMAN & LITTLEFIELD PUBLISHERS, INC.
Lanham • Boulder • New York • Toronto • Plymouth, UK

Published by Lexington Books
A division of Rowman & Littlefield Publishers, Inc.
A wholly owned subsidary of The Rowman & Littlefield Publishing Group, Inc.
4501 Forbes Boulevard, Suite 200, Lanham, Maryland 20706
http://www.lexingtonbooks.com

Estover Road, Plymouth PL6 7PY, United Kingdom

British Library Cataloguing in Publication Information Available

Library of Congress Cataloging-in-Publication Data
Patterson, Eric, 1971–
  Just war thinking : morality and pragmatism in the struggle against contemporary threats
/ Eric Patterson.
      p. cm.
  Includes bibliographical references and index.
  1. International relations—Moral and ethical aspects. 2. War—Moral and ethical
aspects. I. Title.
  JZ1306.P38 2007
  172'.42—dc22

                                                                            2007033844

ISBN: 978-0-7391-1900-6 (cloth : alk. paper)
ISBN: 978-0-7391-1901-3 (pbk. : alk. paper)
ISBN: 978-0-7391-4146-5 (electronic)

⊖™ The paper used in this publication meets the minimum requirements of American
National Standard for Information Sciences—Permanence of Paper for Printed Library
Materials, ANSI/NISO Z39.48-1992.

Printed in the United States of America

For Mary, Spencer, and Jane

Contents

Preface

On the morning of September 11, 2001 I was home with my five month old son, having returned the day before to California from a political science conference in Washington, D.C. What I saw on television that morning was shocking. Although the baby could never have understood the images of falling buildings that played over and over, I immediately turned his back to the screen, which I remained glued to for some time. I had a sense, a deep feeling that I had to guard his impressionable soul from the bitterness of that day.

That autumn was full of surprises, from a united Congress singing on the Capitol steps, the U.S. attacks on Afghanistan, NATO invoking its collective security commitment on behalf of America, and the quick routing of Al Qaeda and the Taliban before Christmas. Nonetheless, the second "shock" that I experienced during that period was an outcry by some, especially in sectors of the academy and the church, that the U.S. response was unjust. I continued to be flabbergasted by charges that America deserved September 11, that crushing the barbaric Taliban was immoral, that the United States was killing tens of thousands of civilians (later disproved by the Red Cross), that America should turn the other cheek (which one—Los Angeles? Chicago?), that perhaps we could learn something from Osama bin Laden, and the like.

One allegation that seemed clearly contrary to my understanding of morality and the use of force was that U.S. action was unjust because the first principle of just war was *last resort*—was it really at the last resort that the United States utilized force? Had all other options failed? More importantly, what made last resort the cardinal principle of (inter)national security? This charge did not square with my modest understanding of the classical just war tradition, nor did it meet the basic requirements of common sense security in international life.

In short, my reflection on this topic—morality in the consideration, conduct, and conclusion of war—was piqued by my own scholarly work on Christian realists in World War II and the Cold War, the legacy of violence in the post-Cold War era, the events of 9/11, and a personal surprise at the position some scholars and churchmen took at the time. What I quickly discerned was that for many, contemporary just war theory had become quasi-pacifism.

My own feeling, which I believe is in accord with the historic just war tradition and classical Christian realism, is that at times the use of force is a moral obligation, not simply a lesser evil. Augustine asserted that just wars righted wrongs, punished evil-doers, and protected the weak. This is the perspective I have argued from in this book.

The manuscript of this book was originally completed just prior to the Fall semester of 2005. The book went through the usual lengthy review and publication process, and as it nears final publication in mid-2007, I was recently asked if I would change my original arguments expressed herein, particularly with regards to Iraq and Afghanistan. After re-reading those passages, the answer is negative: the arguments are sound and therefore stand.

I am grateful to the many I have learned from during the past three years of reflection, including those who have agreed with me, those who have a different point of view, and the many authors whose work I have learned from. Of special note are: George Lucas and Albert Pierce who hosted an NEH-funded symposium on just war theory at the U.S. Naval Academy as well as my classmates in the seminar; my friends Reuben Brigety and Tom Knecht for intellectual stimulation; Dennis McNutt and Shadrach Ludman for reading parts of the manuscript; additional colleagues at Vanguard University who sharpened my thinking on these issues, especially John Wilson, Mike Wilson, and David Marley; anonymous reviewers, those who praised my effort as well as those who did not; my research assistants Mary MacLean, Stephanie Ricardo, Jason Searle, Jackie Isaac, Teresa Casale, Kendra Puryear, and Monique Lopez; and Lexington Books for publishing the book. I am deeply grateful to my beautiful and wise wife Mary for her encouragement and support at every stage of the process.

Eric Patterson

Chapter 1

Old Wars vs. New Wars:
The Challenges of the 21st Century

Is it ethical for the United States military to kill an avowed terrorist? What if the likely "collateral damage" included his wife and children? The events of September 11 and the resulting war on terrorism happened suddenly, shattering old presuppositions and giving us little time to thoughtfully erect new paradigms in their place. Thus, many feel that the United States presently lacks a framework for the ethical and practical resort to force. This may be in part because the scholarly and religious communities, for partisan or ideological reasons, tend to presume against the use of state power and military force. Thus, discussion within those quarters is predictable and often lacks creativity. On the other hand, the policy-making community has had to react to a rapidly changing world since the early 1990s and therefore tends to rely on ethical categories developed in the periods of de-colonization and atomic energy that immediately followed the Second World War.

Some have turned to Just War theory for guidance. For a thousand years Just War theory has been used to limit and critique the decision to go to war and the methods employed upon the battlefield. Unfortunately, however, at the beginning of the twenty-first century most writing on Just War and the contemporary war on terrorism is flawed for at least two reasons. First, those who take Just War seriously, such as scholars operating from a religious worldview, forget the eminent practicality of Just War tenets. Second, proponents of Just War usually fail to reflect on how modern warfare has changed since the time of Augustine.

This book calls for a general rethinking of the intersection between morality and pragmatics in modern warfare and considers how twenty-first century wars differ from the old wars that Just War doctrine was originally designed for. The book argues that the contemporary application of military force should prioritize international security and the protection of human life, reconceptualizes a minimal just war framework for doing so, and evaluates the usefulness of this approach by investigating contemporary cases such as the war on terrorism, the call for assassination of political leaders, and military humanitarian intervention (MHI).

Just War Theory and just war thinking

The notion of justice in war was elucidated by Aristotle, Cicero, and Augustine and was systematized in the thirteenth century by Thomas Aquinas. Over time Just War theory has been refined by a variety of Catholic thinkers, Protestant jurists, and numerous international legal commentators.[1] In the past century many of the institutions of the Western world order such as democratic governments and the United Nations have also embraced the concept of "just war."[2] However, there is a general failure to take into account first principles in all of the debates over the "justness" of a given use of force: What is meant by justice in war? Does the notion of "justice" evolve in tandem with revolutions in political and military affairs? Is Just War theory really an ethical exercise, is it a pragmatic cost/benefit analysis, or some hybrid of the two?

In its strict form, Just War theory provides policy and moral guidance on two issues: under what conditions is it moral to go to war (*jus ad bellum*) and how violence can be employed during war in ways commensurate with our values (*jus in bello*). As will be discussed in chapters two and three, early Just War theorists such as Thomas Aquinas argued that the just decision to use military force (*jus ad bellum*) was based on three criteria: *sovereign authority* acting on a *just cause* with *right intent*. One scholar observes that "over time prudential criteria were added to the original *jus ad bellum* trio: *likelihood of success, proportionality of ends, last resort,* and *comparative justice.* The prudential items are additional practical criteria for judging the wisdom and morality of employing violence."[3] Of course as chapter three suggests, decision-makers the world over have long argued the rightness of their cause in order to justify the use of military power and this lip-service to morality is an important signal that warfare and politics are not separate from normative consideration.

In addition to the *jus ad bellum* criteria governing the resort to force, *jus in bello* suggests that our values can influence and restrain the use of the military instrument in the course of conflict. Today, the Just War creed suggests that wars should be waged with restraint: using means and tactics proportionate (*proportionality*) to battlefield objectives and which limit harm to civilians (*discrimination*).

Although many contemporary applications of Just War theory use these criteria as an exhaustive checklist that must be met in full for a given conflict to be considered "just," this was not always the case. Indeed, some of the most penetrating analyses of the issues of morality and warfare throughout Western history have taken into account the real-world context of threats, security, and violence and attempted to apply concerns about political order, justice, punishment, restitution, and even reconciliation on a case-by-case basis. Certainly this was the case when the sixteenth-century monk and professor Vitoria provided an innovative and damning critique of elements of Spain's empire-building in the New World. Vitoria went beyond the existing Just War doctrine of his day and considered the issues of non-combatant immunity, siege warfare, and Christian proselytization. In the centuries that followed, early international jurists such as Grotius, Pufendorf, and Vattel relied heavily on the "law of nations," rooted in large part on the customs of war defined in terms of Just War categories, in articulating principles of sovereignty, laws of war, and international jurisprudence. In the mid-twentieth century Christian realists such as the theologian Reinhold Niebuhr, the international relations scholar Martin Wight, and the historian Herbert Butterfield defended the use of force against the Nazis in terms of morality and justice without a strict Just War catechism. More recently, Michael Walzer's landmark *Just and Unjust Wars* thoroughly investigates the issues of morality and the contemporary use of force without binding itself to a re-articulation of the Just War creed.

This book follows suit. From the outset the discussion begins not with an exposition of a rigid Just War checklist, but rather with three questions: when is it just to go to war (*jus ad bellum*), how can war be fought justly (*jus in bello*), and how do we engage justice at war's end (*jus post bellum*)? In other words, this is a skeletal or minimalist just war approach. Such an effort aligns with Oliver O'Donovan's assertion that just war thinking is "a proposal for doing justice in the theatre of war" rather than a strict theory of Just War.[4] Furthermore, I am much more concerned with the real-world, contextual application of these principles than adherence to a strict Just War doctrine. I will argue throughout the work that security/order is the essential feature of politics and war and that it must come first before more (and welcome) notions of justice, reparation, punishment, forgiveness, and reconciliation.

Consequently, throughout the work the capitalized "Just War" [theory, doctrine, etc.] will be utilized to designate the historical and contemporary list of *ad bellum* and *in bello* criteria. In contrast, the lower case "just war" thinking [framework, approach] will refer to the approach of this book.[5] This semantic differentiation is important because there are those who would not consider this project to meet the scrutiny of the Just War tradition and because this volume rejects many of the contemporary applications of Just War doctrine which are quasi-pacifistic, utopian, and catechistic.

This chapter suggests that the violence of the past decade presents novel challenges to the international system, to the priorities and security of individual states, to human survival in various locales, and to our notions of morality and war. Instead of canting the refrains of yesteryear we must consider the challenges of "new wars" and develop just war thinking that responds in ways congruent with our security and our values.

Old Wars vs. New Wars

Just War theory developed at a time when conventional wars were fought by hand using the sword, lance, and bow, prior to mechanization and even before the advent of gunpowder. To the popular mind, the sort of battles Just War theory was designed for are the large confrontations one sees in *Braveheart* or *Spartacus*; to the historian the scenario is best represented by traditional military conflicts from the Peloponnesian Wars through the Napoleonic era.

It is important to reconsider the elements that make up the traditional or "old" style of wars prevalent in the West prior to September 11, 2001, and then contrast them with twenty first-century threats. First, old wars were conflicts between legitimate authorities. This means, at least for the past four centuries, that wars were fought between states. This principle for Just War theory attempted to distinguish between corporate acts of criminal violence (e.g. piracy, outlawry) and wars waged by legitimate political entities. Groups of criminals, such as the Barbary pirates and the corsairs of the Spanish Main, were seen as enemies of civilization because they challenged political order and refused allegiance to rightful authority.

Second, old wars between states were generally a dispute over property, defined primarily in terms of land and its attendant natural resources. Thus, even the megalomaniac ambitions of Hitler and Napoleon were primarily territorial, just as most wars in preceding centuries were over possession of a desirable piece of terra firma. In this sense, war was a part of the political process—the furtherance of national policies or the last resort when diplomacy failed. Another way of thinking about this is that old wars, particularly before the nuclear era, were usually constructive in some sense. There is irony here: however destructive the conflict was for the victims, the aggressor usually had a nation- or empire-building project in mind that was justified as the *summum bonum* of that state.

Third, old wars were fought by "combatants." Soldiers (or sailors, marines, or airmen) could take two forms: professionals and conscripts. Nonetheless, in both cases, "real soldiers" or combatants were legitimate purveyors of, as well as targets, in war, distinguishing them from non-combatants and innocents. The rules of war generally held that military uniform was the symbol of belonging to a legally appointed authority, hence the harsh, usually capital, punishment of non-uniformed combatants who were considered to be spies or brigands.

The idea of distinguishing combatants from non-combatants implies the fourth condition of old wars—they were to be fought away from civilians. In a sense, Just War theory represents an archetype, or perhaps a caricature, of a certain type of "civilized" warfare: war fought between two armies on the battlefield, without pillaging the countryside, cities, or non-combatants. In the twentieth century, aerial "dogfights" and the great naval battles such as Jutland and Midway also reflect the battle insulated from civilian centers. Hence, most weapons were intended for and targeted at, though not always successfully, soldiers.

Of course, much of historical warfare does not fit the ideal. The most obvious example is the siege of cities. Urban centers have the distinction of generally being both a vital strategic location (i.e. situated on a waterway or mountain pass) as well as the retreat of large numbers of non-combatants. Consequently, nearly every war has its examples of siege as well as irregular warfare (e.g. guerrillas), be it the twelfth-century Welsh fighting the English, the Russians fighting Napoleon and later the Germans, Sherman's march through Georgia, or the bombings of London, Dresden, and Tokyo. Nevertheless, even in these departures from the norm, the larger battles in such wars were generally fought by armies on battlefields. Thus, we have the model of the correctly fought war and our general distaste for less "civilized" forms of warfare.

Fifth, Just War doctrine was developed over centuries when the tools of warfare were extremely limited by today's standards. Just War theory was developed when soldiers hacked at one another with blades or shot at one another with arrows. This has both a practical and a moral application. Practically speaking, the weapons were limited and limiting in their use and generally could kill but one enemy at a time. On a moral level, the limited "reach" of these weapons meant that those employing them faced a great deal of risk. In other words, face-to-face infantry or cavalry encounters seem "fair" in that combatants were facing one another, using similar weapons, in a defined space.[6]

One final point should be made about "old" wars. Prior to the twentieth-century, war could not be conceived as global or truly total. For instance, it was unlikely that a conflict between Austria and Naples would wreck the economies of China and the Incas. No one thought in terms of an international political or economic system on the scale we have today. Moreover, in old wars, there were no weapons powerful enough to make a region uninhabitable for generations; consequently there was usually little concern for the future of the natural environment.[7] In other words, old wars lacked the destructive power in terms of human life, international economics, and the environment that modern weapons of mass destruction (WMD) can achieve. Hence it is important for us to reconsider what armed threats to the West look like in the twenty-first century.

New Warfare and the War on Terrorism

At the time of this writing, the United States is at "War on Terror" in response to the attacks on the World Trade Center and Pentagon on September 11, 2001. On the one hand, the War can be fought against regimes that support terrorists or terrorist networks. Such wars, such as the recent conflicts in Afghanistan and Iraq, may meet some of the criteria of "old" wars. On the other hand, fighting the "new" war on terrorism departs from traditional warfare in several ways. Many of these innovations are paralleled in the challenges states and international agencies face from the proliferation of WMDs and in confronting armed threats in scenarios of military humanitarian intervention.

Most obviously, old wars were conflicts between states. Those who attacked the United States on 9/11 belong to no traditional political structure—they are fugitives from nearly every government on earth. Indeed, they reject the modern state and the existing political order. However, unlike traditional outlaws, they claim a political and moral legitimacy based on religion and ideology. In a sense, although they represent no popular earthly political authority, they claim to be a legitimate political movement based on theology. The ramification for how war is fought is clear: because they are fighting for a religious cause, not material ends, any weapon is simply a means to an end, even mass murder and suicide bombing. This ideology and method of warfare is eschatological, lacking a clear this-worldly concept of victory in terms of territory or booty. Indeed, many commentators have pointed out that rogues and terrorists have no positive political program, but employ violence out of a keen sense of frustration and hatred.[8] The same chilling application of absolutist violence marks the ethnic genocide of the past fifteen years. What makes such movements terrifying is that they are willing to use the tools of modern warfare to destabilize states around the world using the cover of religion or ideology to justify their barbarism.[9]

A related question is how the terrorist or guerrilla fighter should be defined: as a soldier, a civilian, or a bandit?[10] The answer has become increasingly complex in recent years, with the introduction of female and child "soldiers" and the migration of foreign nationals to serve in far-away causes, as illustrated by the American John Walker Lindh and British subjects among the Taliban. The point is that America's opponents in the war on terrorism choose not to wear uniforms nor behave like traditional combatants. Nevertheless, regardless of how they dress and where they set up headquarters, they use the language of war in their vitriol against the West. This is just as true of Al Qaeda as it is of rogue states like North Korea. Because the enemy declares the conflict a "war" and is delighted to kill to achieve its objectives, the West must respond seriously: "this means war."

Furthermore, terrorists and guerrillas see no distinction between combatants and non-combatants. Al Qaeda and other terrorist organizations view their opponents through apocalyptic lenses which distinguish "holy" from "damned," usually along religious or racial lines. Thus, an American businesswoman or child is as legitimate a target as an American marine because all Americans represent the Great Evil. To the zealot this means that warfare can and should be taken to the heart of the enemy, to their homes and cities, not to barren battlefields. The same is true for guerrilla movements throughout Africa as well as rogue states like North Korea—Pyongyang's explicit threat is not against armed forces on the DMZ but against Seoul and Tokyo.

This loss of non-combatant immunity becomes increasingly grave in the era of WMDs. Such weapons, be they chemical, biological, or nuclear, are tremendous threats for several reasons. At the most basic level, such weapons have an immediate destructive potential several orders of magnitude greater than the World Trade Center attack. However, the threat of these weapons is greater to international security than even killing tens of thousands of civilians. The domestic economic impact of September 11 has been estimated in the tens of billions of dollars—imagine the international economic crisis that would ensue if a nuclear device had taken out not only the World Trade Center but also Wall Street! What would the effect on the world economy be if such a knockout blow was leveled at, say, Tokyo and New York simultaneously?[11] Likewise, in the old wars there was no consideration of the long-term environmental effects of the tools of war. Indeed, until the last fifty years weapons that could render an area uninhabitable for generations were the stuff of fantasy. Today, one can only imagine the present and future environmental, not to mention health, economic, social, and political ramifications of a dirty bomb exploding in Los Angeles or of a biological attack on London.

Likewise, there is the post-Cold War quagmire of crimes against humanity and military humanitarian intervention. Traditional definitions of sovereignty preclude armed intervention and interference of any kind in the affairs of another sovereign state. Nevertheless, innovations to the state system as well as the barbaric cruelty in the former Yugoslavia and Rwanda have made military humanitarian intervention more likely than in the past.

In sum, new wars are often not conflicts with legitimate authorities concerned with the ethics and pragmatics of limited warfare. The new enemy is motivated by ideology, fearless of death, deliberate in attacking women and children, willing to defile the environment, and lusts to destroy the existing political and economic order or another ethnic group. The United States and the international community need to carefully consider how to face these new threats and preserve human beings and their way of life in a manner consistent with their values.

Just War and the Contemporary War on Terrorism

Just War theory used not to be a monolithic, immutable structure. Rather, it evolved slowly over centuries and should continue to do so. Aquinas' thirteenth century formulation of Just War criteria focused exclusively on *jus ad bellum* (just cause, right intent, legitimate authority) and such was the focus of Just War thinking for centuries. Three centuries later Vitoria explicitly discussed the *jus in bello* considerations that we today call proportionality and discrimination. And it was not until the past century that international law has slowly codified the principles of *jus ad bellum* and *jus in bello* in the Geneva and Hague conventions, the UN Charter, the Torture Convention, and other international covenants.

Just War theory took a further turn in the early 1980s in the aftermath of Vietnam and in the context of the nuclear freeze movement when a controversial article followed by a pastoral letter recast Just War doctrine as "presum[ing] against the use of force."[12] Although I disagree with the quasi-pacifist interpretation of Just War theory, the point is that Just War doctrine is a dynamic framework which should be re-evaluated based on context. More than ever what is needed is just war thinking that is parsimonious, flexible, and usable, and which combines moral concerns with pragmatic considerations in the evaluation of twenty-first century threats.

A revised just war thinking for the twenty-first century has at its heart two concerns. First, it should privilege issues of domestic and international security. Security, or Order, is both a pragmatic and a moral good. Security is the necessary foundation for human beings to live in civil society, thus, just war thinking should take threats to that order very seriously, whether they arise from domestic sources (e.g. criminals) or outside agents (e.g. terrorists). The state has an ethical obligation as well as a practical duty to defend itself against threats that seek to degrade the present and future of its populace. The second concern is regard for human life: just war thinking values and protects individual men and women.[13] Human beings are the end of politics and their security is the *raison d'etre* for the state—this is fundamental for any just war approach. In considering just war thinking for the twenty-first century we should reconceptualize the decision to go to war (*jus ad bellum*), how war is fought (*jus in bello*), and how conflict should end (*jus post bellum*).

Presuppositions of this Book

National and international security are ephemeral and must be safeguarded by shrewdly assessing the nature of threats while retaining a commitment to acting in a manner consistent with the fundamental values of Western civilization. This book spends its entirety exploring the application of such an approach to the resort to war, the waging of war, and the resolution of discrete conflicts. No approach to this topic is without fundamental presuppositions about the nature of security, politics, and war. Below are four assumptions that provide a foundation for the chapters that follow. In short, this book argues for the primacy of national security and political order in reflections on conflict and calls for a practical and adaptive approach to just war thinking based on a political ethic of responsibility that can meet the challenges of twenty-first century threats.

Security is the first objective of international politics.

In contrast to idealism and the quasi-pacifist Just War position argued against in chapter three, this book returns order/security to its privileged place when thinking about international relations.[14] Indeed, Augustine premised his claim that some wars can be just on the necessity of political order. The presumption of order is a moral concept. The idea that war should proceed only on the basis of legitimate authority acknowledges that governments and law are the foundation of the good life. This is consonant with the Greek emphasis on the state and the Christian concept of government providing order in social relations as essential to justice and security.[15] Although we may disagree with Aristotle that there is no real morality outside the *polis*, in practice a strong political order is the basis for experiencing security and justice in every day life. In short, the idea of establishing and maintaining security and justice within the political order is essentially a moral consideration.

Of course, security is a modest goal for it says little about justice, charity, or reconciliation. However, for millions of people around the globe security is anything but modest—an orderly socio-political environment would provide them with the first opportunity to better their families and rebuild their societies. Security is the buttress, the bulwark, the keel of justice. Twenty-first century just war thinking must return to its roots, advocate and defend political order, and not sacrifice security to misguided attempts at empathy, appeasement, or rapprochement. In some cases it will be possible to employ a more robust notion of justice and even reconciliation, particularly at the end of war, but such efforts are doomed to fail if not founded upon guarantees of security.

Responsibility motivates state considerations of the use of force.

Augustinian Just War theory was supposed to be guided by *caritas* (charity), the love of one's neighbor. As sovereignty was then located in a single ruler (e.g. emperor, queen), it was fairly easy to meet the *jus ad bellum* criteria of *right authority* and *just cause*. Consequently, theorists attempted to evaluate the intentions of sovereigns in order to fully ascertain the justness of their cause. More recently, contemporary Just War advocates answer "when is it just to go to war?" with a longer checklist of considerations based on the Just War paradigm: just cause, just intent, right motives, last resort, etc. Such academic efforts, however noble, are not the best way to consider whether or not states should utilize violence in international politics in the twenty-first century.

The old framework presupposed that the primary threat to national security came from other states and that the objective of most warfare was material gain. Neither assumption is correct in the war on terrorism, the global WMDs counterproliferation effort, or military humanitarian intervention. When considering whether or not to go to war, policy makers should begin from the premise that the state has certain ethical and practical responsibilities. Instead of prevaricating over the old notions of right intention and likelihood of success, in the aftermath of 9/11 policy makers should ask "what is our responsibility to our citizens?" and "what is our responsibility to the international system?"[16]

A political ethic of responsibility recognizes that political and social life is made up not only of rights, but of responsibilities. Chief among such responsi-

bilities is the protection of one's citizens. In other words, the state's first responsibility is to self-defense. Of course, the desire to "save our own skins" is pragmatic, while at the same time valuing human life and international security is an
ethical good. A doctrine of responsibility is thus at the intersection of practicality and ethics. It is the moral obligation of the state to take every reasonable step
to protect the life, livelihood, and way of life of its populace. It is also pragmatic
for states to be alert to threats, actual and potential, and consider appropriate
action.

The twenty-first century security dilemma is that we live in an uncertain
environment even if war is not being actively waged. Consequently, in an era of
multiple, often undeclared threats to national security, states must take responsibility for preparing for and at times prosecuting a war against those threats to
their security. In short, it is irresponsible, an abdication of responsibility, for
states to not protect humanity by thoughtfully waging a war against terror.

The old Just War concept of legitimate authority was similar to this idea of
responsibility, but was limited in that it implied a conflict between states. In the
new century most conflicts are either illegitimate regimes harming their own
people or non-state actors perpetrating terrorism against the citizens of legitimate governments. In either case, the authority for response comes not from an
artificial conception of dueling belligerents but from the legitimate right of self-
defense. Governments are the authorities responsible to protect the lives and
futures of their citizens from the depredations of rogue states and terrorists.

Just war guidance should be pragmatic and evolutionary.

Today, the most common use of Just War theory is as a checklist—if one
can notate that all of the *jus ad bellum* criteria have been completely met, then
one can begin to consider the *jus in bello* principles. Such an approach is
sophomoric and does not provide the rigorous analysis married to a sense of
responsibility necessary to meet the dilemmas of the twenty-first century. Just
war thinking used not to be so canonical. Augustine, Aquinas, Vitoria, and other
theorists applied their normative concerns to real-world exigencies, and when
novel situations developed they expanded or relaxed the "theory" as necessary.[17]

Thus, just war thinking was once evolutionary and that it should continue to
be so. As chapter two demonstrates, just war thinking developed in tandem with
the socio-political environment of its day. For instance Augustine's letters, from
which are drawn some of his Just War principles, consider the issue of war in
the context of barbarian invasions of Rome. Aquinas wrote against the backdrop
of a true clash of civilizations: Islam versus Christian Europe. More recently and
in contrast to much of the simplistic analysis by most contemporary Just War
users, Michael Walzer's *Just and Unjust Wars* carefully considered issues of
justice and violence in the context of the Vietnam War and the larger Cold War
struggle.[18]

The dawn of the twenty-first century suggests new challenges to the old notions of state sovereignty, non-intervention, the war convention, and just war thinking itself. For example, do "failed" states have a right to non-intervention? Do their neighbors have a responsibility to intervene to promote international security? How should we think about apocalyptic terrorists like Osama bin Laden and the now deceased Abu Musab al Zarqawi? Are they criminals or soldiers or something else? Should they be treated differently if they utilize jet liners rather than if they threaten to detonate a dirty bomb? How should states respond to those within their publics who consistently violate the laws of war and threaten their neighbors? This book suggests that a concern for justice in war—at its outset, during its commencement, and at its conclusion—can evolve to meet such novel conditions.

Likewise, just war thinking must be pragmatic. By pragmatic it is meant that just war thinking is useless unless it provides us with sensible policy alternatives that are commensurate with Western mores.[19] Historically, the value of just war thinking was that it did provide a realistic assessment of war and politics while at the same time pointing to the ideals of justice and charity. This is exactly how it should be. Just war thinking should force us to move from our platitudes about justice and reconciliation to no-nonsense, down-to-earth policy prescriptions that are at once hopeful and realistic.[20] Just war thinking, to paraphrase Supreme Court Justice and Nuremberg prosecutor Robert Jackson, should not be a suicide pact—it does not call on states to give up their responsibility to self-defense in pursuit of utopian goals.

Some things are worse than war.

In the Catholic bishops' "Harvest of Peace" and their earlier missive, "The Challenge of Peace," they assert that Just War doctrine maintains a "presumption against the use of force." James Turner Johnson rightly argues that this position is an innovation to Just War thinking. Nonetheless, the spirit of the bishops' letter is one to be found in much of contemporary Just War scholarship as well as the larger realm of organized Christianity and the academy. One of the critical ideas of the "presumption against force" line of reasoning is that war has become so destructive that there are almost no conditions under which such violence should be employed. A second assumption of this position is that global society has evolved ("grown up") beyond having to fight to adjudicate differences between peoples.

Unfortunately, this is a misguided view of war, values, and political policy. It is often associated with political prescriptions that seek to empower international bodies like the United Nations at the expense of states. It is a viewpoint that is grimly aware of how terrible war can be on civilians but forgets that the so-called peace can be even worse. Recent history should remind us that the use of arms in military humanitarian intervention may be far less "evil" than genocide, practices of mass rape and mutilation, the expulsion or destruction of "undesirables," the employment of hundreds of thousands of child soldiers and camp followers in Third World struggles, and the like. It is also preferable to preempt and prevent aggression, whether by states or by individuals, to protect our own citizenry.

Certainly war is terrible. However, slavery, rape, torture, mass murders— these are worse than war. There are times to fight a war and just war thinking should give policy makers clear guidance about how to respond to threats and aggression rather than constantly impeding effective security policies. This book will address several questions asked of twenty-first century just war thinking such as: how should we consider the decision to employ force against non-states? How should we respond to the violence of international criminal cartels and terrorists? Under what set of policies and laws should terrorists be tried? What principles should undergird efforts at ending a conflict?

Overview of the Book

This is a book about war and policy. Although it uses historical examples, it is not a history of Just War doctrine. There are already excellent volumes on the development of Just War theory noted earlier. Similarly, it is not political science analysis of the causes of war or an extended philosophical treatise on humanity and conflict. Again, works of superb quality already exist on these topics and can be found among this book's references.

Instead, this monograph is an attempt to reignite a dialogue about the meaning of security and the nexus of morality and conflict, and urges policies commensurate with our interests and our values. Thus, chapter two suggests that some of the assumptions that traditional Just War theory rested on may be out of date. For instance, for the past several centuries sovereignty has rested with the state. Prior to that an individual—a king or empress—was sovereign. Consequently the *jus ad bellum* considerations regarding legitimate authority and right intent focused on the motivations of an individual human being. This is no longer the case. Democratically-elected representatives have far less autonomy in the exercise of sovereignty than their autocratic predecessors did, and the former must respond to public opinion—whether the cry is "Remember the Maine!" or "We Will Never Forget (the World Trade Center)!"

Chapter two observes that Just War theory used to be dynamic and adaptive to the milieu in which it was applied. The same should be true today— just war thinking should not be bound to a narrow script but part of a larger analysis of the changing face of human conflict. Chapter two provides an analysis of some of the changes the twenty-first century presents to Just War theory, such as non-state actors, WMDs, military humanitarian intervention, and apocalyptic terrorism. Chapter two concludes that the evolution from "old wars" to "new wars" requires new thinking about what is just in war.

Chapter three considers the decision to use military force, *jus ad bellum*, especially after September 11. Chapter three echoes a philosophical assumption presented in this introduction: that state responsibility to self-defense and the defense of international security should be the primary foundation upon which a policy implementing force is based. It also discusses some of the more contentious issues for U.S. foreign policy, including the role of the UN in determining when to go to war, the possibilities and pitfalls of prevention and preemption, and whether or not to dispense with the elaborate *jus ad bellum* requirements such as "last resort" and "right intent" when employing force. Finally, the chapter concludes with mini-case studies analyzing the American resort to war in Afghanistan and against Iraq, finding that U.S. action was commensurate in both cases with its responsibility for security.

Chapter four takes an equally critical look at *jus in bello*, the conduct of war. Traditional Just War doctrine focused on two criteria: proportionality and discrimination. This chapter suggests reframing both of them in the context of twenty-first century conflicts. For example, when considering proportionality in a case of military humanitarian intervention, the chapter argues that the force employed be commensurate with the perceived threat. Thus, massive force is appropriate in potential cases of genocide like Bosnia. Similarly, the chapter argues that the clandestine nature of terrorism calls for a rethinking of discrimination. Terrorists and those who support them tangibly, including family members and associates, are enemy combatants and should be treated as such. This may mean that we should expect greater numbers of civilian, or quasi-civilian, casualties in the war on terrorism. The chapter provides mini-case studies including a look at targeted killing of terrorists (al Qaeda) and heads of state (Iraq), dealing with enemy combatant prisoners in Afghanistan, and applies the revised model of proportionality to stopping the genocide in Rwanda.

Chapter five provides a logical extension to just war thinking, a principle of justice at war's end or *jus post bellum*. As chapter five shows, it is both surprising and unsurprising that traditional Just War doctrine neglected war's ending, but this chapter presents a framework for settlements based on privileging security, calling for justice when appropriate, and considering reconciliation when possible. The chapter looks at the end of World War II and the Korean Conflict and grapples with the issue of international reconciliation.

Chapter six concludes the book with reflections on changes in warfare and politics and forecasts areas where further research is needed. The chapter suggests that democracies may find the issues of justice and war particularly difficult because elected leaders must be responsive to their constituents. It is entirely possible that an introverted public will refuse to act for security or justice, as the Allied powers procrastinated before confronting Hitler in 1939–1940. On the other hand, the public may demand blood, regardless of the justness of the case. Chapter six also suggests that the postmodern philosophical approaches in the academy are directly at odds with the normative presuppositions of classical and contemporary just war thinking. Additionally, with the evolution of sovereignty to supra-national agencies and its increasing devolution to democratic publics, Just War doctrine and its sibling the international legal paradigm are on new footing in the twenty-first century. In sum, how can just war thinking adapt in the era of democracy, moral pluralism, and evolving notions of supranational governance?

In sum, just war thinking should reflect a commitment to security and to practical measures to defend our lives, livelihoods, and way of life. Just war thinking must be minimalist in its design, adaptive in application to changing circumstances, and privilege order in international life. Just war thinking does not presume against war—it seeks to illuminate policies that preserve our interests and that are consistent with our values.

Notes

1. The history of Just War doctrine is well known. An excellent introduction that relies heavily on antique and medieval literature is Frederick H. Russell, *The Just War in the Middle Ages* (Cambridge: Cambridge University Press, 1976). Also see James Turner Johnson, Ideology, *Reason, and the Limitation of War: Religious and Secular Concepts, 1200–1740* (Princeton: Princeton University Press, 1975) and Johnson's *The Just War Tradition* (Princeton: Princeton University Press, 1981).

2. See Philip A. Crowl, "The Strategist's Short Catechism: Six Questions Without an Answer" in Reichart and Sturm, eds. *American Defense Policy*, fifth edition. (Baltimore, MD: Johns Hopkins University Press, 1982); Dan Smith, "Just War, Clausewitz, and Sarajevo" in *Journal of Peace Research* 31, no. 2 (1994). Also see Richard B. Miller, *Interpretations of Conflict: Ethics, Pacifism, and the Just War Tradition* (Chicago: University of Chicago Press, 1991).

3. James Turner Johnson, *Morality and Contemporary Warfare* (New Haven, CT: Yale University Press, 1999), 34.

4. Oliver O'Donovan, *The Just War Revisited* (Cambridge: Cambridge University Press, 2003), vii.

5. Peter Temes uses a similar language, using several concepts that he distinguishes such as "just war thinking" and "just war philosophy." However, his use of the terms is not identical with their usage in this work. See *The Just War: An American Reflection on Morality in Our Time* (New York: Ivan R. Dees, 2004).

6. A discussion of the ethical framework within which such wars was conducted is Robert A. Kann, "The Law of Nations and the Conduct of War in the Early Times of the Standing Army" in *The Journal of Politics* 6, no. 1 (February, 1944).

7. Of course, some invading armies did attempt to denude the land to spite future generations, such as the Roman strategy in Palestine and Carthage. However, sowing the earth with salt is hardly the equivalent of long-term radioactivity.

8. One such argument is that Islamic civilization has failed in modernity, hence Islamists like Bin Laden operate from a tremendous sense of frustration and rage. See Muhammad Oueiny, "Why should the Middle East be turned upside down?" available online at http://freelebanon.org/articles/a313.htm (accessed January 6, 2003). A not dis-

similar assessment was made in Bernard Lewis, *What Went Wrong?* (New York: Perennial, 1993).

9. This book is primarily about war defined as violence. Imagine, however, in the integrated global economy, what a terrorist hacker might achieve—the shut down of water purification plants, the erasure of financial records, perhaps the meltdown of a nuclear reactor—all from the relative safety of cyberspace.

10. One could further distinguish terrorists from guerrillas and from insurgents based on their motivations for violence. However, at this point of this work such non-state violent actors have much in common—they fight asymmetrically against the legitimate authority of a sovereign state and generally attempt to blend in to the populace rather than risk open confrontation. Usually such groups lack widespread political legitimacy, so they try to achieve by arms what they cannot hope to win at the ballot box.

11. Consider also how public opinion might respond. It is not unlikely that Western publics would react violently toward the entire Muslim world: "you have gone too far . . . ." The value of rethinking American strategic doctrine in light of a reconceptualized just war thinking is precisely this: it might provide a realistic but invaluable framework and boundaries within which to work should such a crisis occur.

12. See James F. Childress, "Just-War Criteria" in *War or Peace? The Search for New Answers*, Thomas A. Shannon, ed. (Maryknoll, New York: Orbis Books, 1980); the Catholic Bishops letter *The Challenge of Peace* (1986) and its successor *The Harvest of Justice* (1993).

13. A thoughtful article that argues for human rights and justice but recognizes the limitations of the international system is Geoffrey Best's "Justice, International Relations, and Human Rights," the 21st Martin Wight Memorial Lecture, London School of Economics and Political Science (March 9, 1995), printed in *International Affairs* 71, no. 4.

14. Consequently this work uses "order" and "security" interchangeably in ways congruent with the idea of "domestic-," "national-," and "international-" security in the social sciences literature. This work does not adumbrate an elaborate notion of individual security in terms of quality of life issues (employment, healthcare, etc.).

15. For instance see Aristotle, *Politics*. Ernest Barker, ed. (Oxford: Oxford University Press, 1946): Book I, chapter 2 and Book III, chapters 6-7. Also, Augustine, *The City of God*, tr. Marcus Dods. (New York: The Modern Library, 1950): xix. 13, xxii 22.

16. There is an emerging but poorly known body of work applying just war thinking to cases of humanitarian intervention, including Kjell-Ake Nordquist, *From 'Just War' to Justified Intervention* (Uppsala: Department of Theology Publications, 1998); Dean K. Chatterjee and Don E. Scheid, *Ethics and Foreign Intervention* (Cambridge: Cambridge University Press, 2003); Robert L. Philips and Duane L. Cady, *Humanitarian Intervention: Just War vs. Pacifism* (Lanham, MD: Rowman and Littlefield, 1996); Terry Nardin, "The Moral Basis of Humanitarian Intervention" in *Ethics and International Affairs* 14, no. 1 (2002).

17. My primary argument is against the plethora of op-eds, magazine and journal articles, editorials, petitions, interviews, and other media that take the checklist approach. This is not to say that there are not decent introductory works that apply the Just War criteria to individual conflicts. Two of the best recent ones are A. J. Coates' *The Ethics of War* (Manchester: Manchester University Press, 1997) and Richard J. Regan's *Just War: Principles and Cases* (Washington, D.C.: Catholic Institute of America Press, 1996).

18. Just War "users" is used from time to time in this work to denote the popular utilization of Just War criteria in ways that are quasi-pacifistic or overly rigid. "Users" usually utilize media interviews, speeches, op-eds, or other editorial avenues to express simplistic and narrow applications of Just War criteria to current events. Such "use" may border on misuse or abuse.

19. This work is neither in the pragmatic philosophical tradition of Charles Peirce and William James nor the utilitarian tradition of Jeremy Bentham. In contrast, "pragmatic" is used herein in its popular rendition to be synonymous with "practical" and "utilitarian," meaning useful, practical, efficacious, and having real-world utility.

20. Throughout this book the argument is made that we need to identify what is practical as well as what is moral in just war thinking. This bifurcation does not sit well with many philosophers who prefer a more unified ethical framework. However, it is fundamental to my argument that in addition to moral concerns, what makes just war thinking implementable in the real world is its utility. Just war thinking is not head-in-the-clouds, pie-in-the-sky sophistry for the salon. Rather, it is feet-on-the-ground, meat-and-potatoes, rubber-meets-the-road tools for grappling with real-world phenomena.

Chapter 2

The Triumphs, and Failings, of
Just War Thinking

Different cultures in different eras have thought about war in contrasting ways. War has alternately been defined in terms of a masculine right of passage, a sport "played" by kings and their knights, an opportunity for glorious sacrifice on behalf of the Fatherland, the crèche of "the people," the opportunity for national cleansing, a vehicle for conversion, and a political stratagem. In the past century officers have been taught by Clausewitz that "war is the continuation of politics by other means" and by Mao that "political power grows out of the barrel of a gun." However, soldiers who endured Gettysburg, the Ardennes, the siege of Stalingrad, the Chosin Reservoir, the Hanoi Hilton, or the break-up of the former Yugoslavia would more likely concur with General William Tecumseh Sherman that "War is Hell."

The violence of the last decade more resembles Sherman's definition of war than that of Clausewitz. The communal violence between religious and ethnic groups such as in Bosnia, Rwanda, and Congo has taken on new proportions as enemies attempt to "cleanse" their nation of impure ethnic elements. Genocidal policies are enhanced by modern technologies of communication, logistics, and weaponry. Similarly, the attacks of international apocalyptic terrorism in Africa, Asia, Europe, and even the United States portend a new, absolutist type of conflict between the representatives of states and violent opponents to the Western system.

The big questions surrounding any war are those of a moral nature. Can the advent of war be justified to spread religious or other normative ideals? Is there an ethical way to conduct war? Can something so destructive result in good? Are we fooling ourselves to think that we can write laws and treaties that limit warfare? Do foreigners have some responsibility to victims located continents away when violence breaks out? What about pacifism?

As the previous chapter suggested, these questions are increasingly complicated when states are fighting non-uniformed groups, when religious leaders rather than political leaders declare war, when governments fail leaving their territory prey to warlords, brigands, and zealots, when rogue states sneer at international law, when weapons of mass destruction (WMDs) are added to the mix, and when one considers the potential of hackers destroying the global financial infrastructure.

Just War theory is one way that the individuals in the Western philosophical tradition have sought to answer these questions. Just War theory attempts to constrain war by limiting when the state has recourse to war and by restraining the conduct of battle. Just War theory rightly asserts that there is a place for morality in every human endeavor, even war.

The purpose of this book is not to apply Just War doctrine strictly to the war on terrorism and other contemporary conflicts. Indeed, this work asserts that such syllogistic treatment of traditional Just War criteria is problematic. Instead, the changing nature of warfare compels us to rethink how we apply what this text calls "just war thinking:" an approach to warfare that takes into consideration normative concerns and the practical realities of security and politics. In other words, one objective of this book is to remind the reader that just war approaches are not monolithic but can be refreshed and applied to novel circumstances in the twenty-first century. This chapter initiates the discussion by introducing historic Just War doctrine and its philosophical competitors, and then considers the state of Just War theory today, ultimately laying the groundwork for a revised approach for just war thinking in light of apocalyptic terrorism, rogue states, military humanitarian intervention, and WMDs.

Pacifism, Just War, and Holy War

In the Western Christian tradition, there have been at least three ways to think about war: pacifism, crusaderism, and Just War doctrine.[1] All three have strong roots in organized Christianity's first millennium and are in tension with one another. Today they have secular siblings such as humanistic pacifism and ethno-nationalistic holy war which share most of the essential assumptions and policy prescriptions.[2] Consequently, the three remain the basic frameworks for considering the normative content of warfare in the West. Understanding the philosophy of the pacifist and the crusader illuminates their shortfalls and suggests the enduring value of just war thinking.

Pacifism

As J. Daryl Charles reports, history provides no evidence that the early Church took a unified pacifist position although many second and third century Christians were apparently pacifists.[3] Although there is some debate about why this is the case because Christ offered no explicit teaching on war, it is nevertheless clear that one compelling motive was a rejection of sinful Rome.[4] Christians, like Jews, repugned the idolatry and emperor cult of Rome and were persecuted by taxation, imprisonment, crucifixion, and performances in the arena.

In this milieu Christian pacifism was a rejection of the idolatrous claims of the state on the individual.[5]

Over time Christian scholars such as Augustine and Aquinas differentiated between the citizen's duty to the state, including military service, and the pacific duties of the churchman. The latter were to devote themselves entirely to spiritual service and therefore could not take up the sword. It has recently been suggested that Vatican II's dissolution of the chasm between laity and clergy applies this pacifism to all believers.[6]

More broadly, pacifism is a commitment against violence and an allegiance to peace defined as nonviolence. In practice, Christian pacifists were motivated by Christ's commission to love one's neighbor and secular pacifists often parallel this injunction with their own: "Do no harm." Moreover, Christian pacifists have looked back on Christ's example of self-abnegation and resignation to his fate as the archetype for their position. The pacifist faces war with two questions: 1) how could I, an agent of peace, be so presumptuous as to take someone else's life, and 2) how could I be so vain as to employ violence in self-defense rather than resign my fate to God? In short, the pacifist asserts personal responsibility for his or her own actions, and nothing more.[7]

In the fourth century Augustine responded to Christian pacifism in a way which laid the foundation for Just War theory. Whereas pacifists focused on employing the transcendent values of Christ's millennial kingdom, Augustine attempted to balance the realities of a fallen world (*civitas terrena*) with the values of the *civitas dei* (City of God).[8] Interestingly, Augustine's notion of just war also relied heavily on "love your neighbor as yourself." In domestic society as well as international life, how does one go about loving one's neighbor? Augustine argued that within a society, adherence to the rule of law, including punishment of lawbreakers, was one way of loving one's neighbors. When one loves his neighbor, he refrains from harming him and supports the authorities in their efforts to provide security to the citizenry. Moreover, Augustine noted that *caritas* means protecting one's neighbor when they are attacked, even if one is forced to employ violence to protect that individual. For Augustine, the law of love includes punishment (consequences for immoral behavior) and justice (restoration of what was taken, righting past wrongs).

A second critique of pacifism from within the Christian tradition comes from Christian realist Reinhold Niebuhr. Niebuhr was an ardent pacifist until the march of militarism and fascism in Europe and Asia made him abandon it in the 1930s. Niebuhr respected the "witness" of absolute pacifists who refused to support a war effort in any way, including service in the medical corps or through their taxes, but he denounced those he called "political pacifists." For Niebuhr, political pacifists are those who refuse to make moral distinctions about political categories and to make "lesser evil" choices when confronted with political evils. He attacked those in his day who argued that going to war in 1939–1940 was immoral because both sides, the British Empire and the Third Reich, were equally evil. Niebuhr castigated this "neutrality" as conceited, irresponsible, and naïve because pacifists failed to accept their individual responsibility to thwart evil whenever possible.[9]

In sum, the pacifist position is as old as Christianity itself, and it has found renewed vigor since the Reformation among Anabaptists, Quakers, Mennonites, and some other Protestants. Since the 1980s Catholic pacifism may be at its strongest point since the second century and varieties of pacifism are flourishing in mainstream Western society, especially in European publics and among American intelligentsia due to the legacies of the Vietnam War, nuclear weapons, and recent U.S. action in Iraq. Although Just War and Christian realist perspectives are critical of pacifism, the holy war position seems to be most at odds with it.

Holy War

The crusade, or holy war, assumes the polar opposite of pacifism. The crusader believes that violence can be employed in defense of or to further eternal values. In practice, holy wars are often reactions to threats which seem to undermine the basic ideals and existence of one's civilization. Thus, the medieval Crusades and the *reconquista* of the Iberian peninsula were perceived at the time as "holy" in repulsing the onslaught of heretical Islam in its religious and political forms. Similarly, some contemporary proclamations to violent jihad in the Middle East are a response to perceived Western cultural and political domination.

What inspires the individual holy warrior? Of course, as skeptics like to note it is entirely possible that material gain might stimulate participation, as it did for many during Islam's early wars of conquest or the creation of Spain's empire in the New World. Nevertheless, many holy warriors are motivated by other concerns. For one, crusaders are provoked to action by righteous indignation. Their most personal convictions have not only been questioned, but affronted and defiled. The jihadi feels compelled to action in defense of those ideals held most dear—faith in God and country. The holy warrior may also seek an eternal reward. This does not necessarily indicate a "death wish," rather that the individual is convinced that his or her actions are in pursuit of transcendent ends and that such behavior will please the deity he or she worships. Of course, some holy warriors seek glory in both the here and hereafter in the tradition of early martyrs of their faith.

More could be said about crusaders and jihadis, but the basic principle is that holy war can be based on zealous love for one's faith and that this justifies employing violence. What concerns most critics of holy war is that if the end is absolute—the defense of God's name—then it is difficult to provide any ethical rationale for limiting the means employed. Crusaders are not content with a "settlement" because they are attempting to inaugurate God's kingdom on earth.

Hence, the "excesses" of holy war: the extermination of entire cities during the rapid expansion of early Islam and the reactionary Christian crusades, the Inquisition and wars of the Counter-Reformation, the quasi-religious philosophy of the *kamikaze*, and the *fatwas* of Osama bin Laden resulting in al Qaeda's attacks on civilian populations. For the holy warrior, the end justifies any means.

In the sixteenth century a Catholic friar and professor at the University of Salamanca, Francesco de Vitoria, responded to European defense against the Turks as well as Spain's activities in the New World using an expanded Just War criteria based on Augustine and Aquinas. Vitoria argued that wars can be just if fought by legitimate authorities with right intent on behalf of a just cause. However, Vitoria asserted numerous limits on the prosecution of war, even on behalf of faith. For instance, Vitoria argued that it is wrong to kill noncombatants such as women, children, "harmless agricultural folk," "clerics and members of religious orders," and even enemy prisoners who are no longer a threat. Vitoria writes,

> The reason for this restriction is clear: for these persons are innocent, neither is it needful to the attainment of victory that they should be slain. It would be heretical to say that it is licit to kill them. . . . Accordingly, the innocent may not be slain by (primary) intent, when it is possible to distinguish them from the guilty.

Vitoria's use of Just War theory suggests limits on the resort to and the prosecution of war, even in defense of the faith against infidels.[10]

Just War Theory

Just War theory has evolved into an ethical framework for evaluating the decision to go to war (*jus ad bellum*) and the way war is fought (*jus in bello*).[11] It is not the purpose of this book to either disregard or scorn the formal Just War criteria as it exists today. However this book criticizes the application of Just War theory in two ways. First, most applications of Just War theory are rigid, formulaic, and quasi-pacifistic. The application of just war thinking in chapters three through five of this work offers an alternative to such writing.

The second critique is that Just War theory used to be what this text calls "just war thinking:" it evolved over time in tandem with the political developments and security environment of the day. This assumption underlies the approach of this book. The historical record is clear—just war thinking was useful in responding to the real-world dilemmas of politics. For example, Augustine and Ambrose were not theoreticians cloistered away from society. The latter had been a Roman provincial governor in Milan and both wrote about justice, punishment, order, and war while all that was good about *Pax Romana* was disintegrating due to barbarian invasion. Ambrose justified Roman power on the one hand while criticizing his friend, the emperor Theodosius, for the massacre at

Thessalonica. Similarly, Augustine's *The City of God* is founded on the dual citizenship of the Christian, to the heavenly kingdom as well as the mundane world, and trumpets the responsibility of individuals in this world to work for order and justice. Augustine thus defended the use of force by legitimate authorities on behalf of the common good. Augustine's letters are full of references to his concerns not only about the dangers of heresy within the Christian church, but of his concern regarding the violence and lawlessness perpetrated by various tribes overwhelming the empire.

As discussed in the next chapter, Thomas Aquinas wrote with the Crusades and medieval warfare in mind. Vitoria and Suarez responded to Spain's imperial wars in the New World. Indeed, it is Vitoria and Suarez who went beyond Aquinas' three *jus ad bellum* criteria to explicitly limit war-making in terms of *jus in bello*: proportionality and discrimination. This was the basis of their critique of Spaniards killing and enslaving Indians in the Americas. Hugo Grotius responded to the world war of his day, the Thirty Years War, by articulating just war principles in his *The Law of War and Peace* (1625) as part of the "law of nations."[12]

The evidence that creative just war thinking evolves in the context of complex international situations of high politics and war continues to the present. Perhaps the best known recent examples are Paul Ramsey's considerations of nuclear deterrence during the Cold War, Michael Walzer's magnum opus *Just and Unjust Wars*, and Jean Bethke Elshtain's recent evaluation of the first year of the war on terrorism and the coalition campaign in Afghanistan.[13] What is most striking about these last three is that none of them use a rigid Just War theory checklist to evaluate war and morality. Rather, they focus on questions of justice, order, and morality more broadly in the context of the contemporaneous dilemmas.

This, however, is not the case for the application of most Just War doctrine in recent decades. Most discussions of Just War theory are formal applications of the Just War existing criteria. Although there are slight variations in the explication of Just War principles, the list below is representative and probably the best well-known.[14] The following statements are taken verbatim from the widely-circulated pastoral letter of the (American) National Council of Catholic Bishops, "The Harvest of Peace is Sown in Justice."[15]

> First, whether lethal force may be used is governed by the following criteria (*jus ad bellum*):
>
> > •*Just Cause:* force may be used only to correct a grave, public evil, i.e., aggression or massive violation of the basic rights of whole populations;
> >
> > •*Comparative Justice:* while there may be rights and wrongs on all sides of a conflict, to override the presumption

against the use of force the injustice suffered by one party must significantly outweigh that suffered by the other;

- *Legitimate Authority:* only duly constituted public authorities may use deadly force or wage war;
- *Right Intention:* force may be used only in a truly just cause and solely for that purpose;
- *Probability of Success:* arms may not be used in a futile cause or in a case where disproportionate measures are required to achieve success;
- *Proportionality:* the overall destruction expected from the use of force must be outweighed by the good to be achieved;
- *Last Resort:* force may be used only after all peaceful alternatives have been seriously tried and exhausted.

Second, the just-war tradition seeks also to curb the violence of war through restraint on armed combat between the contending parties by imposing the following moral standards (*jus in bello*) for the conduct of armed conflict:

- *Noncombatant Immunity:* civilians may not be the object of direct attack, and military personnel must take due care to avoid and minimize indirect harm to civilians;
- *Proportionality:* in the conduct of hostilities, efforts must be made to attain military objectives with no more force than is militarily necessary and to avoid disproportionate collateral damage to civilian life and property;
- *Right Intention:* even in the midst of conflict, the aim of political and military leaders must be peace with justice, so that acts of vengeance and indiscriminate violence, whether by individuals, military units or governments, are forbidden.

In short, traditional Just War theory in one sense provides a middle ground between holy war and pacifism. The Just War advocate agrees with the pacifist that war is a costly, brutal endeavor and should be avoided. However, Just War theory concurs with the crusader that there can be moral content to war, although the former strongly disagrees with the normative characterization of the latter. However, in other ways it would be better to say that just war approaches have offered a third vector, an independent focus, for contemplating the resort to force based on issues of security and justice rather than absolutism of any sort. Moreover, just war thinking has a certain pragmatism that makes it useful to the policymaker for it applies not only to the individual's choices but to those of the statesman as well. This is because it has historically been applied to real-world political contexts and evolved in tandem with the evolution of international law, sovereignty, and the society of states.[16] Finally, although both the pacifist and the jihadi are solely concerned with the resort to war (*jus ad bellum*), the Just War paradigm is likewise concerned with the conduct of war. Hence, just war thinking has been useful both as a guide to policy and in restraining war for centuries. The question this work addresses is whether just war thinking has the resources and the flexibility to encounter the new world of non-state terrorist actors, failed states, military humanitarian intervention, and the proliferation of nuclear technology.

The State of Just War Theory Today

The Triumph of Just War Theory

Michael Walzer recently published an article entitled "The Triumph of Just War Theory."[17] Walzer rightly argues that by the 1970s thinking about justice and war triumphed over the amoral *realpolitik* characterized by some forms of the realism which dominated U.S. foreign policy during the first decades of the Cold War.[18] Walzer's claim that Just War theory has triumphed is true in another sense as well.[19] As he and James Turner Johnson have argued elsewhere, much of the foundation of international law, or what they call "the international legal paradigm," is rooted in Just War theory.[20] For example, international jurists like Pufendorf and Grotius used the notions of *legitimate authority* and *just cause* (e.g. self-defense) in their juridical writings. The cardinal principle of sovereignty in international affairs, codified in the Peace of Westphalia (1648), is the offspring of the Just War idea of authority. Similarly, the *jus in bello* criteria have been fleshed out in the Geneva and Hague conventions, the UN Charter, and various other international covenants that protect non-combatants, prisoners of war, and the wounded. Proportionality and non-combatant immunity are formal components of the military doctrine of Western countries. Moreover, one of the historical antecedents for contemporary human rights norms comes from the valuing of human life ultimately rooted in historical Just War theory.[21] Indeed, we should rejoice in the triumphs of the theory.

Just War theory influences international affairs in many ways at the start of the twenty-first century. James Turner Johnson recently concurred with Michael Walzer on the ubiquity of Just War theory, but suggests that the Just War theory which is triumphing today is a problematic innovation. He writes that Just War doctrine "as it was" is not Just War theorizing "as it is."[22] Johnson argues that much of contemporary Just War writing has strayed from the original assumptions of the traditional paradigm. Most importantly, he asserts that "the presumption against war" articulated in the Jesuit journal *Theological Studies* (1978), by the National Council of Catholic Bishops in 1983, and reasserted in the bishops' 1993 pastoral letter, is at odds with historic Just War theory.[23] Johnson cites several critical mutations in the "presumption" doctrine which distinguish it from classical Just War theory. Most importantly, he argues that the "presumption against force" is actually "just war pacifism" or "*jus contra bellum justum.*"[24] In addition to being quasi-pacifistic Johnson observes that the "new" Just War theory privileges supranational entities over the state in determining *jus ad bellum*. In other words, the "presumption against" position usually identifies the appropriate venue for decisions about war as the United Nations, not the capitals of sovereign states. In sum, a doctrine which places legitimate authority in the hands of the UN and not individual governments, makes all seven *jus ad bellum* requirements mandatory in employing force, and generally presumes against force is a significant departure from traditional Just War theory. In the end, Johnson calls for renewed reflection on the institution of just war thinking and thoughtful scholarship that respects the intellectual commitments of the tradition.

Johnson is also correct that in the past generation there have been some scholars who have extended the boundaries of how one should think about just or "justified" war, most notably Michael Walzer and Paul Ramsey. Moreover as the bibliography for this work demonstrates, there are numerous other short works which are a contribution in elucidating just war thinking in specific contexts. Unfortunately, however, most of the recent application of Just War theory has been doctrinaire, simplistic, quasi-pacifistic, and lacking realistic policy-orientation.

The Failings of Just War Theory

Just War theory has been useful for the better part of two millennia in guiding both philosophers and practitioners in their thinking about war. The primary argument of this work is that twenty-first century decision-makers can and should continue to think about conflict in ways that stay true to Western values and yet offer practical policy alternatives on and off the battlefield. Hence, just war thinking stands apart from the uncompromising positions of holy war and pacifism, be they religious or secular, calling for real-world policies that are commensurate with our normative commitments. The real-world nexus of morality and practicality is the chief feature not only of just war thinking but of any ethical system.

Unfortunately, late twentieth-century Just War theory became increasingly less helpful in thinking through the dilemmas of international security. As shown below there are numerous reasons for this, but most of the problem stems from the revision of Just War theory by contemporary advocates into a form of quasi-pacifism.[25] Any notion of "just war" doctrine is irrelevant to the twenty-first century if it cannot offer practical policy guidance that is founded on a moral commitment to responsibility and security.

So, what's wrong with Just War theory today? As discussed in the previous chapter, a significant flaw in Just War scholarship is the lack of attention to how wars have changed. Old wars were fought between states for land, territory, or prestige. The agents of states were uniformed soldiers fighting under conditions of some moral equality—using similar weapons and for centuries fighting in hand-to-hand encounters. Although war was still terrible and hardships as well as treachery occurred, the guidelines of proportionality and noncombatant immunity were often adhered to.

Traditional Just War theory made sense in such a world. However, today many conflicts are internal conflicts—civil wars, the dissolution of failing states, long-term insurgencies. How should one think about sovereignty in a failed region, like Somalia? Who was "responsible" for intervention in Yugoslavia and Rwanda—a state, a coalition, an alliance, the UN? Indeed, it is unclear that Just War theory compels states to act on behalf of victims in far-away places. Twenty-first century just war thinking must address the changing faces of responsibility and sovereignty.

The same is true for dealing with combatants. Non-state actors such as drug cartels and international terrorist networks have started deploying weapons traditionally reserved to states—how should they be treated? Are they criminals, soldiers, or something else? Furthermore, the advent of not only WMDs but satellites, unmanned aerial vehicles, precision missiles, and robots locate the human perpetrators of violence thousands of miles from their targets. What does *jus in bello* have to say when soldiers lose their battlefield equality or when asymmetric warfare becomes the norm?[26]

Contemporary Just War scholarship also often seems out of tune with the novel political environment and opportunities characteristic of the twenty-first century. The practical reality is that Western decision makers are no longer isolated from public opinion but must respond to it in their foreign policies. How should a foreign policy based in part on public opinion change the way one thinks about justice in war? Does this mean that public schools should educate the citizenry in Just War doctrine so that they can provide input to their representatives?

Similarly, the locus of authority has changed and contemporary Just War doctrine does not clearly provide thinking on how to deal with agencies like the UN, NATO, and the European Union. For instance, it was relatively easy to ascertain the intention and justness of the cause of a sovereign ruler, but how does one measure the motives of "a coalition of the willing" or the UN Security Council? Likewise, just war thinking must respond to the changing organization of international life, such as the UN, the European Union, and international covenants which reframe state sovereignty and international authority.

In recent years the most common application of Just War theory has been articles and lectures which enumerate the extended *jus ad bellum* model and then painstakingly examine each criterion in light of the proposed conflict. This is checklist Just War theory—if one cannot check off all of the Just War theory boxes on one's clipboard, then the war in question must not be "just." One critic of this approach calls it "ticking off a list" and writes, "such attempts have a disconcertingly legalist feel to them, ticking off the principles, as it were, one by one."[27] This approach is most commonly applied to the decision to go to war. Although Aquinas only proffered three *jus ad bellum* criteria—legitimate authority, just cause, and right intent—these have multiplied to seven. Moreover, all must be met simultaneously or the war is judged "not just." One can imagine how difficult it is for any use of force to meet this standard, particularly when one considers the subjective nature of the principle of last resort.

An example of this is an essay examining whether or not the U.S. should participate in an invasion of Iraq, written just prior to the 2003 invasion.[28] In his exposition the author exhaustively considers each *jus ad bellum* criteria: he conjectures about the intentions (right intent) of President Bush and his Administration, suggests that lawful authority to go to war resides in the United Nations (right authority), and concludes that the United States was far from the moment of last resort. Although the paper is a valuable academic exercise, it unfortunately repeats a simplistic Just War catechism without considering how issues such as state sovereignty over issues of national defense, borderless WMDs, and the rise of military humanitarian intervention, all of which demand rethinking traditional Just War theory.

Some of the recent application of *jus in bello* seems to be similarly out of touch with contemporary realities. Perhaps the best example of this is the unswerving commitment of some to the distinction between combatants (soldiers in uniform) and noncombatants. The first lesson of September 11 should be that enemies disguised as noncombatants and camouflaged within the civilian populations are an active threat and will continue to be so, not only in Tel Aviv and Kandahar but also in New York, London, and Madrid. Also, until very recently Just War scholarship had little to say about *jus in bello* in cases of military humanitarian intervention.[29] We need to rethink Just War theory based on the principle of the state's responsibility to its own security and think about aggressive, practical steps that are congruent with our values in dealing with such threats.

Another reason that Just War theory has become primarily an unfruitful exercise in theoretical ethics rather than flexible and useful in a changing world is due to its abandonment by social scientists. In the academy, those disciplines that one would expect to find Just War theory most useful in their contemplation of war—political science and international relations—have largely washed their hands of normative endeavors, seeking instead to build parsimonious "scientific" theories based on survey data and other forms of observable evidence. Fortunately, philosophers and ethicists have continued to contemplate the morality of war, but the present state of scholarly reflection on just war considerations is out of balance due to the lack of engagement by scholars and practitioners of international relations. A recent four-week institute on Just War theory, sponsored by the National Endowment for the Humanities, is a case in point. Of the nearly thirty academics in attendance, eighty percent were philosophers and only a handful represented history or political science. We need philosophers thinking about justice and war but we also need politicians and political scientists to give it more than lip service.

Furthermore, a real problem for Just War scholarship over the past half century is its clear relocation away from a middle ground between crusaderism and pacifism toward the latter. In practice, many contemporary Just War theorists demand that all of the *jus ad bellum* criteria must be met before a war is just. What this really does is collapse all or nearly all occasions of violence into a single category ("unjust") rather than respect the nuances of individual cases. Similarly, the demands of *jus in bello* have become so constraining, especially that of non-combatant immunity, that it has become almost impossible to fight a war, even in self-defense, that meets these fortified criteria. One can see in cases of military humanitarian intervention that onerous rules of engagement so restrain peacekeepers as to actually incite the belligerents to greater bloodshed.

Traditional Just War theory has been silent on a doctrine of critical importance—how war's end. Amazingly, there is no time-honored account of *jus post bellum*. In other words, while Just War theorists have quibbled about whether or not such and such historical case met the standard of "last resort," they neglected to develop what might have been a singularly useful contribution of Just War theory—a framework for providing security at war's end that establishes a better status quo which makes a resumption of conflict unlikely.

There may be another reason for the neglect of *jus post bellum*. The combination of the moderate pacifism of many Just War thinkers and the ethical relativism of the Western academy make the implementation of justice at war's end difficult. A just end to conflict would likely result in punishment for wrongdoers. This was the unique denouement of World War II—some of those responsible were held accountable and punished for their actions. However, in the postmodern world one must wonder if it is truly possible to assign blame for wrongdoing in international politics. The conceptual confusion which surrounds issues of justice and punishment in international relations is regrettable, and chapter five argues for a robust *jus post bellum* that embraces security as well as restitution and punishment when possible.

Finally, the concept of just war thinking is in danger of being stretched beyond its natural limits. The term "conceptual stretching" is a methodological indicator suggesting that concepts can be distended, or misused, in ways incommensurate with their fundamental meanings.[30] For example, when we speak of an authoritarian regime that allows a modicum of freedom in municipal elections it is simply not the same "democracy," regardless of what people call it, as the national systems of Canada or the United States. Similarly, "Just War" has been used in numerous ways without clearly articulated conceptual boundaries and has been applied in recent years not only to hot wars, the Cold War, military humanitarian interventions, post-war occupations, and proxy instruments of violence such as economic sanctions regimes, but even to environmental degradation and intelligence collection.[31] If scholars are not careful in defining their terms and defending their application of a paradigm assuming armed violence to different venues, the legacy of just war thinking may dilute into terminological vapidity.

Conclusion

Just War doctrine has traditionally stood between the poles of holy war and pacifism. The purpose of both *jus ad bellum* and *jus in bello* was to provide criteria for establishing the normative and practical context within which war might have to be waged. Just war thinking agrees with the pacifist that war is destructive but concurs with the crusader that war does not occur in a moral vacuum. This book suggests that this basic idea—that our values must underlie efforts to fight against other states, terrorists, and cases of crimes against humanity—is as true today as it was for Augustine. This book rests on the assumptions that states are responsible to promote their own security as well as the security of the international state system and that considerations of the use of force must be both pragmatic and normative. Moreover, as we consider the threats of apocalyptic terrorism, failed states, and WMDs one must conclude that there may be scenarios worse than war.

The following chapters begin with a minimal framework for just war thinking: what considerations of morality and utility should guide the resort to war? The practice of warfare? The settlement at war's end? The framework provided loosely follows the original Just War canon—*jus ad bellum* and *jus in bello*, but makes several innovations, including the addition of *jus post bellum* considerations to the end of conflict. However, before one can consider war's end, one must start at the beginning—the consideration of a twenty-first century *jus ad bellum* that takes into account the changed world symbolized by September 11, 2001.

Notes

1. There are some works that make comparison of these schools their primary aim. For instance, Richard B. Miller, *Interpretation of Conflict: Ethics, Pacifism, and the Just-War Tradition* (Chicago: University of Chicago Press, 1991). A brief summary is made in J. Darryl Charles, *Between Pacifism and Jihad: The Christian and the Just War* (Colorado Springs, CO: Intervarsity Press, 2005).

2. A slightly different approach is applied by A.J. Coates who contrasts four "images of war:" pacifism, just war, militarism, and realism. See his *The Ethics of War* (Manchester: Manchester University Press, 1997).

3. Charles reports on the historical context and position of early church fathers such as Tertullian (who thought that political and military service were forms of pagan sacrifice) and Origen—both of whom admit that Christians were serving in the Roman military. J. Daryl Charles, "Presumption against War or Presumption against Injustice? The Just War Tradition Reconsidered" in *Journal of Church and State* 48, no. 3 (Fall 2005). Charles points out that even the Quaker pacifist Roland Bainton suggests that the occupation of soldiering was likely not completely off-limits to early Christians in Bainton's *Christian Attitudes Toward War and Peace* (New York: Abingdon, 1960), 66, 81.

4. Frederick H. Russell discusses how the limited teaching of Christ on violence ultimately resulted in early Church leaders, such as Origen and later Ambrose and Augustine, having to define a Christian position on military service, allegiance to the state, and war in general. See his *The Just War in the Middle Ages* (Cambridge: Cambridge University Press, 1975), chap. 2.

5. A somewhat one-sided view of the historic Christian pacifist position is Geoffrey Nuttall, *Christian Pacifism in History* (Berkeley, CA: World Without War Council, 1971). For a thoughtful look at historical and contemporary Christian pacifism from its most famous contemporary defender, see John Howard Yoder, *The Original Revolution: Essays on Christian Pacifism* (Christian Peace Shelf Series) (Philadelphia, PA: Herald Press, 2003). A history of the application of pacifism in American politics is Theron F. Schlabach, et al, *Proclaim Peace: Christian Pacifism from Unexpected Quarters* (Urbana and Chicago, IL: University of Illinois 1997).

6. For a brief introduction to this entire controversy, see James Turner Johnson, "Just War, As it Was and Is" in *First Things* 149 (January 2005): 19.

7. John Langan, S.J. takes a slightly different approach to varieties of pacifism. He distinguishes those withdrawn from the controversy surrounding a given war from those who take an activist and ideological or politicized pacifist stance. "Just War Theory After the Gulf War" in *Theological Studies* 53 (1992), 99-100.

8. Augustine's *The City of God* is his famous treatise contrasting the *civitas dei* and the *civitas terrena*. However, we gather much of his just war thinking from his voluminous correspondence such as "To Publicola" and "To Marcellinus." Many of these letters are available in classic compilations from Catholic University Press or in a new series by New City Press.

9. See Niebuhr's "An Open Letter to Richard Roberts," *Christianity and Society* 5 (Summer 1940). This argument is updated in thoughtful chapters by Paul Ramsey, William V. O'Brien, and Jean Bethke Elshtain in the latter's edited volume *Just War Theory* (New York: New York University Press, 1992).

10. Qtd. in Richard Shelly Hartigan, "Francesco de Vitoria and Civilian Immunity," in *Political Theory* 1, no. 1 (1973): 83. This discussion can be found in Vitoria's work is *De Indis et de Iure Belli Reflectiones*, Ernest Nys, ed., J.P. Bate, trans. (New York: Oceana/Wildy and Sons, 1964), n.d.a: 449, LXIII.

11. Some have recognized that Just War theory can by misused to justify holy war. If for example, medieval clerics declared the cause of war just, then Just War usage could be "a prescription for the intensification of ideological struggle rather than for its moderation." Ian Clark, *Waging War: A Philosophical Introduction* (Oxford: Oxford University Press, 1988), 12. However, such abuse clearly falls within the rubric of crusade/jihad discussed above.

12. Thomas Aquinas' famous discussion of war is in Question 40, Secunda Secundae of the *Summa Theologica*. Vitoria's work is *De Indis et de Iure Belli Reflectiones*, ed.

Ernest Nys, trans. J.P. Bate (New York: Oceana/Wildy and Sons, 1964). Suarez's work on this issue is found in his "The Three Theological Virtues," 3.8.1. See James B. Scott, *The Spanish Origins of International Law: Lectures of Francisco de Vitoria (1480–1546) and Francisco Suarez (1548–1617)* (Washington, D.C.: Georgetown University Press, 1929).

13. Paul Ramsey, *The Just War: Force and Political Responsibility*, rev. edition (Lanham, MD: Rowman and Littlefield, 2002) and *War and the Christian Conscience/ How Shall Modern War Be Conducted Justly?* (Durham, NC: Duke University Press, 1961, 1985); Michael Walzer, *Just and Unjust Wars*, third ed. (New York: Basic Books, 2000); Jean Bethke Elshtain, *Just War Against Terror* (New York: Basic Books, 2003).

14. A slightly different framework is provided by the leading historian of Just War theory. *Jus ad bellum*: just cause, right authority, right intention, proportionality of ends, last resort, reasonable hope of success, aim of peace. *Jus in bello*: proportionality, non-combatant protection/immunity. See James Turner Johnson, *Morality and Contemporary Warfare* (New Haven, CT: Yale University Press, 1999), 28–29.

15. The dedication of the document reads, "In commemoration of the tenth anniversary of the bishops' pastoral letter, *The Challenge of Peace: God's Promise and Our Response*, and the thirtieth anniversary of Pope John XXIII's encyclical letter, *Pacem in Terris*, an ad hoc subcommittee of the Committee on International Policy drafted and approved a statement on peacemaking in a post-Cold War world. This statement, *The Harvest of Justice Is Sown in Peace*, was approved by the NCCB Administrative Board in September 1993, was submitted to and approved by the full body of bishops on November 17, 1993 and is authorized for publication as a reflection of the National Conference of Catholic Bishops by the undersigned. . . " (Washington, D.C.: U.S.C.C., 1983). The document can be found at http://www.nccbuscc.org/sdwp/harvest.htm (accessed January 1, 2007).

16. A complementary argument is made by William P. George who calls on theologians to respect and engage in the development of international law rather than cloister themselves away and theorize within their own subculture. See "Looking for a Global Ethic? Try International Law" in *The Journal of Religion*, 76, no. 3 (July, 1996).

17. The article's full title is "The Triumph of Just War Theory (and the Dangers of Success)" and was published first in *Social Research* (Winter 2002). The essay is reprinted as chapter one in his *Arguing About War* (New Haven, CT: Yale University Press, 2004).

18. Of course, political "realism" as Walzer calls it is often used as a straw man by various forms of moralism. A more nuanced approach to the nexus of morality and political realism which draws on Hans Morgenthau and Reinhold Niebuhr is John C. Hulsman and Anatol Lieven, "The Ethics of Realism," *The National Interest* (Summer 2005).

19. Not everyone agrees that Just War theory has triumphed. Although Chris Brown acknowledges the very important work of Michael Walzer, he is critical that there is a void of larger theories of international justice in the international relations literature. "Theories of International Justice" in *British Journal of Political Science* 27, no. 2 (April, 1997).

20. Walzer describes a six-part "legalist paradigm" that accurately sketches international law on the issues of state sovereignty and war. See his *Just and Unjust Wars*, 61–62. Johnson fleshes out the history of Just War theory and its progeny, the international legalist paradigm, as they grow independently yet in dialogue in the early modern era. Thus we have Just War theory rooted in Church doctrine and natural law scholarship as

distinct from early international law based in large part on customary law and the law of nations (*jus gentium*). See James Turner Johnson, *The Just War Tradition and the Restraint of War* (Princeton: Princeton University Press, 1981), esp. chaps. 1 and 5.

21. See William P. George "Looking for a Global Ethic? Try International Law" in *Journal of Religion* 76, no. 3 (July, 1996); Kenneth Watkin, "Controlling the Use of Force: A Role for Human Rights Norms in Contemporary Armed Conflict" in *The American Journal of International Law* 98, no. 1 (Jan., 2004).

22. James Turner Johnson, "Just War, As it Was and Is" in *First Things* 149 (January 2005).

23. James F. Childress, "Just-War Theories" in *Theological Studies* 39 (1978). The bishops' letter, *The Challenge of Peace* can most easily be found at http://www.osjsp m.org/cst/cp.htm (accessed January 1, 2007).

24. Oliver O'Donovan observes this trend slightly differently. He suggests that during the late Cold War many pacifists and Just War advocates appeared to "be on the same page" due to their opposition to elements of nuclear deterrence, but that this perception of shared perspective was false. Oliver O'Donovan, *The Just War Revisited* (Cambridge: Cambridge University Press, 2003), 8–9.

25. William V. O'Brien made a similar criticism of the Catholic bishops and the quasi-pacifism of "new" Just War theory in "The Challenge of War: A Christian Realist Perspective," in *The Catholic Bishops and Nuclear War*, Judith A. Dwyer, ed. (Washington, D.C.: Georgetown University Press, 1984). In contrast, Richard B. Miller defends the position of the Catholics bishops based on the notion of prima facie duties in "Aquinas and the Presumption Against Killing and War," *The Journal of Religion* 82, no. 2 (April, 2002).

26. A case study that introduces this question is Michael Ignatieff's *Virtual War: Kosovo and Beyond* (New York: Picador, 2001). Ignatieff treats the ethical issue of distance between combatants in technological warfare more fully in his *The Warrior's Honor: Ethnic War and the Modern Conscience* (New York: Henry Holt, 1998). A look at the how dehumanizing the enemy creates an "emotional distance" between combatants is Lieutenant Colonel Dave Grossman, *On Killing: The Psychological Cost of Learning to Kill in War and Society* (Boston: Little, Brown & Company/Back Bay Books, 1995).

27. O'Donovan, 13.

28. Gary Chartier, "Just War Theory and the Resort to Force in Iraq." Paper presented as part of Global Issues Forum, February 2, 2003 at Vanguard University, Costa Mesa, California.

29. Two of the insightful works on this are the edited volume by philosophers Dean K. Chatterjee and Don E. Scheid, *Ethics and Foreign Intervention* (Cambridge: Cambridge University Press, 2003) and Simon Chesterton's *Just War or Just Peace? Humanitarian Intervention and International Justice* (Oxford: Oxford University Press, 2003). A thought-provoking article is Tony Pfaff, *Peacekeeping and the Just War Tradition* (Carlisle Barracks, PA: Strategic Studies Institute, U. S. Army War College, 2000).

30. The famous broadside on conceptual stretching is Giovanni Sartori, "Concept Misinformation in Comparative Politics," in *American Political Science Review*, vol. 64, no. 4 (Summer, 1970). For a thoughtful application of this problem with regards to the concept of democracy, see David Collier and Steven Levitsky, "Democracy with Adjectives: Conceptual Innovation in Comparative Research," *World Politics* 49, no. 3 (April, 1997).

31. Again, the argument is not that all such work is bad, but that we risk stretching just war concepts beyond their fundamental meanings by applying them to everything. A thoughtful article applying traditional Just War criteria to economic sanctions in the case of Haiti is Albert G. Pierce's "Just War Principles and Economic Sanctions" in *Ethics and International Affairs* 10 (1996). Other pieces on sanctions using a slightly different approach to justice are Joy Gordon's "A Peaceful, Silent, Deadly Remedy: The Ethics of Economic Sanctions" in *Ethics and International Affairs* 13 (1999); Thomas G. Weiss' "Sanctions as a Foreign Policy Tool: Weighing Humanitarian Impulses" in *Journal of Peace Research* 36, no. 5 (September, 1999). An ecological application is Gregory Reichberg and Henrik Syse's "Protecting the Natural Environment in Wartime: Ethical Considerations from the Just War Tradition" in *Journal of Peace Research* 37, no. 4 (July, 2000). A recent application to the world of spies is Angela Gendron, "Just War, Just Intelligence: An Ethical Framework for Foreign Espionage" in *International Journal of Intelligence and Counterintelligence* 18 (Fall, 2005).

Chapter 3

Political Responsibility and the
Decision to go to War (*jus ad bellum*)

The summer and fall of 1862 were marked by reverses and defeats for the Union Army in the American Civil War: the ill-fated Peninsula campaign, the second Battle of Bull Run, Antietam, Fredericksburg. In this context Abraham Lincoln delivered a message to Congress on December 1, 1862 that elaborated his motivation for fighting America's bloodiest war.

> Fellow citizens, we cannot escape history. . . . We say we are for the Union. The world will not forget that we say this. We know how to save the Union. The world knows we do know how to save it. We— even we here—hold the power, and bear the responsibility.[1]

Lincoln argued that the motivation for fighting the war was the responsibility he had as Commander in Chief of the Union. Interestingly, one finds again and again in Lincoln's speeches references to his duty, obligation, and responsibility for the preservation and defense of his country. Although Lincoln clearly saw this charge as a moral imperative, and although from time to time he used the word "just" in his speeches, he never publicly defended his decision to go to war based on a detailed consideration of the modern Just War checklist. For Lincoln, the imperatives of national security and preserving the values of the American republic were a just cause.

The Civil War was a desperate and devastating conflict. Nonetheless, the principle of *jus ad bellum* suggests that there are some things worse than fighting a war. In other words, there are causes commensurate with our values which are worth employing violence for, such as self-defense, the security of one's home, and the defense of human life. This chapter looks at the foundations of *jus ad bellum*—the just decision to employ violence—and critiques the current state of quasi-pacifist Just War advocacy. This chapter advances a twenty-first century *jus ad bellum* that is both practical and moral, suggests a minimalist *jus ad bellum* based on a political ethic of responsibility, and argues that contemporary states should base their security decisions not on elaborate ethical catechisms, but on the moral imperative of state responsibility to domestic and international security.

The Historical Development of *Jus Ad Bellum*

Excellent volumes have been written on the history of Just War theory making a full presentation here redundant.[2] However, it is worth investigating the following question: is the *jus ad bellum* of today congruent with the original principles and intent of the patriarchs of Western Just War theory, Augustine and Aquinas? The answer is clearly no—much of the contemporary application of Just War doctrine is far more restrictive than that of the early Church fathers and tends to lack their practical concern for political order in the form of national security, responsibility for standing up to aggression, and the notions of justice and punishment in motivating the use of force.

Augustine

At the end of the fourth century, Augustine (354–430 A.D.) pondered the conditions for when it was just to employ violence in political life. Augustine's formulation of the just use of force relied heavily on the notion of *caritas*, or charity: "love your neighbor as yourself." In domestic society as well as international life, how does one go about loving one's neighbor? Augustine argued that within society adherence to the rule of law, including punishment of lawbreakers was a way of loving one's neighbors. When one loves one's neighbors one refrains from harming them and supports the authorities in their efforts to provide security to the citizenry. Moreover, Augustine noted, *caritas* means protecting one's neighbor when they are attacked, even if one is forced to employ violence to protect that individual. Augustine used Romans 13:1-5 to argue that sovereign authorities have a responsibility to order and to justice, including the use of the sword:

> Let every soul be subject unto the higher powers. For there is no power but of God: the powers that be are ordained of God. Whosoever therefore resists the power, resists the ordinance of God: and they that resist shall receive to themselves damnation. For rulers are not a terror to good works, but to evil. Wilt thou then not be afraid of the power? Do that which is good, and thou shalt have praise of the same. For he [the government official] is the minister of God to thee for good. But if thou do that which is evil, be afraid. For he beareth not the sword in vain: for he is the minister of God, a revenger to execute wrath upon him that doeth evil. Wherefore ye must needs be subject, no only for wrath, but also for conscience sake.

Augustine suggested that this is also true with regards to foreign threats: loving our neighbor can mean self-defense of the polity. Likewise, loving our foreign neighbors may mean using force to punish evildoers or right a wrong. He writes, "true religion looks upon as peaceful those wars that are waged not for motives of aggrandizement, or cruelty, but with the object of securing peace, of punishing evil-doers, and of uplifting the good."[3] In his recent book, theologian Oliver O'Donovan comments that Augustine's typology suggests "defensive, reparative, and punitive objectives" of the decision to go to war.[4]

In addition to *caritas*, Augustine's writings suggest a second reason for *jus ad bellum*: order. Augustine consistently privileged political order over disorder. The Augustinian conception of the universe is one in which God is the ultimate Creator, Judge, Arbiter, and End. Although God allows sin and imperfection in this world, he nonetheless sustains the universe with a divine order. This order is mirrored in society by the political order with its laws and hierarchy. Augustine argued that although the City of Man is a poor reflection of the City of God, nonetheless it is the political principle of temporal order which most approximates the eternal order.[5] During his lifetime Augustine witnessed the alternative: the breakdown of *Pax Romana*, the looting of Rome, and ultimately the sacking of his home in North Africa in the final days of his life. Thus, Augustine's fear of political disorder was more than a distaste for regime change, it was dread of losing civic order with all of its attendant moral duties and opportunities.

Today, most religious Just War theorists want to focus on the law of love but neglect Augustine's presupposition that political order is the foundation for society.[6] Augustine's argument is that the state has a responsibility to both domestic and international security—a responsibility that it must uphold, even if the state dirties its hands in the process of securing the realm.

Thomas Aquinas

Aquinas (1225–1274 A.D.) was the great Scholastic expositor of Augustine. He argued that a war was just when it met three requirements: sovereign authority, just cause, and right intent. It is noteworthy that Aquinas began not with just cause or right intent, but with *sovereign authority*:

> In order for a war to be just, three things are necessary. First, the authority of the sovereign by whose command the war is to be waged. For it is not the business of a private individual to declare war. . . .And as the care of the common weal is committed to those who are in authority, it is their business to watch over the common weal of the city, kingdom or province subject to them. And just as it is lawful for them to have recourse to the sword in defending that common weal against internal disturbances, when they punish evil-doers. . . so too, it is their business to have recourse to the sword of war in defending the common weal against external enemies.[7]

In short, Aquinas saw most violence as criminal and lawless. The fundamental purpose of the state was to provide a counterpoise to lawlessness. *Ergo*, the legitimate use of force should only be in the hands of the rightful authorities in order to promote security.

Aquinas also argued that states should be concerned with *just cause*. He writes: "Secondly, a just cause is required, namely that those who are attacked, should be attacked because they deserve it on account of some fault." He quotes Augustine, "Wherefore Augustine says: 'A just war is wont to be described as one that avenges wrongs, when a nation or state has to be punished, for refusing to make amends for the wrongs inflicted by its subjects, or to restore what it has seized unjustly.'"[8] Aquinas' conception of just cause is richer than the contemporary debate on self-defense because it includes punishing wrongdoing and restitution of some sort to victims. Indeed, it seems that Aquinas' just cause would support the use of force to curb aggressive non-state actors, protect individual human life via humanitarian intervention, and punish rogue regimes that disrupt the international status quo.

Third, Aquinas said that the just resort to force required *just intent*. Scholars and churchmen alike have long pointed out the dilemmas of ascertaining right intent. For the average soldier, the medievals solved this problem by providing absolution to their troops before battle and sometimes providing it again after the battle for the survivors. This did not completely solve the problem of rage and bloodlust on the battlefield, but sought a spiritual solution to a very human dynamic.

However, this says little about the sovereign's motivation. Contemporary politics makes the situation even more complex because most state decisions are not made by a sovereign individual such as a king or empress. Western governments are pluralistic, representing multiple voices and acting based on a complicated set of interests and ideals. However, Aquinas' focus on right intent did not necessarily call for agonizing over one's ethical motivations. He wrote, "Thirdly, it is necessary that the belligerents should have a rightful intention, so that they intend the advancement of good, or the avoidance of evil." In other words, Aquinas' idea of right intent is that states should seek to advance the security of their people and avoid wars based only on greed or vengeance. Aquinas again cites Augustine: "Hence Augustine says: 'The passion for inflicting harm, the cruel thirst for vengeance, an unpacific and relentless spirit, the fever of revolt, the lust of power, and such like things, all these are rightly condemned in war.'"[9] Aquinas would likely agree that in contemporary international politics, the right intent of states is to seek their own security and then promote human life around the world.

Contemporary Just War Theory

As demonstrated in chapter 2, Augustine and Aquinas' minimal *jus ad bellum* criteria have been added to over time. For all intents and purposes *jus ad bellum* has become a checklist which includes proportionality of ends, last resort, comparative justice, and likelihood of success.[10] This work refers to such as a "checklist" because for many Just War users, unless a conflict can meet all of these requirements simultaneously, involvement in the conflict is unjust.[11]

James Turner Johnson has taken a more nuanced approach to *jus ad bellum*. He suggests that there is a hierarchy of values within the contemporary Just War framework. He calls the traditional three criteria (just cause, right intent, right authority) deontological, meaning that they are based on moral obligation. He argues that the other criteria (e.g. last resort, likelihood of success) are "all prudential criteria to be applied as additional checks when the above deontological requirements have been met. All are derived historically from Roman practice and they refer to political prudence at any time and in any culture."[12] In other words, traditional *jus ad bellum* has a moral foundation and additional practical considerations which can be prudently applied on a case-by-case basis.

Johnson takes issue with the "presumption against the use of force" which has become a popular refrain among many Just War proponents.[13] He asserts that the increasing stress of the Catholic bishops and other contemporary Just War theorists on the prudential criteria as normative is really "*jus contra bellum justum* . . . just war pacifism. . . . It begins with a presumption against war, and it employs certain dogmatic assumptions about modern weapons to attempt to undercut the possibility of any contemporary use of force, on the grounds of the just war principle of proportionality."[14]

Johnson's observation parallels one of the primary arguments of the present work—that thoughtful concerns about morality, political order, and war of the Augustinian tradition have often given way to the laborious, adolescent process of checking off the long list of *jus ad bellum* criteria. This new Just War theory, what Johnson terms "just war pacifism," lacks the creativity and flexibility necessary to deal with twenty-first century threats and aggression.

Re-examining the Foundations of *Jus Ad Bellum*

Jus ad bellum is not a perfectionist moral system. Rather, it is an attempt to bridge the gap between the problem of violence and the ideal of a peaceful and secure order. The utility of just war thinking is that it calls for moral accounting in the imperfect world that we live in. Hence, twenty-first century just war thinking must be both ethical and practical in order to be a useful guide for policy when confronted with the decision of whether or not to employ military force.

The Morality of *Jus Ad Bellum*

So, what can possibly be moral about the decision to go to war? We should not simply rely on the moral fiber of just war thinking because of its association with a major religion nor because it is employed by many well-meaning people.

Simply put, *jus ad bellum* is grounded in moral concerns regarding restraint, motivation, and responsibility. First, *jus ad bellum* articulates the principal of restraint. War is terrible: *jus ad bellum* calls for careful moral consideration of and limits on the material and human destructiveness of such an enterprise. This does not necessarily mean that war should be fought on the cheap or in slow phases of escalation. Such approaches were tried in Kosovo and accelerated the ethnic cleansing, rather than curtailing it. Nonetheless, the idea of restraint in the decision to go to war regards our analysis of the real cost of war and our desire to restrain not only the violence of the battlefield but the collateral damage to human beings, infrastructure, the environment, and the long-term prospects of rapprochement. We practice restraint because we envision peace and security; restraint is evidence that war is not an end to itself.

Second, *jus ad bellum* is moral in that it calls for accountability for one's motives. This is true for individuals and for collectives. At a fundamental level the onus is the state's to be responsible for acting on the interests of and to promote the security of its citizenry—such is right intent. When attacked, defending ourselves can take many forms, from repelling the invaders to utterly destroying their homeland. The former is certainly just, the latter may well be vengeful genocide. Such policies are a choice. Regardless of the provocation, *jus ad bellum* argues that we are ethically responsible for how we choose to respond to aggression.

Moreover, *jus ad bellum* suggests that not every cause is just, thus problematizing not only our intentions but also the conditions of each specific conflict. Just cause is contextual: it is inextricably linked to dynamic features of specific conflicts. In addition, just cause is moral in that it does not grant complete absolution for using violence but it recognizes that the resort to force, such as in self-defense or to promote international security by helping a neighbor, is appropriate when compared to the tacit approval of evil demonstrated by quietude, inaction, and appeasement.

Finally, just war thinking's presumption of order is a moral concept. The idea that war should proceed only on the basis of legitimate authority acknowledges that governments and law are the foundation of "the good life." Political order is the first step towards more expansive notions of justice and well-being; the breakdown of order in the context of violence highlights this dynamic. In short, establishing and maintaining security and justice within the political order are essentially ethical considerations: *jus ad bellum*.

The Practicality of *Jus Ad Bellum*

In addition to its normative presuppositions, *jus ad bellum* is founded on practical considerations. The notion of *legitimate authority* is a case in point. Because legitimate authority, at least in the modern world, means primarily states or their representatives (e.g. UN, NATO), only members of this exclusive club can "legitimately" go to war. Thus, the notion of authentic authority buttresses not only the entire international system of independent states as we have it today, but also legitimates the domestic status quo within states. Legitimate authority is a pragmatic tool labeling internal threats to the state, regardless of their popular appeal, as illegitimate. Thus, groups that might be real "freedom fighters" (e.g. Chechens, Kurds) are likely to be branded as guerrillas, insurgents, rebels, or terrorists. Furthermore, the call by most Just War theorists for a formal declaration of hostilities reifies the statist nature of the system. While there may be some ethical value in not surprising your enemy's army, if that is even possible in contemporary warfare, nonetheless formal declarations of war are really the centerpiece of a legalistic paradigm that defines war as the legitimate enterprise of states only.

A second practical device for any government, especially a democratic one, is *just cause*. As Lincoln noted, both sides will claim their cause is just and pray that God reward them with victory. Political leaders who can frame their war aims in terms of the moral high ground are much more likely to receive the necessary support of their constituents and the international community.[15] Military leaders know that when their troops believe in the "rightness" of their cause, they will fight better, longer, and harder against the enemy.

The other "prudential" *jus ad bellum* tenets are essentially cost/benefit analyses. The injunction to consider the *likelihood of success* suggests that if a war is not winnable, it should not be fought. This is pure utilitarianism. Certainly many, Winston Churchill or Nelson Mandela for example, would argue that there are causes worth fighting for even if the probability of victory seems to be very unlikely. *Proportionality* in the decision to go to war is similarly sensible: deciding whether a provocation warrants a forceful response is largely a political and strategic calculation. Furthermore, the admonition to resort to war only in the *last resort* is equally pragmatic. Of course in its extreme form, should leaders really not employ force until the very last, the enemy will most likely be at the gates. It is irresponsible to wait to act until it is too late. In reality, *last resort* is a judgment call made by politicians about the costs and benefits of action at any given time, and therefore it is a dynamic and contextual.

Jus Ad Bellum: Responsibility

Much of contemporary Just War advocacy has lost the practical policy orientation of the past. Indeed, when asked, "when is it moral to employ violence?" many of today's Just War users would likely answer "probably never." I disagree. A twenty-first century framework for *jus ad bellum* should be founded on the concept of *responsibility*. When considering whether or not to go to war, policy makers should begin from the premise that the state has certain ethical and practical responsibilities. Instead of prevaricating over the old notions of right intention and likelihood of success, in the aftermath of 9/11 policy makers should ask "what is our responsibility to our citizens?" and "what is our responsibility to the international system?" The post-September 11 context is that an enemy has attacked and promises to attack again and the West's responsibility should be clear: national security and the protection of human life.

A political ethic of responsibility recognizes that political and social life is made up not only of rights, but of responsibilities. Chief among such responsibilities is the protection of one's citizens. In other words, the state's responsibility for self-defense motivates the U.S. to fight the war on terrorism. Of course, the desire to "save our own skins" is pragmatic, while at the same time valuing human life and international security is an ethical good. A doctrine of responsibility is thus at the intersection of practicality and morality. It is the moral obligation of the state to take every reasonable step to protect the life, livelihood, and way of life of its populace.[16] It is also pragmatic for states to be alert to threats, actual and potential, and consider appropriate action. The nature of new wars—the war on terrorism, engagement of rogue states, military humanitarian intervention in failed states, technological attacks on Western economies via the anarchic internet—is that they are a return to the Hobbesian state of war:

> For war consisteth not in battle only, or the act of fighting; but in a tract of time, wherein the will to contend by battle is sufficiently known: and therefore the notion of time, is to be considered in the nature of war; as it is in the nature of weather. For as the nature of foul weather, lieth not in a shower or two of rain; but in an inclination thereto of many days together: so the nature of war, consisteth not in actual fighting; but in the known disposition thereto, during all the time there is no assurance to the contrary.[17]

The twenty-first century security dilemma is that we live in an uncertain environment even if war is not being actively waged on a battlefield. Consequently, in an era of multiple, often undeclared threats to national security, states must take responsibility for preparing for and at times prosecuting a war against those threats to their security. This means that states need to think about a robust, multi-dimensional security agenda that includes defensive and offensive operations in terms of finance, diplomacy, covert operations, propaganda, and at times military force. Such calculation in the face of threats may resemble the Cold War policy of containment. In other contexts, it may justify preemptive or preventive war as well as military humanitarian intervention. In short, it is irresponsible, an abdication of responsibility, for states to not act.[18]

The old *jus ad bellum* concept of legitimate authority was similar to this idea of responsibility, but was limited in that it implied a conflict between states. In the new century most conflicts are either illegitimate regimes harming their own people or non-state actors perpetrating terrorism against the citizens of legitimate governments. In either case, the authority for response comes not from an artificial conception of dueling belligerents but from the legitimate right of self-defense. Governments are the authorities responsible to protect the lives and futures of their citizens from the depredations of rogue states and terrorists.

Such a view of responsibility is decidedly statist and therefore eminently practical. It acknowledges states' responsibility to protect human life, both within and beyond their borders. States are the guarantors of domestic and systemic security. Furthermore, this view of responsibility asserts that international institutions, such as the UN and NATO, are legitimate primarily as the expression of states. Thus, if the UN champions the security of human citizens, it is acting correctly at the behest and on the authority of its member states. On the other hand, if the UN fails to protect human life and security, it is the failure of [some of] its constituent members. When the UN (or NATO, EU, OSCE, AU, OAS) fails to act in accordance with its peculiar mandate, this does not mean that individual states have lost their essential responsibility to act on behalf of security.[19]

Of course, another question arises: does the U.S. have some responsibility as the lone superpower to protect life and the international order outside its borders?[20] It is beyond the boundaries of this chapter to discuss this question at length, but the answer is a qualified "yes" on at least two levels. First, in order to protect its citizens and its way of life in the long run, at times the U.S. will have to act against threats such as rogue states and international terrorist organizations, even if the threats only indirectly affect the U.S. but directly challenge the security of our allies and partners.

Second, the contemporary international order with all its flaws is based on *Pax Americana*. It is an epoch of unprecedented interaction, freedom, and security. Few countries around the globe need fear conquest by the global hegemon making this is a truly unique historical moment. The current peace is far better than the "stability" of the Cold War or eras that preceded it. This peace is worth preserving.[21]

In evaluating how to meet such responsibility the U.S. and the West should be pragmatic: "Do we utilize organizations such as the UN or not? How do we prioritize our involvement in a world of limited resources? How do elected officials balance their responsibility for security with the institutional and popular checks of representative government?" In the end, a political ethic of responsibility requires resistance and containment of threats to security and human life.

Applying an Ethic of Responsibility: Two Cases

Jus ad bellum based on a political ethic of responsibility is the starting point for evaluating the use of American military force in recent years. The hard question is whether U.S. attacks on Afghanistan (2001) and Iraq (2003) meet this criterion. Was the decision to go to war appropriate based on the state's moral responsibility to international security and protecting human life?

September 11 and the War in Afghanistan

On Sunday, October 7, 2001 the U.S. military began a devastating assault on Afghanistan. The incursion was a deliberate response to the airliner attacks on New York and Washington, D.C. three weeks earlier and was designed to decimate the al Qaeda terrorist organization and its leader Osama bin Laden as well as topple the ultra-orthodox Taliban which had ruled Afghanistan by a strict interpretation of the *shariah* since 1996.   The details of the war are well known. After the Taliban refused the U.S. demand to hand over Osama bin Laden and dismantle its terrorist training camps, massive aerial bombardment followed by the insertion of American and some British troops began. The hottest fighting of the war lasted approximately two months, until the Taliban and its al Qaeda associates had been pushed from most of the country by a combination of commandos, American airpower, and Northern Alliance fighters. On December 7 the Taliban Leader, Mullah Muhammed Omar, fled Konduz and at that point all of the major cities of Afghanistan—Kandahar, Jalalabad, Herat, Kabul, Mazar-i-Sharif—had fallen to coalition forces. Although considerable security operations continued, such as at Tora Bora and later the "Anaconda" campaign, the hot war was effectively over by Christmas.

The average American, and many other citizens in the West, considered the fighting in Afghanistan against the Taliban and al Qaeda to be a just war. After all, fanatics who had trained there had murdered over 3,000 civilians and the Taliban itself was a diabolical regime. In addition, the U.S. was fighting alongside the Northern Alliance, a motley assemblage of "freedom fighters" striving to liberate their country from its oppressors.

Perhaps this is too simplistic a portrait of the actual justification for war against Afghanistan. Certainly, there is more to the story: political calculations, the revenge factor, unfinished business from the tail-end of the Cold War, the personality of George W. Bush, the horror of the Twin Towers attacks. Nevertheless, as we reflect back to September 11 and the subsequent intervention in Afghanistan, we are left with questions regarding how just war thinking might apply. Does the military action by the U.S. and its allies in Afghanistan meet all of the contemporary *jus ad bellum* checklist as elucidated by the Catholic bishops? The answer is probably "no." However, I submit that this demonstrates a problem with the rigid manner in which Just War criteria are typically applied, not the quality of the decision to use force in Afghanistan. The following section looks at those critiques of U.S. intervention and the Just War pacifism now in vogue. In contrast to the critics, this chapter counters that U.S. intervention was justified, and just, based on the U.S. government's responsibility to pursue the security of its citizens as well as to punish the wrong-doers and their associates in Afghanistan.

An Unjust War?

So was the decision to go to war in Afghanistan just? There are numerous individuals in the church and in the academy who assert that the war did not meet the contemporary *jus ad bellum* standards. How can this be? This is often the case because the application of *jus ad bellum* is confused, misused, or abused. What is striking about these gripes is the misuse of the traditional Just War principles in their denigration of U.S. action. For instance, the fundamental tenets of just cause and right authority are not invoked, rather, the whimsical criteria of last resort seems to have become the cardinal virtue, and the legitimate responsibility of a democratic government pursuing its security is neglected altogether.

Traditional *jus ad bellum* begins with legitimate authority. Many contemporary Just War users, like those associated with the statement below, would like to remove the power to make war from states altogether and place it in the hands of the "international community"—the UN. For example, on September 12, 2001 the Catholic organization Pax Christi USA posted a statement on its website warning the U.S. to not engage in unjust war.

> We must find the courage to break the spiral of violence that so many in our nation, we fear, will be quick to embrace. We therefore call for restraint on the part of our nation's civilian and military leaders. The appropriate response to this despicable act is not a despicable act of violence in kind. Vengeance is not justice. The only kind of justice that will honor the memory of all those who lost their lives is a justice based on international law, not reckless retribution. [22]

This is a radical departure from the traditional notion of state sovereignty and the authority of governments to act on their own interests and their own definitions of security. The Bush Administration did not seek UN authorization for its action and would have undoubtedly acted despite General Assembly opposition. Although a sovereign government was responding on behalf of its own security situation, to multilateralist, contemporary Just War pacifists the U.S. was spurning their revised legitimate authority for the new millennium—the UN—and embarking on an illegal crusade. Moreover, the Pax Christi missive said little positive about what constitutes a just cause and it had nothing to say, in the tradition of Augustine and Aquinas, about punishing evil-doers.

Was there a just cause? Some argue that the September 11 attacks, perpetuated by rogue Saudi individuals, were an inappropriate cause for the massive U.S. bombardment and invasion of Afghanistan. Indeed, the cause was not clearly self-defense, at least not in the traditional sense, because Afghanistan-the-state had not attacked the United States. The attackers were criminals, thugs, and or terrorists. In fact, some suggested that this was a case for law enforcement, or better for introspection regarding U.S. foreign policy. A Christian theologian, responding to a question from an internet blog, considered the possible justice and injustice of the U.S. attacks on Afghanistan.

> Our ostensible purpose, bringing to justice the chief suspect in the terrorist attack on the World Trade Center and the Pentagon, had a good chance of success through negotiations which we refused. Our bombing caused many civilian deaths and unexploded bombs are likely to kill more over the years. Far more deaths may be caused by the war's interruption of famine relief. Almost certainly the number of deaths resulting from the war will vastly exceed all the deaths

caused by all terrorist attacks to date and in the foreseeable future.
There is no assurance that the new government will, over the years,
bring peace and justice to Afghanistan.[23]

Again, surprisingly, the author said little about the traditional three *jus ad bellum* criteria such as just cause and entirely neglects the issue of state responsibility for the security of its public.

Undoubtedly, the U.S. response displayed elements of punishment and
vengeance. Although early Just War theorists like Augustine called punishment
a moral motivation, punishment has long since been abandoned by those like
Pax Christi as too haughty and overbearing. And vengeance, the Old Testament
"eye for an eye," can have no place in just war pacifism.

More bizarrely, there are those who claim that the acts of al Qaeda align
with justice. Princeton theologian Mark Taylor bemoaned "organized terror experienced by ever larger numbers of world communities today as a result of US-
led, sponsored, or supported activities in its so-called 'war on terrorism.'" Taylor went on to liken Osama bin Laden to Jesus Christ and Christ's opposition to
the Jewish religious authorities of his day to the September 11 destruction of the
World Trade Center, the Jerusalem of bin Laden's era.[24]

Thus, for some critics the United States fails the Just War standard as to the
justness and intent of its resort to force. So too, for U.S. critics, did America fail
the prudential criteria. Certainly, there was some likelihood of success, at least
in deposing the Taliban and disrupting al Qaeda. Indeed, how could the United
States not succeed when it was, allegedly, carpet bombing both the Taliban and
the civilian population of Afghanistan?[25]

More strangely, some users of the Just War criteria turn *jus ad bellum* on its
head and began with the prudential criteria. For example in December 2001
Boston College ethicist Lisa Sowles Cahill took the amazing position that the
first Just War criteria to be applied to conflict is *last resort*, although it is not
one of the historic Just War trinity. Moreover, she suggested a utilitarian position that there is no *jus ad bellum* whatsoever, at least not until the conflict is
over and one can do a cost/benefit analysis of the damage done.

> I don't think we can know that it really is a just war until it's over and
> done with and all of the information has surfaced about what actually
> happened. At this point in time, I find it very premature to say that
> this is a just war, particularly considering the reports that residential
> areas in Afghanistan have in fact been bombed. . .One of the founda-
> tions of the church's tradition of just-war theory is that it begins with
> the fundamental assumption that war is *not* justified. . .It's true that
> the common good of the international community is threatened by
> terrorism. So it is an issue of defending the common good, but even
> after you look at that "cause," you have to make sure that a violent
> response that takes human lives is really a "last resort."[26]

This is similar to the previous complaint the war was far from a last resort because only a few weeks of lackluster negotiations had been tried and the Bush Administration seemed uninterested in diplomatic and nonviolent solutions to bring al Qaeda to justice.

Critics of the U.S. attack such as Dr. Cahill argue that the U.S. B-1 bombers, Stealth aircraft, and Special Operations teams were disproportionate both to the nature of the injury received (20 dead suicide bombers with box cutters) and the nature of the Taliban regime itself. Indeed, at the time it was somewhat unclear at the time who al Qaeda was, what they were responsible for, and what the relationship between them and the Afghan government was. Nevertheless, the Bush administration acted with the mighty tools of its twenty-first century arsenal against the irregular forces of the Taliban. To what end? The end of peace? To his detractors, Bush-the-cowboy seemed to lack the vision of his father's New World Order.

Unfortunately the above is an accurate portrayal of some of the views of those who utilize Just War theory to deconstruct the normative content of the Afghan conflict. The simple truth is that such practitioners have created a Just War dogma which is doctrinaire, quasi-pacifistic, and unrepresentative of both the tradition of just war thinking as well as the dilemmas of real world politics. These protests rarely consider the principle of political order which undergirds Augustine's writing, the need for legitimate government authority, and that a just cause should consider the punishment of wrong. Rather, they are characterized by just war pacifism as well as what Jean Bethke Elshtain calls *ressentiment*, self-loathing of their country, to denigrate U.S. action.[27] In contrast, a *jus ad bellum* based on state responsibility for security would view the conflict in Afghanistan very differently.

A Revised *Jus Ad Bellum*: Responsibility and Afghanistan

Considerations of the morality of going to war should begin with state responsibility. The essential obligation of the state is the protection of its citizens. This is the basis of the fundamental social contract—security for acquiescence to state authority. Political and social order is a moral good, the basis of the good life and the first portal to individual autonomy in society. Moreover, a robust national security policy is concerned not simply with direct threats to the existence of its inhabitants, but is also steadfast in evaluating and acting against threats to their livelihood and way of life. Consequently, threats or attacks on the socio-economic well-being of the citizenry and/or the fundamental American values of civil liberties and human rights must be guarded against.

This talk of responsibility, of duty and obligation, has fallen into disfavor in the era of "rights." We are told that individuals have rights, nations have rights (e.g. self-determination), that there are a host of social, economic, and political rights due individuals and their collectives.[28] In the past two decades we have even been told that corrupt governments who drive their own populace into poverty and despair have rights to non-intervention and deserve hand-outs from the

West (North). Although I adamantly affirm the existence of fundamental human rights, the simple fact of political life is that individual rights in the real world are little more than a pipe dream without an effective state charged with the protection of those rights. Therefore, in international politics and the context of twenty-first century threats we must rely on the state to carry the moral burden of national security and act on the best interests of its citizenry with the tools at its disposal.

Just war thinking that begins with state responsibility considers the September 11 attacks in the larger context of principles of security, self-defense, and justice. How should the United States respond in self defense? And, how should the United States act in order to promote justice and punish aggressors?

Peter Temes argues that the historical context behind the September 11 attacks extends far back: to the Israeli-Palestinian conflict, to the end of World War II and the creation of Israel, to the era of Western imperialism, perhaps to the Crusades.[29] Although the muddled historicism that suggests that the September 11 massacres really had anything to do with the Balfour Declaration or the Crusades is objectionable, nonetheless a look at recent history is telling. According to the 9/11 Commission al Qaeda was at war with the United States for a decade.[30] Osama bin Laden's notorious fatwa trumpeted:

> The ruling to kill the Americans and their allies—civilians and military—is an individual duty for every Muslim who can do it in any country in which it is possible to do it. . . .We—with God's help— call on every Muslim who believes in God and wishes to be rewarded to comply with God's order to kill the Americans and plunder their money wherever and whenever they find it. We also call on Muslim ulema, leaders, youths, and soldiers to launch the raid on Satan's U.S. troops and the devil's supporters allying with them, and to displace those who are behind them so that they may learn a lesson.

Moreover, the Commission reports that bin Laden's network was linked to attacks on U.S. troops in Yemen as well as the Manila airline plot in the early 1990s, that early al Qaeda elements were part of the destabilization campaign in Somalia in the early 1990s, that al Qaeda butchered thousands in attacks on American embassies in Tanzania and Kenya and bombed the USS Cole while it was refueling in Yemen.[31] Since September 11 al Qaeda continues to prosecute its war against the West by attacks on a popular tourist spot in Bali, in Madrid, throughout the Arab world, and most recently in London.

The September 11 slaughter of civilians was only the most recent, at that time, assault on U.S. civilians by al Qaeda and by radical Islamic terrorists more generally (e.g. the Shiite-Hezbollah attack on Khobar Towers in 1996). Thus a forceful response in self-defense was called for. Of course, part of the dilemma at the time was how should the U.S. respond: by treating this as a military campaign or a law enforcement initiative?[32] And, should the U.S. only target individual terrorists or act against state sponsors and the geographical refuges of terrorists?

These questions are important because al Qaeda is not the typical terrorist organization. It is not a secessionist movement or national liberation front dedicated to throwing out a local tyrant. Indeed, al Qaeda attacked civilian targets far from its base of operations and demonstrated a sado-masochistic disregard for human life, not only in its pattern of suicide bombings on non-combatant targets, but in its ruthless treatment of women, children, and those of other faiths.[33] In a sense, it is appropriate that observers have called al Qaeda "apocalyptic" or "nihilistic" in its terrorism because of the lack of a constructive political program.[34] Indeed, to Western values of civilization and the Western political order, al Qaeda's politics can only be seen as destructive.[35]

The U.S. attack in October 2001 was not only against a non-state terrorist network, but happened in geographical context: Afghanistan. This brings forth the issues of international law, sovereignty, and non-intervention. Nonetheless, the U.S. response met just war thinking's standard of state responsibility for security because Afghanistan had become a notorious haven and training ground for radical Islamists and their project to use violence to destabilize parts of Asia and beyond. The Taliban was a rogue government recognized by only three other states, but the important point here is not that they were primitive in their thinking and barbaric in their behavior to their own people, but that as a refuge for terrorists they constituted an active threat to U.S. and international security. The United States did ask questions first and attack later: it specifically requested that Osama bin Laden be handed over for his involvement with the 9/11 affair. The Afghan government refused. The United States then deployed force against the al Qaeda ally just as it might the ally of any foreign belligerent with which it was at war.

Thus far I have argued that al Qaeda was not a legitimate government, yet it declared war on the United States in the 1990s and acted on that threat. Moreover, al Qaeda aligned itself with a rogue regime and in tandem the two presented a clear threat to American security following September 11, if not considerably earlier. The use of deadly force was tardy based on al Qaeda's earlier attacks on U.S. interests and civilians, but appropriate as an immediate reaction to September 11 and as an effort to defeat a menace and thereby prevent future attacks.

Just war thinking about the decision to go to war should consider national security as a moral imperative first and foremost. But it can, whenever appropriate, also take into consideration the issues of justice, reparation, and punishment. Justice begins with the notion that there are moral standards in political life and that there should be consequences for wrongful behavior. Following the September 11 attack it was legitimate for the United States, the aggrieved party, to prosecute the violent acts of al Qaeda and its accomplices with the political and military tools at U.S. disposal. Justice demands an accounting for the murder of thousands of citizens and therefore the U.S. response was congruent with just war thinking. In international life, where there is no judge, jury, nor even the legal tools for adequately addressing non-state terrorist actors and semi-functional rogue regimes like the Taliban, the public trust is located not in Geneva, the Hague, or Brussels, but with the leadership of one's own state who is responsible for the present and future security of the populace.[36]

Targeting Weapons of Mass Destruction: The Second Iraq War

The Iraq war presents a second and more complicated case regarding the just decision to go to war and political responsibility. In March 2003, the United States and its coalition partners invaded Saddam Hussein's Iraq. After a breathtakingly quick military campaign in which much of the Iraqi army melted away before the allied assault, the Iraqi government disintegrated, key figures of the Baathist regime went into hiding, and hundreds of thousands of ordinary Iraqi civilians danced in the streets celebrating the end of the brutal dictatorship.

The Bush Administration built its case that Iraq should be checked almost exclusively on the belief that the regime had and was enhancing a stockpile of weapons of mass destruction. For instance, in October 2002 President Bush suggested, "Iraq could decide on any given day to provide a biological or chemical weapon to a terrorist group or individual terrorists."[37] Several weeks later British Prime Minister Tony Blair made public a dossier of evidence regarding Iraq's alleged weapons of mass destruction, arguing, "His [Saddam] weapons of mass destruction program is active, detailed and growing. The policy of containment is not working. The weapons of mass destruction program is not shut down. It is up and running. . . ."[38] Colin Powell's famous February 2003 address to the UN reported, "Our conservative estimate is that Iraq today has a stockpile of between 100 and 500 tons of chemical weapons agents. That is enough agent to fill 16,000 battlefield rockets."[39]

Interestingly, most European capitals, from Paris to Moscow, did not dispute the existence of chemical and biological agents in the Iraqi arsenal, although they did dispute that Baghdad had an active nuclear weapons program. The main disagreement between Washington/London and the rest of Europe was whether military intervention was the appropriate course of action, or, in its stead, what steps should the international community take to constrain and ultimately disarm the Iraqi threat.

It is apparent today that although the Iraqi regime possessed the know-how to produce weapons of mass destruction, that they were far less successful in doing so. The Duelfer Report suggests that Saddam Hussein cleverly dissembled about his WMD programs in order to create uncertainty and fear among his enemies. The Report goes on to say that there is no doubt that Hussein wanted to create weapons of mass destruction, but that he faced various international constraints on renewing such programs.[40]

At the time much of the world community believed that Iraq did possess weapons of mass destruction. Moreover, it is clear that Saddam's senior leadership did as well. After interviewing dozens of high-ranking Baathist leaders, a finding of the USJFCOM Iraqi Perspectives Project is that Saddam's closest

henchmen all believed that the regime had an aggressive WMDs program un-
derway.[41] In short, the real debate at the United Nations (and elsewhere) was
never over whether Hussein had such an arsenal (of biological and chemical
weapons) and the desire to augment it with nuclear weapons. Rather, the controversy was about what means should be utilized to neutralize or contain the threat
Hussein posed.[42]

Consider then, the counterfactual: coalition forces discovered Iraqi weapons
of mass destruction in the spring and summer of 2003. They discovered not only
mobile chemical and biological labs, but also bunkers filled with nerve agents,
missile technology for delivering them throughout the great Middle East, and
operational plans for their use on Israel and Western interests in Saudi Arabia,
Kuwait, the United Arab Emirates, and Turkey. Perhaps a rudimentary nuclear
weapons facility had been created, buried in a bunker deep below one of Saddam's opulent palaces.

Would such a war have been just? It is likely that most of world opinion that
has criticized U.S. policy regarding Iraq would have been muted or vanished
altogether had the weapons of mass destruction been found. This is not to argue
that public opinion should be our guide in making moral judgment calls, indeed,
the opposite is true. Chapter six analyzes the tension between what the public
wants and moral thinking. Nonetheless, we should recognize that much of the
debate over the "morality" of the Iraqi invasion is consequentialist: "See, no
weapons of mass destruction were found, thus the decision to go to war was
immoral."

Such reasoning, although somewhat natural due to our 20/20 hindsight vision, is poor from a moral point of view. The real question about the war in Iraq
is this: did the United States, and perhaps other countries, have a responsibility
to their own citizens to restrain, constrain, and perhaps punish Iraq? What is the
basis of such responsibility?

In the contemporary international system, the primary focus of the state
should be adherence to its responsibility to secure its own citizenry, both domes-
tically and internationally. This is the basis for a twenty-first century *jus ad bellum* based on a political ethic of responsibility. Second, *jus ad bellum* suggests
that it may be just to go to war to protect human life in a larger context. In the
Iraq case, the international intelligence community believed that Hussein had
weapons of mass destruction and by 2003 he had violated numerous international covenants, including sixteen UN resolutions. Probably the best policy
would have been "inspections with force" in 1998. Had the UN demanded that
inspections continue and put military force on the ground to enforce their access,
the 2003 war would probably never have happened. Such a policy would have
been clearly justified as the moral responsibility of states to promote international security.

Similarly, U.S. military action in 2003 was clearly based on a conception of
government responsibility in the post-9/11 context. From the American vantage
point, Iraq had attacked its neighbors and Baghdad had become the hideout for
numerous international terrorists after the fall of Afghanistan. Although there

were no clear links between the Hussein regime and al Qaeda, Saddam's past associations with terrorists, including making Baghdad a sanctuary for notorious killers, combined with his supposed arsenal of weapons of mass destruction made Iraq a unique threat. Moreover, Saddam's regional bullying against Iran, Israel, Kuwait, not to mention threats against Saudi Arabia and the UAE, made Iraq a clear threat to international security.

American strategic interests, from the protection of Israel to vital oil supplies, were also part of the decision to go to war. These are American vital interests, and it is ethical for the state to protect them and thereby promote the lives, livelihoods, and lifestyle of its citizenry. Of equal importance to many of us was the suffering of the Iraqi people.[43] Although the Bush Administration said little about this prior to the invasion, many observed before the war that Saddam's regime was responsible for the torture and deaths of hundreds of thousands of his own citizens, the internal displacement of 900,000 people, and a system of *de jure* segregation that marginalized the Shia majority as well as the Kurds and other minority groups.

Did the United States have some responsibility to the people of Iraq? Is national liberation a just cause for war in the twenty-first century? The answer is not necessarily—liberating an oppressed people is not always a sufficient cause for military intervention in contemporary international life.[44] However, the liberation of the Iraqi people was a compelling motivator for many Americans, particularly after a failed decade of poorly enforced and scandal-ridden economic sanctions. When the humanitarian dilemma is added to the exigencies of international security, it seems clear that the decision to go to war against Iraq war was justified.

In sum, a sovereign state went to war with an international coalition against a rogue state clearly breaking the international covenants the latter had agreed to. The primary intent of the campaign was the promotion of American security interests—a legitimate motivation for the responsible state. The purpose, to modify Augustine, of the Iraq war was to "advance the good" and "avoid evil" by limiting a rogue state with weapons of mass destruction. Hussein and his regime were candidates for punishment in international life as lawbreakers and threats to their own citizens and their neighbors. Certainly the United States was justified in acting. A better way of putting this which reflects the core principle of political responsibility is that the U.S. decision to employ force was commensurate with its responsibilities to international security and the well-being of its populace, not to mention the safety of the majority of Iraq's repressed population.

Did the United States have to act? In the words of the Christian tradition that Just War theory is based on, would inaction have been a "sin?" Perhaps not. The dilemma of state responsibility is that states must make decisions about what actions are commensurate with their ideals and their interests. Thus, the moral course of action, at the least, was to consider the cost of action, the various possible modes of action (e.g. continued diplomacy, ignore Iraq, nuclear war, etc.), and then make a decision. Responsibility demands a decision, but that decision is based on the unique context of events and world politics.

Conclusion

Just war thinking brings ethical and practical considerations to the table when considering the use of force. The problem with some Just War theorizing today is that it and many of its defenders are mired in the presuppositions of an ancient world. It was a world of swords and slow-moving armies with decisions made by sovereign individuals. At the outset of the twenty-first century, it is time to consider how just war thinking can be useful in mitigating contemporary conflicts which involve rogue states, non-state actors, and WMDs.

This chapter argues that a place to start is *jus ad bellum*—the decision to go to war. Augustine and Aquinas argued that it was just to go to war not only for self-defense, but for justice, punishment, and restoration. I agree. In the twenty-first century states (right authorities) should be concerned about domestic and international security as well as human life around the globe (right intent). Such concern may motivate the use of force not only for immediate self-defense when attacked, but to curb violent non-state actors, restrain rogue states, and diminish the threat of weapons of mass destruction (just cause). I am not arguing that the tripartite categories of Aquinas be applied to every war in international politics.[45] Rather, Western policy makers should begin by asking the question about their responsibility for securing the lives, livelihood, and way of life of their citizenry.

Such twenty-first century just war thinking begins with the idea that states are the primary actors of international politics, and consequently have a responsibility to promote domestic and international order. This responsibility motivates thoughtful deliberation and sometimes action, be it diplomacy, engagement, sanctions, or the use of military force. The question now before us is when the decision to employ force has been made, how can twenty-first century just war thinking based on a political ethic of responsibility be us useful in the deployment of military force?

Notes

1. It is in this address that Lincoln calls for remunerative manumission of slaves. *Great Speeches by Abraham Lincoln*, Dover Thrift Edition (New York and London: Dover, 1999), 15.

2. Two of the best are Frederick H. Russell, *The Just War in the Middle Ages* (Cambridge: Cambridge University Press, 1975) and James Turner Johnson, *The Just War Tradition and the Restraint of War* (Princeton: Princeton University Press, 1981).

3. This famous quote from Augustine is referred to in Aquinas' statement following Objection 4. *Summa Theologica*, Part II, II, Question 40.

4. Oliver O'Donovan, *The Just War Revisited* (Cambridge: Cambridge University Press, 2003), 53.

5. Roger Epp, "The Augustinian Moment in International Politics," International Politics Research Papers, No. 10 (Aberystwyth, UK: Department of International Politics, University College of Wales, 1991).

6. This debate—how to employ the law of love in a violent world—turned many Christian pacifists such as Reinhold Niebuhr away from pacifism and toward "Christian realism" in the 1930s and 1940s. The Christian realist argument reflects Augustinian's call for this-worldly policies to thwart evil, even if such policies dirty the hands of those engaged in fighting for justice and order. See Eric Patterson, ed., *The Christian Realists* (Lanham, MD: University of America Press, 2003), especially chap. 1.

7. Aquinas, *Summa Theologica*, Part II, II, Question 40.

8. This continues Augustine's quote from above in Aquinas' Question 4. *Summa Theologica*, Part II, II, Question 40.

9. Aquinas, *Summa Theologica*, Part II, II, Question 40.

10. See the statement by the US Catholic Bishops "The Harvest of Justice is Sown in Peace," available at http://www.nccbuscc.org/sdwp/international/justwar.htm (accessed January 1, 2007).

11. As noted in chapter one, there are good introductory works that apply the Just War criteria in a systematic fashion to individual conflicts. See A. J. Coates' *The Ethics of War* (Manchester: Manchester University Press, 1997) and Richard J. Regan's *Just War: Principles and Cases* (Washington, D.C.: Catholic Institute of America Press, 1996).

12. James Turner Johnson, *Morality and Contemporary Warfare* (New Haven: Yale University Press, 1999), 34.

13. For a rebuttal to Johnson, see Richard B. Miller "Aquinas and the Presumption Against Killing and War" in *The Journal of Religion* 82, no. 2 (April, 2002).

14. James Turner Johnson, "Just War, As it Was and Is" in *First Things* 149 (January 2005): 18–19.

15. A superb critique of this phenomenon is Kathleen M. McGraw's "Manipulating Public Opinion with Moral Justification" in *Annals of the American Academy of Political and Social Science* 560, "The Future of Fact," (November, 1998). McGraw suggests that it is extremely difficult to detect deceptive moral justifications because of public ignorance of political issues as well as due to the taboo among politicians of explicitly calling one another liars.

16. Neta C. Crawford argues that responding in self-defense after an attack is a poor definition of self-defense. She suggests "a thicker sense" of self-defense which incorporates our "free and prosperous existence." "Just War Theory and the US Counterterror War" in *Perspectives on Politics* 1, no. 1 (March 2003), 14.

17. Thomas Hobbes, *Leviathan*, Edwin Curley, ed. (Indianapolis, IN: Hackett, 1994), chapter 13, par. 8.

18. A new literature is developing that applies just war thinking to humanitarian intervention. See Kjell-Ake Nordquist, *From 'Just War' to Justified Intervention* (Uppsala: Department of Theology Publications, 1998); Dean K. Chatterjee and Don E. Scheid, *Ethics and Foreign Intervention* (Cambridge: Cambridge University Press, 2003); Terry Nardin, "The Moral Basis of Humanitarian Intervention" in *Ethics and International Affairs* 14, no. 1 (2002).

19. A related point is that failed or repressive states—those who do not or cannot protect their citizens— forfeit their sovereignty to possible international intervention for the sake of human life and security.

20. Jean Bethke Elshtain argues that all human beings should be dignified with "equal regard" and that this application of the Golden Rule invites the US and other powers to engage in military humanitarian intervention to protect human life. See her *Just War Against Terror*, 168. Geoffrey Best points to the tensions between our aspirations of justice and human rights with the political realities of intervention in "Justice, International Relations, and Human Rights," the 21st Martin Wight Memorial Lecture, London School of Economics and Political Science (March 9, 1995), printed in *International Affairs* 71, no. 4: 785. A more general approach based on English School and quasi-constructivist approaches is Nicholas J. Wheeler's *Saving Strangers: Humanitarian Intervention in International Society* (New York: Oxford University Press, 2001).

21. This point echoes Jean Bethke Elshtain's *Just War Against Terror* (2003). President Bush's much-maligned *National Security Strategy* similarly calls for preserving, defending, and extending "the peace" (www.whitehouse.gov/nsc/nss.html, accessed October 17, 2005). Moreover, it seems that only the United States seems to have the will to act on behalf of promoting human life and security. We saw in Bosnia, Kosovo and elsewhere that the international community will almost never act unless the US does.

22. "Pax Christi Statement on the Devastation of September 11," September 12, 2001. Available http://www.paxchristiusa.org/news_events_more.asp?id=100 (accessed May 2, 2004).

23. Dr. John B. Cobb, Process Theologian, responding to an online question about the justice of the war in Iraq. Available at http://www.ctr4process.org/pandf/cobbfaq/ just-war.htm (accessed November 21, 2005).

24. Quoted in Elshtain, 83.

25. Numerous scholars have pointed out that despite the allegations that the US targeted and killed massive numbers of civilians in Afghanistan, the truth was somewhat different. As reported by the International Committee of the Red Cross and the Los Angeles Times, far less than 2,000 civilians were killed collaterally in this was by summer of 2002 (7 months after the hot war had finished). See David Zucchino, "The Untold War" in the *Los Angeles Times*, June 1-2, 2002.

26. Interview with Lisa Sowles Cahill, Boston College ethicist, *US Catholic* (December 2001), available at http://www.uscatholic.org/2001/12/cov0112.htm (accessed July 19, 2004).

27. Elshtain argues that much of the response to the war on terrorism from the pulpit has lacked theological rigor settling rather for emotionalism, evocations of Western guilt, and ideological tirades. She cites Nietzches *ressentiment* or "self-loathing" as a cultural crisis among American scholarly and religious elites, resulting in the position that September 11 was the fault of the US due to its policies and character. Jean Bethke Elshtain, *Just War Against Terror*, 117.

28. A superb introduction to the issue of the rights of ethnic communities to claim political sovereignty and national self-determination is Dan Smith's "Ethical Uncertainties of Nationalism" in *Journal of Peace Research* 37, no. 4 (July, 2000). Smith calls the rights advanced under nationalism "morally ambiguous."

29. See chapter 3 of Peter Temes' *The Just War: An American Reflection on Morality in our Time* (New York: Ivan R. Dees, 2004).

30. Also see Richard A. Clarke, *Against All Enemies: Inside America's War on Terror* (New York: Free Press, 2004), especially chaps. 4, 6.

31. *9/11 Commission Report: Final Report of the National Commission on Terrorist Attacks Upon the United States*, authorized edition (New York: Norton, 2004). See pages 109–110, 115, 190–191.

32. Some scholars have suggested that the way to deal with an armed and deadly non-state actor is the traditional application of international law on piracy. This means a vigorous military approach to extirpating the threat because pirates behave outside the laws of war and transgress the norms of civilization. Neal A. Pollard, "Globalization's Bastards: Illegitimate Non-State Actors in International Law" in *Low Intensity Conflict and Law Enforcement* 11, no. 2 (Winter 2002): 210–238; Joseph McMillan, *Apocalyptic Terrorism: The Case for Preventive Action,* Institute for National Strategic Studies (November 2004).

33. There is a wide ranging literature on the motivations and aspirations of terrorists which go far beyond the scope of this paper. An introduction would include Martha Crenshaw's important "The Logic of Terrorism: Terrorist Behavior as a Product of Strategic Choice" in *Origins of Terrorism: Psychologies, Ideologies, Theologies, States of Mind,* ed. Walter Reich (Washington, DC: Woodrow Wilson Center Press, 1990); Eli Berman and David D. Laitin, "Rational Martyrs: Evidence from Data on Suicide Attacks." Paper presented for the Conference on Suicide Bombing, center for Democracy, Development, and the Rule of Law, Standford University (September 2003); Sean L. Yom and Basel Saleh, "Palestinian Violence and the Second Intifada: Explaining Suicide Attacks." Paper presented at the 19th Middle East History and Theory Conference, University of Chicago (2004); Eli Berman, "Hamas, Taliban, and the Jewish Underground: An Economist's View of Radical Religious Militias." National Bureau of Economic Research (NBER) Working Paper 10004 (2003); James D. Fearon and David D. Laitin, "Ethnicity, Insurgency, and Civil War" in *American Political Science Review*, 91, no. 1 (2003); and Andrew Kydd and Barbara F. Walter, "Sabotaging the Peace: The Politics of Extremist Violence" in *International Organization*, 56, no. 2 (2002).

34. There are those who disagree. In a provocative treatment Michael Scheuer argues that al Qaeda makes some simple requests of the U.S., such as closing US military bases in Saudi Arabia and ending support for Israel. He suggests that the US would not be facing the al Qaeda threat if it were to disengage or try different engagement tactics in the region. See Anonymous (Michael Scheuer), *Imperial Hubris: Why the West is Losing the War on Terror* (Washington, D.C.: Potomac Books, 2004).

35. Many writers have tried to adequately describe the novelty of an international terrorist network based on radical Islamist principles that glorifies martyrdom and is disassociated from any state-building or national liberation enterprise. Michael Ignatieff calls al Qaeda's form of terror "nihilistic" whereas Joseph McMillan and others call it "apocalyptic terrorism." See Ignatieff's *The Lesser Evil: Political Ethics in an Age of Terror* (Princeton: Princeton University Press, 2004); Joseph McMillan's monograph *Apocalyptic Terrorism: The Case for Preventive Action,* Institute for National Strategic Studies (November 2004).

36. Not everyone agrees. In an editorial written for a scholarly audience immediately following the September 11 attacks and US counter-response, Jonathan I. Charney opined that the US' muscular response should have occurred only after prolonged diplomatic initiatives to the international community. See "The Use of Force against Terrorism and International Law" in *The American Journal of International Law* 95, no. 4 (October, 2001).

37. Remarks by President Bush on Iraq at the Cincinnati Museum Center October 7, 2002. Transcript available at http://www.whitehouse.gov/news/releases/2002/10/2002 1007-8.html (accessed June 4, 2004).

38. Statement of Prime Minister Tony Blair air to emergency session of the House of Commons, January 14, 2003. Available at http://archives.cnn.com/2002/WORLD /europe /09/24/uk.iraq/ (accessed June 4, 2004).

39. Statement by Secretary of State Colin Powell to the United Nations 5 February 2003. Transcript available at http://www.cnn.com/2003/US/02/05/sprj.irq.powell.trans cript.06/ (accessed June 4, 2004).

40. Charles Duelfer, *The Comprehensive Report of the Special Advisor to the DCI* (the "Duelfer Report"), (September 30, 2004), available at http://www.cia.gov/cia/report s/iraq_wmd_2004 (accessed November 21, 2004).

41. Reported by Kevin Woods, James Lacey, and Williamson Murray in "Saddam's Delusions: The View From the Inside" in *Foreign Affairs* 85, no. 3 (May/June, 2006).

42. Many suggest that there was an alternative to violence—economic sanctions. George Lopez and David Cortwright argue that the UN sanctions program of the 1990s, combined with rigorous inspection until 1998, resulted in crippling Saddam Hussein's WMDs capacity ("Containing Iraq: Sanctions Worked," in *Foreign Affairs* (July/August, 2004). However, the authors concede that the sanctions were a form of force and that the effects were largely felt by the general public, as Saddam's elite skimmed billions from the oil-for-food program, diverting some to the national security apparatus and millions to their own pockets. Sanctions are a form of forceful coercion—they can result in physical harm and even death, as allegedly happened to many of Iraq's poor during the sanctions period. In fact, the conditions surrounding the sanctions regime certainly strengthened Saddam Hussein's power in comparison to the under-class in Iraqi society during that time period.

43. It has been suggested that this is a post hoc analysis. I carefully outlined my argument for intervention in Iraq based on these principles prior to the invasion in a panel discussion, "Global Issues Forum: War in Iraq?" on February 2, 2003 at Vanguard University, Costa Mesa, California.

44. Although many in religious quarters agree that some form of military humanitarian intervention is appropriate *in extremis*, not all do so. Duane L. Cady argues forcefully against intervention based on pacifism. See Robert L. Philips and Duane L. Cady, *Humanitarian Intervention: Just War vs. Pacifism* (Lanham, MD: Rowman and Littlefield, 1996).

45. One could argue that the argument thus far regarding Just War theory and "old wars" is disingenuous. On the one hand this chapter argues about going back to the approach of Augustine and his successors but on the other hand it argues against being mired in the "presuppositions of the past." The position of this book is that the flexible, contextual, evolutionary *approach* to the questions of resort to war, war-fighting, and war's end is what we should preserve and promote in international relations study. However, the formulaic use of a specific *criteria* for every conflict based on the old model is what is not necessarily helpful.

Chapter 4

Fighting to Win:
The Nexus of Morality and Practicality
(*jus in bello*)

One of the reasons that the Vietnam War scarred the American psyche was the wide range of tactics utilized by both sides during the conflict. The American public had a difficult time coming to terms with the Administration's schizophrenic mix of policies, from the use of Agent Orange and massive aerial bombardment on the one hand to treating the Viet Cong with the courtesies of the Geneva conventions on the other. Similarly, the heinous treatment of American POWs, who were denied the protections of the war convention and suffered every hardship and humiliation imaginable, as well as the guerrilla and terroristic tactics of insurgents, seemed to dissolve all strictures governing how war was fought (*jus in bello*).

This state of affairs stood out in stark relief due to the fact that in the twentieth century the focus of international law and Just War theory was often on the ethical conduct of war. *Jus in bello* principles, especially proportionality, are not really new to warfare, although they were secondary in traditional Just War doctrine, because battlefield commanders for millennia have concerned themselves with pragmatic proportionality. However, the case of Vietnam reminds us that the two well-known criteria for *jus in bello*, proportionality and discrimination (non-combatant immunity), do not have universal provenance.

Twenty-first century just war thinking must reconsider how restraint is defined in terms of the battlefield. For instance, in an era of weapons of mass destruction states must reframe proportionality not in terms of harm incurred but in terms of threats perceived. Similarly, militaries must reconsider the issue of discrimination based not on an artificial conception of non-combatancy but on an evaluation of battlefield threats, from traditional soldiers to child soldiers to non-uniformed insurgents. This chapter looks at provocative cases, from the Taliban prison uprising in Mazar-i-Shariff to the attempted decapitation strike against Saddam Hussein, to apply just war thinking to the use of force.

The Moral and Practical Bases of *Jus in Bello*

Jus in bello, strictly speaking, means to fight war justly. What does it mean that the conduct of war should be just? Just war thinking presupposes that war can be fought *well*: decently, with propriety, lawfully. We want not only to win battles, but also to win in ways that are commensurate with our values and we want our troops to be well behaved. In others words, *jus in bello* is about restraint because, for ethical and practical reasons, the immediate and long-term destructiveness of war should be limited.

A skeptic might ask, "War is Hell—do you really think you can restrain it?" My answer follows Michael Walzer: "If war is Hell, we must restrain it."[1] The truth is that societies have long restrained the "dogs of war." Before moving to what *jus in bello* should look like in the war on terrorism and beyond, it is important to consider the pragmatic and the ethical reasons for restraining the conduct of conflict.

Jus in Bello is Practical

Military necessity is a cardinal principle of war fighting. It is the idea that the practical aspects of battlefield scenarios must be taken into account in light of the imperatives of troop protection and victory. Not surprisingly, just war thinking is often in tension with military necessity because of the former's ethical claims. Thus, for *jus in bello* principles to ever be widely accepted on the battlefield, they must demonstrate some utility, some practical relationship to the complexities associated with military necessity. It is not enough to claim the morality of such a principle and hope that it will become military doctrine, because in war someone will always use their adversary's self-limitations to their advantage. Therefore, for *jus in bello* to work the principle must have practical value in addition to its normative content.

There are numerous sage reasons to avoid the tactics of total war. By total war I mean the attitude that "all's fair in war."[2] For this discussion the pole of just war is total war, the idea that "anything goes" on and off the battlefield and at war's end one can expect at the minimum some form of unconditional surrender of the enemy, and likely more than that (e.g. slavery, ethnic cleansing, imposed ideology).

So, why practice *jus in bello*? It is worthwhile to avoid total war by limiting the means and prosecution of war and thereby constrain war's destructiveness, both during and after conflict. In other words, there are two practical reasons for *jus in bello*: to limit the conduct of war during its engagement and to make a lasting peace easier to achieve.

The primary pragmatic reason for not engaging in a crusade is to avoid the destructiveness of battle-to-the-death between societies. Total wars, such as the three Punic Wars, cost an incredible sum in human life, devastated property, and financial expense. The loser, Carthage, was razed in 146 B.C. The city was totally denuded of humans, beasts, and agriculture, the Romans sowing the earth with salt to make it uninhabitable. And the cost of decades of war on the Roman empire is impossible to tabulate with certainty.

Wars fought without restraint are too risky and too costly, unless waged against a significantly weaker foe. They are imprudent because they can result in a cycle of increasingly vicious retaliations during the war. For instance, German cities and civilians would likely have been spared the raids of Bomber Command had Hitler not first expressly targeted the people of Coventry and London. In short, the pragmatic reason to avoid total war is that it usually exacts the ultimate price: quid pro quo.

Not only is it wise to limit the conduct of war because that helps shape the immediate response of the enemy, but also because how a war is fought affects the likelihood of settling the war. As Clausewitz wrote, "It had ceased to be in harmony with the spirit of the times to plunder and lay waste the enemy's land. . . . It was rightly held to be unnecessarily barbarous, an invitation to reprisals, and a practice that hurt the enemy's subjects rather than the government—one therefore that was ineffective and only served permanently to impede the advance of general civilization."[3] In short, total wars, ones that target the lives and livelihoods of the enemy's citizenry, are difficult to conclude. Who wants to settle, except *in extremis*, with an enemy who employs rape, pillage, and torture? At the least it seems dishonorable to settle with such foes; at the most it may mean societal suicide. Political leaders feel compelled "to never give up" rather than settle with enemies who brazenly violate *jus in bello*.[4]

A third reason to avoid total war is that it inflames the passions, particularly of the citizenry. Political and military leaders usually want to limit war. However, the victorious government of a total war, especially if it was attacked first, may find it difficult to limit the destruction of the enemy when its citizens demand vengeance and retribution from the aggressor. For those who cannot understand the U.S. policies of unconditional surrender and the dropping of the bomb in the Pacific theater, one should call to mind not simply Pearl Harbor, but also the Bataan Death march and the treatment of U.S. POWs throughout the Pacific war. Unlimited wars—where one or both sides employs scorched earth and eradication campaigns—result in longer, costlier, and uglier conflicts than are generally necessary or cost-efficient.

Jus in Bello is Moral

The essential morality of *jus in bello* is the same as the pragmatic calculus: it is moral to restrain the conduct of war to limit destruction and make eventual peace easier. At its most basic level, this is the principal of Order. Order is an ethical category— without a minimal level of order and restraint all the other features of "the good life" we expect from community are impossible. The same is true in war. In most wars civilians can go on living their lives to some degree: most people continue to work, marry, and worship. However, in the chaos of a

Rwanda all order is abrogated and the rules of engagement become "do anything which debases and violates my enemy."

The related contemporary principle from the international legal paradigm is "lawfulness."[5] Most countries have signed documents limiting the use of force such as the UN Charter, the UN Declaration of Human Rights, the Geneva Convention, and the International Protocol on Torture, thereby acknowledging and reinforcing that at least some behaviors in war are illegal. To break such laws is illegal, the abrogation of one's contract, in other words, a crime.

To violate *jus in bello* also violates the principle of stewardship. The principle of proportionality is in part about stewardship: the calculated husbanding of resources. War should be waged in a manner that is miserly in expending human life and military materiel. This is not to say that militaries should be resourced on the cheap, but that there is a moral element to the use, or waste, of manpower and machinery. Hence, our terrible fascination with Masada, the Light Brigade, Gettysburg, and the Somme. *Jus in bello* applies to numerous decisions regarding the environment, the utilization of weapons systems, our tactics, and the like. The key focus of stewardship is regard for human life. When just war thinking is boiled down to its essential features, one is a commitment to the preservation of human life whenever possible. Thus, when policy makers and commanders are making decisions about how and where battle is to be enjoined, at some level their task should be constrained by a valuing of human life. The principle of discrimination is one way that *jus in bello* calls for such restraint.

A moral approach to how war is fought must also take into account how the means used will affect the end of the war. The goal of war should be a "just and durable peace." Such a peace is "just" in that it should be, ideally, a normatively superior environment to the one in which the war broke out in the first place. It should also be a durable, or stable and secure, context that addresses the war's causes and promotes a stronger peace. The means and methods of fighting, or better, restraint on means and methods, can make the settlement of conflict be focused on either collaboration between combatants toward a secure peace or something else. That something else is often vengeance and retribution. A war fought in unjust ways will invariably lead to a desire for vengeance that makes the termination of conflict extremely difficult, at least short of unconditional surrender. In other words, the prosecution of some wars leads to hatred, although to fight is not necessarily to hate. In conflicts where ethnic cleansing, torture, or other repeated violations of *jus in bello* have been employed, the loss of ethical restraint usually results in the prolongation of conflict into increasingly vicious cycles of retaliation. In sum, disregard for *jus in bello* can result in both sides forgetting what they were initially fighting for (*jus ad bellum*) and make *jus post bellum*—a just peace—seem impossible.

Jus in Bello: **Proportionality**

Jus in bello in classical Just War theory is made up of two criteria: proportionality and discrimination. Although in recent years great attention has been paid to discrimination, proportionality was traditionally the preeminent criterion.[6] The standard statement of proportionality for *jus in bello* goes something like this: the specific application of force in any given situation must be proportionate to the nature of the target and the immediate military objective. Hence, one often hears scenarios such as the following: "it violates proportionality to drop a 2,000 lb bomb on an individual when some less powerful means, such as a machine gun, is available." This is said to especially be the case when the individual dodging the ordnance is surrounded by noncombatants. A second common anecdote of proportionality is the following: "American dropping of the atomic bombs violated proportionality if the objective was to intimidate the Soviets."[7]

Proportionality has long been an ethically and practically useful principle for battlefield commanders. However, during the Cold War many tried to use the principle of proportionality to promote Just War pacifism by claiming that the means of war had simply become disproportionate to any conceivable human security. One shrewd observer notes,

> Any conflict undertaken as proportional means to the end of just peace will become disproportionate in the end, by virtue of two facts: it will have failed, or it will have succeeded. . .Those, then, who like to employ the categories of Just War to disallow every attempt at judgment by armed conflict know what they are about. . .Like the stopped clock which is sure to tell the correct time two times in twenty four hours they only have to go on saying that it is disproportionate for long enough and sooner or later events will catch up with them.[8]

The sophistry of those who would turn Just War theory against all war should not deter the application of proportionality in just war thinking, however, in an era of terrorism, rogue states, and genocide the conception of proportionality needs rethinking. Instead of thinking of proportionality in terms of means, governments should think of it in terms of threats. A revised statement of proportionality that is appropriate for the twenty-first century is the following: *the means employed should be proportionate to the gravity of a) actual harm incurred and/or b) the perceived threat.*

The first criterion seems intuitively obvious, unless one accepts the pacifist position. When one is attacked, proportionality is a tool for regulating response. It provides a limit on retaliation based on the seriousness of the injury sustained. Thus, a lone Ecuadorian soldier crossing their neighbor's border illegally is not grounds for an air strike. In contrast, the U.S.-led campaign in Afghanistan in 2001 in response to attacks on New York and Washington, D.C. at first glance seem to meet the first criterion.

It is to the second criterion that we turn. In the era of old wars threats were usually quite clear—either the enemy's army was in the barracks or on the march. Today this is not necessarily the case. Missile technology, the portability of weapons of mass destruction, and the violent agenda of some non-state actors and rogues states make the nature and imminence of the threats they pose far less easy to discern.

Furthermore, these days Western soldiers are more likely to enter a combat zone as peacekeepers than as belligerents. In a case of humanitarian intervention, what exactly is the threat? The threats are multi-dimensional: to international order and security, to human life in general, to our troops. We need to consider how threat is defined in situations of civil war, peacekeeping, and genocide. If a response is called for, then actions should be taken in ways that are proportionate to the threat.

When one thinks about the intricate conflicts of the contemporary world, the principle of proportionality defined in terms of threat is both useful and flexible. For instance, what is a proportionate response to a child soldier with a hand grenade in Liberia? To a female terrorist in Algeria or a suicide bomber in Tel Aviv? What is a proportionate military response to the forced expulsion of 500,000 Kosovars by the Serbian Army directed by a democratically elected president? What is proportionate to the slaughter of 800,000 in Rwanda? Congo? Sudan? Iraq?

The following mini-cases are an attempt to suggest the application of proportionality-as-threat principle. The underlying assumption is that proportionality begins with threat assessment in the context of conflict, and need not simply be a reaction to violence. Consider Pearl Harbor: certainly the ensuing battles were proportionate to the injury, but would not also forceful interdiction of the Japanese fleet have been a proportional response to the threat . . . before Hawaii was ever bombed?

Proportionality and al Qaeda

Proportionality is the idea that the means employed in conflict are proportional to the gravity of the actual harm incurred or the perceived threat. Obviously, the notion of threat is extremely difficult to quantify, and a "perceived threat" is even more ambiguous. A simple rule of thumb is, "Does my adversary wish to participate in harm to my life, way of life, or livelihood?" If the answer is yes, then the threat is real and should be guarded against, analyzed, and reduced.

Al Qaeda is a group of criminals and ideologues who not only promise violence, but also have indiscriminately killed men, women, and children, both in their own neighborhood and abroad. They promise security only to those who will live according to their arcane authoritarian system. Moreover, they have actively sought to procure and develop WMDs.

In the aftermath of 9/11, what is a proportionate response to terrorism? In the past the West has dealt with most terrorists as criminals, not as combatants.

Consequently, in the twentieth century the United States usually limited its response to terrorism to law enforcement activities. However members of al Qaeda, whether or not they wear a uniform, have clearly declared war on the U.S. and its allies. They see themselves as soldiers, as an army of Allah. They certainly are not civilians and therefore should be classified as soldiers, enemy combatants, or better, pirates.[9] They represent a sustained threat and the response to that threat should be proportional to the catastrophes that they openly hope to wreak on the US.[10]

Therefore, in prosecuting the war on terrorism the U.S. should utilize all of its tools to counter this enemy—hard and soft power in the form of diplomacy, economics, politics, and at times, military force.[11] As it did in the Cold War, the U.S. must be flexible in is responses and not rely solely on military power to win. Because terrorists have attacked in the US, Yemen, Bali, Afghanistan, Iraq, Madrid, London, and elsewhere, the West should recognize that the war has commenced and that the proportionate response to this threat is its elimination. In other words, the use of force involved should be adequate to contain or destroy the threat.

For example, what actions would be proportionate in fighting the war on terrorism if Osama Bin Laden's base camp was finally discovered? What about if an al Qaeda chemical weapons lab was discovered? If Osama bin Laden's lair was found or if an al Qaeda cell was working on a chemical device in an isolated bunker in a Malaysian jungle or the Yemeni desert, we should have no doubt that U.S. forces would attack in one way or another, either by sending in elite units to capture and collect the suspects and materials, or by massive aerial assault to demolish the compound and weapons. Such actions would be proportionate to the threat to Western lives, livelihoods, and way of life.

What if the chemical lab was under a village on the outskirts of Islamabad? Or under a mosque? What if Osama Bin Laden's compound included the wives and children of al Qaeda leadership living there? The nature of the threat is such that overwhelming force, if necessary to neutralize the threat, is appropriate. Commanders and civilian leaders must think about what force or forces are proportionate to the necessity of eradicating the threat. Does this mean that massive aerial attacks should always be used? Certainly not. If effective force can be used to capture, contain, and collect the terrorists and neutralize the weapons system, while preserving the lives of local family members, then that is the best scenario. But in the end, the most important objective is neutralization of severe threats.

Proportionality and Weapons of Mass Destruction

Weapons of mass destruction are particularly horrific threats because they endanger not only our present population, but the people and environment of the future. The devastation of a nuclear attack or dirty bomb could last for years. If an adversary's ideology dehumanizes its opponents, the probability that such weapons might be used increases dramatically.

Again, proportionality is the idea that we should respond proportionally to threats based on the likelihood and potency of the threat. In the case of non-state terrorist actors, there is no doubt that states would prosecute nuclear, chemical, or biological terrorism zealously after the fact. However, the threat is so dire that a proportionate response to the threat may include a long list of preventive strategies, from economic sanctions to military intervention. The two most controversial are military intervention against a state and the torture of an individual.

The U.S. invasion of Iraq in 2003 is a case of the former. The Bush Administration justified its intervention almost entirely on the argument that Saddam Hussein was violating international law and UN resolutions by an emerging WMD program. The U.S. argued that military intervention was preferable to the alternative: increased stockpiles of deadly agents, their proliferation to terrorists, and their future use against Saudi Arabia, Israel, Turkey or Western powers. Although there was tremendous international pressure against U.S. intervention, the Bush Administration nonetheless attacked Iraq. The question is whether the response was proportionate, as part of the ongoing war on terrorism, to the threat. Interestingly, the Duelfer Report concluded that Saddam Hussein wanted the world to think that he was redeveloping his arsenal and planned to do so at the first opportunity. In any event, if the United States really acted against Iraq because it believed that Iraq was an imminent threat, then in the context of the previously made decision to fight a war on terrorism against non-state actors and proliferation by rogue regimes, U.S. action was justified based on proportionality.[12]

A similar case can be made for torture. I abhor the thought of torture as a tactic in the context of war. However, as Michael Ignatieff and Alan Dershowitz have argued separately, there may be "ticking bomb" cases where the use of torture is proportionate to the threat.[13] Consider the doomsday scenario of an al Qaeda cell deploying a nuclear device to London or Tokyo. If authorities happened to capture one of the ringleaders hours before the bomb's timer went off, they would rightly stop at nothing to extract the necessary information about its whereabouts and components. In the context of the war on terrorism—a real struggle against a committed albeit unconventional foe, torture would be appropriate in this case. The act, although ugly, would be proportional to the threat. The harm to a mass murderer would be far outweighed by saving countless individual human beings and their property. In the end this is not to say that torture is a good *in bello* tactic, but that it is a "lesser evil" when compared to the loss of thousands or millions.

Proportionality and Humanitarian Intervention

Since the end of the Cold War, Western military forces have been called upon more and more frequently to serve as peacekeepers and/or to intervene with military force in situations of extreme human hardship or violence directed at civilians. The most notable recent examples are Haiti, Somalia, Bosnia, Kosovo, and Liberia. However, the West is also haunted by places where it acted too late (Srebrenica) or not at all (Rwanda, Democratic Republic of Congo (DRC)).

Most people, at least in the West, tend to agree that in some cases military humanitarian intervention is justified. The same people also generally believe that in a smaller subset of cases, military humanitarian intervention is not only justified, but called for.[14] Interestingly, although the *moral* argument for military humanitarian intervention is the saving of human lives, the usual argument against military humanitarian intervention is *political*: military humanitarian intervention violates the sovereignty of the state in question.

The issue of sovereignty, however real in legal circles, is a moot one here. This discussion is about proportionality *in bello*, not *ad bellum*. It is assumed that the decision to intervene has been made, thus the question before us is: how do we decide which "on the ground" measures are proportionate to the ends in military humanitarian intervention?[15]

The case of Rwanda provides a case in point. Rwanda is located in a dangerous part of Africa where tribal rivalries have endured for centuries. One such conflict in neighboring Burundi resulted in 50,000 dead the year before. In Rwanda, parallel violence between ethnic Tutsis and Hutus ended with the UN-brokered Arusha Accords in 1992. That violence reignited in 1994. Over a six-week period an unknown number of Rwandans massacred 800,000 of their fellow citizens.[16] During this time the world refused to intervene in force.

I have argued elsewhere that it is nearly impossible to conceive of any actor or actors in the international community acting on behalf of the Rwandans in April or early May of 1994.[17] What would have been a proportional military humanitarian intervention? Certainly not the rump contingent of 250 UN peace-keepers essentially abandoned on the ground at the end of the first week of the killing.

Again, if the international community decided to intervene after the killing had started, what actions would have been proportionate to the threat? What was the threat? The threats were multiple. First, the fundamental threat was to individual men, women, and children who were citizens of Rwanda and its neighbors. Likewise, the insecurity caused by massive refugee flows and the attendant disease, crime, and chaos that ensued was a local and regional threat. And of course there was the threat to the lives of the peacekeepers themselves, few of whom joined their national militaries to protect foreigners in UN peace-keeping operations in the Third World.

So, what use of force would have been proportionate to the gravity of such threats after the killing had started? Say in the second or third week of April, what use of force would have been proportionate to the daily massacres of thousands? In the period of hot conflict I assert that a large military force with robust rules of engagement would be appropriate. Such a military force would have the authority to impose martial law, be authorized to "shoot to kill," establish and defend safe havens, police communities, separate combatants, defend places of refuge, and imprison political and military leaders causing conflict.

Consider the counterfactual of May 7, 1994: 10,000 British, French, and U.S. troops deploy with armor across Rwanda. They impose martial law and secure safe havens. Citizens carrying weapons are immediately detained; those perpetrating violence are imprisoned or killed. This scenario would be heavy-handed, resulting in the detention of thousands and the deaths of hundreds, if not thousands. It would also likely mean the death of dozens of peacekeepers and perhaps even a forcible UN-backed partition plan based on ethnicity for both Rwanda and Burundi and perhaps eastern DRC (then Zaire), including resettlement of large parts of both populations.[18] The financial cost would be expensive, but the dividend of such an investment would be the saved lives of hundreds of thousands of individual human beings, as well as a practical political plan for the future.

Why overwhelming, rather than gradually escalating, force? There are two reasons. The first is troop protection. Peacekeepers generally joined their national militaries to defend their own countries, not peacekeep in international danger zones. Their governments should be cautious about their employment and use. Overwhelming force with expansive rules of engagement is most likely to protect both the credibility and well-being of those peacekeepers. Second, the goal is a quick end to the conflict, and rapid, massive demonstrations of force are the most likely way for this to occur.

The response I am describing not only did not happen in Rwanda, it has never happened anywhere.[19] That is because world leaders consider proportionality at the *ad bellum* level (what would induce us to violate sovereignty?) instead of at the *in bello* (what action is proportionate to this genocide?) level. Moreover, as discussed in chapter six, the UN uses an approach of gradual escalation that rarely works in situations of mass violence. This is because the UN wants to seem impartial and to restore the status quo. Proportionality in military humanitarian intervention should be about security—decisive action in the midst of human crisis to stop the killing, not a return to the conditions that led to the conflict in the first place. A revised doctrine of proportionality will commit interveners to a far more powerful military force and more aggressive rules of engagement to impose order and save lives and property.

In sum, the preceding argued that states should reconceptualize the old principle of proportionality based on not only harm incurred but the gravity of the threat. This chapter suggests that a new framework can inform the rules of engagement in the fight against terrorists, in countering weapons of mass destruction, and in military humanitarian intervention. The critical principle for the commander is the protection of his troops' and their homeland's lives, livelihoods, and way of life. Proportionality is about using restraint when appropriate but also about acting powerfully and decisively when necessary.

Jus in Bello: **Discrimination**

Classical Just War theory had two primary *jus in bello* criteria: wars were said to be fought justly when a) the means employed are proportionate to the ends of the conflict (proportionality) and "innocents" are protected from battlefield violence (discrimination). Traditionally, the definition of "innocents" has been "civilians" or "non-combatants" to distinguish them from soldiers on the battlefield.[20] However, the conflicts of the post-Cold War era such as intra-state guerilla warfare and terrorism problematize these distinctions. For example, how should soldiers respond to a child walking toward them with a large stuffed animal? In Vietnam Americans witnessed, to their horror, that such innocent displays sometimes hid a bomb sewn into the toy. The recent terrorist attack of 9/11 and the international war on terrorism will witness more cases of the blurring of distinctions between combatants and non-combatants. I argue that we must reformulate the principle of discrimination to accord with the times by focusing on active threats rather than settling for traditional military/civilian distinctions.

Discrimination: Making Right Distinctions

The recent language employed in discussing discrimination or non-combatant immunity is prone to terminological and conceptual confusion.[21] Are we talking about innocents, non-combatancy, or a distinction between military and civilian? Traditionally, Just War theorists have distinguished between combatants (fighters) and the "innocent." The concept of *innocence* in war comes from the original Latin, *nocēre*, meaning "to harm."[22] An innocent was one who was causing no harm, and meant women, children, and the elderly. However, a standard of "innocence" is not very helpful in making distinctions in the war on terrorism, for without traditional battlefields, it is less and less clear as to who is "causing no harm." Indeed, terrorists largely rely on familial, tribal, and other kinship networks within the civilian population for intelligence, respite, and resources.

More recently, a term used in discussions of discrimination is *non-combatant immunity* which contrasts "lawful combatants" from recognized "noncombatants." Traditionally, soldiers, sailors, marines, and today airmen, belong to the former whereas everyone else is assumed to belong to the latter. Again, this is a term that is largely outdated. Historically, combatants wore the uniform of a sovereign, legal entity, but in the past decade we have seen non-state actors declare war on states (Taliban, al Qaeda) as well as the rise of armies in failed states where there is no legitimate authority. Moreover, the contemporary challenges to the old notion of noncombatant immunity, including kinship networks harboring terrorists, child soldiers, the rise of private security firms, and economic and technological warfare such as "hacking" make the old distinction between combatants and noncombatants archaic.

A third set of terms that poorly reflect modern realities of war are patriarchal definitions of non-combatants as *women and children*. Since the First World War females have slowly been introduced into modern militaries. Recently we have also witnessed the first female suicide bombers in the Israeli-Palestinian imbroglio and in Iraq. The same is true of children. Adolescents and children are regularly recruited, or kidnapped into, rebel armies and paramilitary organizations in Africa and Asia either as soldiers, workers, "camp followers," or "trophy wives." Indeed, it is estimated that there are 300,000 children serving in armies around the globe today.[23] It is no longer adequate to think of men as warriors and women and children as non-combatants.

Similarly, the old distinction between *military* and *civilian* has broken down in some areas. Western jurisprudence defines the civilian as an "outsider" to military affairs, or better, considers warfare to be a breakdown of the civil order. Indeed, Western political theory, from Hobbes through the twentieth century, usually sees war as belonging to an atavistic world outside the bonds of civil society. This is changing. How should one think about the cases of "civilian contractors" supporting the U.S. military and intelligence communities in Afghanistan and Iraq? How should private security firms which have developed their own elite armies in Africa be classified? In places like Rwanda, Iraq, and the Palestinian territories we have seen increasing violence perpetrated by civilians against their neighbors. Again, old distinctions seem to be falling apart.

Reconceptualized just war thinking articulates a principle of *discrimination* rather than one of *non-combatant immunity*. Discrimination simply means making a choice about who constitutes an active threat as distinguished from those who do not. "Active" threats are those, whether in military uniform or not, who are actively waging or materially supporting conflict. Thus, the Sunni girl carrying munitions to insurgents is a threat, whereas the Pashtun male protesting against the government is not.[24]

Discrimination in this sense is at once a more liberal and a more conservative principle than the traditional category of non-combatant immunity. It is more liberal because in some conflicts it broadens the definition of combatant beyond those wearing a uniform to include any individual actively threatening the troops. This means that anyone directly involved in the war effort, from a political leader supervising the war effort to the suicide bomber, should be discriminated against as combatants. On the other hand, such a principle is decidedly conservative in that it protects people in and out of uniform who constitute no active threat. For instance, in the war on terrorism some rogue regimes should not be targeted because they do not constitute an active threat (e.g. Cuba, Myanmar). Likewise, it may be more discriminating to launch a decapitation strike against a target's leaders than to carpet bomb an outlaw regime's conscripts.

Most importantly, the notion of discrimination, or thoughtful distinctions in context, is far more realistic than universal non-combatant immunity in today's world. The reality is that Western soldiers and peacekeepers discriminate against threats to their mission and personnel every day. Real world platoon and company commanders decide daily in places like Afghanistan and Iraq every day whether various groups or individuals constitute a threat. Unfortunately, in modern conflict more and more fighters are putting on civilian garb to use the general population as a shield from within which to strike. Military leaders should practice restraint and discretion in their response.

Discrimination in Practice

Discrimination is the principle of distinguishing active threats in the context of conflict. In general, Western troops should attempt to hold to the old principle of non-combatant or civilian immunity while recognizing that in new wars danger may be hidden behind a child's smiling face or underneath baggy civilian attire. Careful consideration of actual cases will help us consider how prudent discrimination may be employed in dangerous environments.

POWs and the Taliban Uprising

Historically, prisoners have received different treatment from combatants on the battlefield. There is a sort of implicit contract between prisoners taken in war and their captors: decent treatment for compliance (or at worst passive resistance). It is this convention which allows for parole of officers, limited freedoms "in-camp" for POWs in structuring their life and hierarchy, and the like. In the twentieth century, specific international covenants were signed, namely the first and second Geneva Conventions, which specifically protect prisoners captured on land or sea. The heart of these protections is the idea that upon surrender, both captives and captors relinquish their right to employ deadly force. In other words, the relationship changes from battlefield equality and mutual combatancy to one of hierarchical obligation between captor and prisoner.

Such restrictions are valuable because they protect human life by discriminating the new non-combatants (POWs) from battlefield combatants. In order for this change of status to work, however, both sides must play by the rules of the game. Prisoners must cooperate and behave like prisoners (they can resist and attempt escape, this is different from massacring the guards). And captors must behave like law enforcement rather than battlefield soldiers (warriors). If either side violates this relationship, not only does the immediate system crash, but also this sets a precedent for similar scenarios throughout the duration of the war.

In the war on terrorism, the United States is fighting and capturing individuals who have no training in the law of war. They do not subscribe to the international convention between captive and captor. Indeed, we have seen how some Islamic fundamentalists treat their captives in Iraq and Afghanistan: torture and beheading. Regardless of the rules of war and the conventions of detainment, it is likely that irregular troops in captivity may rebel given the opportunity as happened in Afghanistan.

In late November 2001 Taliban prisoners revolted against coalition forces at the Qala-e-Jhangi fort, near Mazar-i-Sharif in northern Afghanistan.[25] Even today, some details of the uprising at the makeshift battlefield prison are uncertain, but it is clear that the prisoners, disarmed Taliban fighters, looted local arms caches and killed some of their captors, including an American CIA interrogator and high ranking Northern Alliance officers. The prison grounds, an old fortress, made an extremely strong defensive position and in the context of the larger Afghanistan war, was a crucial setback for the Alliance and its American and British allies. The reversal seemed to shift the local balance of power. The United States response was powerful, including aerial bombardment, leaving over two hundred of the Taliban dead.[26]

My primary purpose is neither to laud nor condemn the Allied response to the prison uprising, but to highlight how twenty-first century wars should provoke new thinking about discrimination. Discrimination means that an enemy "soldier" may not wear a uniform but nonetheless be an enemy combatant. Discrimination means realizing in advance that captive enemies may have little knowledge or appreciation of the war convention as well as distinguishing active threats within the prisoner population. This may mean tight regulations on prisoner conduct and other policies.[27] It may result in the use of powerful and even lethal force in cases of the breakdown of order. Moreover, discrimination means that when an enemy becomes a prisoner, he or she is treated like a prisoner, but than when they revolt and return to the fray, that law enforcement procedures are inappropriate in a war zone. A military response seems to have been *a propos* in Mazar-i-Sharif case.

Suicide Bombers

In the past decade suicide bombers have attacked American targets in Saudi Arabia, Tanzania, Kenya, and the United States in New York City and Washington, D.C. Suicide bombings do not only occur on land. For instance, on October 12, 2000 the USS Cole was attacked by suicide bombers who brought a small boat alongside the ship during a refueling stop in Aden, Yemen. The blast tore a hole forty by sixty feet wide in the ship's hull, resulting in the death of seventeen and an additional thirty-nine crew wounded. Although it was initially thought that the attackers blended in with harbor craft assisting in the ship's refueling, the evidence indicates that the attack was brazen, coming hours after the Cole docked and commenced fueling. However, the suicide bombers were not deterred by action from the ship's crew because the crew simply did not act. Interestingly, the Defense Department review of the attack recommended keeping the existing ("standing") rules of engagement for American war vessels, but advocated a change in posture from reaction to deterrence when considering threats and increased training.[28]

How can this be the case? Why no substantive change to rules of engagement which appear to have failed? The reason is because the Navy, like the other branches of service, has rules for engaging potential threats like the suicide bombers. The rules are clear: there is a geographic point at which an approaching individual leaves the civilian world and enters a war zone. In the case of the USS Cole, the sailors should have deterred the suicide bombers from approaching. However, in the past soldiers and sailors alike have been reluctant to prosecute those rules because more often than not the perpetrators were unwitting civilians, not terrorist masterminds. A response of lethal force against a car, or presumably boat, has earned the U.S. military the scorn of the media on numerous occasions in Iraq.

Suicide bombers turn the logic of war on its head in at least two ways. First, the Western conception of the warrior is one who wants to survive the battle. This made the Japanese samurai code, *bushido*, incomprehensible to American GIs. Suicide bombers, be they kamikazes or jihadists, see personal annihilation as an opportunity for heroic martyrdom. Western troops want to finish the job and go home.

Second, suicide bombings are generally sneaky and purposely target non-combatant populations or soft military targets such as the places where civilians or troops eat and relax. This was the effective tactic of the Algerian FLN in the 1960s and is the choice of some Palestinian militants and Iraqi insurgents today. Again, this is counter to Western policies designed to keep battles on the battlefield and limit collateral damage.

The truth of the matter is that there is no absolute security from suicide bombers. Anyone willing to sacrifice their life in the course of destructive activity will likely wreak some havoc on their target. Nevertheless, the principle of discrimination provides options. Discrimination means making thoughtful distinctions to identify active threats. In most conflicts today, that decision is going to be made by a low-ranking enlisted person at a roadblock or checkpoint as an unidentified person or vehicle approaches.

Consequently, pre-planning and training are essential. One way to discriminate threats is by creating buffer zones between the civilian and military sectors. Military commanders are perfectly justified in clearly delineating zones of danger that non-combatants should not approach. This includes roadblocks, signs, checkpoints, markers, and the like. When unauthorized civilians pass those warnings or enter the military sector, they have shed noncombatant immunity. The same is true at sea. Sailors on the USS Cole should have enforced existing nautical markers, even if it meant destroying the incoming boat, because the boat left a zone of noncombatancy and entered a battle zone when it approached the warship.

In short, discrimination calls for assessing threats. One way to counter the unpredictable threat of suicide bombers is to differentiate and enforce zones of security. Individuals who approach these boundaries are in a sense leaving the realm of non-combatant immunity and putting themselves at risk. The principle of discrimination allows for thoughtful yet robust rules of engagement, including the use of lethal force, against suspected suicide bombers.

Targeted Killing

Assassination has a long history in domestic and international politics. In theory, assassination is the politically instigated killing of a political leader through some form of treachery.[29] I distinguish politically motivated assassinations from the legitimate use of force directed against specific enemy combatants.[30] Targeted killings are the latter: force directed against enemy combatants in hostile overseas environments. Targeted killings are analogous to the use of marksmen on the battlefield—designed to eliminate specific enemy combatants who have already initiated violence against the United States. Moreover, targeted killing is congruent with just war thinking in the context of twenty-first century conflict.[31]

The United States has used targeted killing against some terrorists since September 11. For example, in November 2002 a U.S. Predator drone fired a missile into a truck in the Yemeni desert, killing al Qaeda lieutenant Abu Ali al Harithi and four other terrorists. However, a more controversial case is that of targeting a foreign head of state.[32] On March 20, 2003 the United States opened the military campaign against Iraq with an aerial attack aimed directly at Saddam Hussein. Military officials called the operation a "decapitation strike" aimed at top Iraqi command centers and President Bush described the action as "striking selected targets of military importance to undermine Saddam Hussein's ability to wage war."[33] After receiving intelligence reports that Saddam and other top Iraqi officials would be meeting in a bunker under a private home in Baghdad, President Bush authorized the strike, requiring last-minute changes in plans for initiating the conflict. Three hours after the command was given, two bombers dropped four precision-guided 2,000-pound bombs on the private home reported to be housing Saddam Hussein and his officials.

The targeting of Saddam Hussein prior to the "shock and awe" aerial bombardment was a legitimate attempt at targeted killing. The United States had not only openly declared its intent to attack, but also clearly signified that such an assault could be averted by the "departure" of Saddam Hussein. Hussein was a tyrannical dictator with personal oversight over the Iraqi military and security agencies, making him an enemy combatant.[34]

Did this attack meet the standard of *jus in bello*? Yes. The targeted strike against Saddam Hussein was justified in that it was proportionate to the threat of weapons of mass destruction and as an attempt to save lives. Had Saddam been killed, there is little doubt that his military and security apparatus would have melted away, as indeed they did after about two weeks of fighting. A successful targeted killing would have prevented civilian casualties and saved the lives of common soldiers in both armies, including large numbers of Iraqi conscripts who did not want to fight in the first place.

Targeted killing is proportionate and discriminating The case of Saddam Hussein was a legitimate attack on an enemy combatant—the individual controlling the Iraqi war machine. The attempt at "decapitation" was a strike against a foreign head of state in the context of war which could have saved the lives of thousands of troops on both sides of the conflict. [35] Striking against political leaders who support terrorists or who jeopardize international security, instead of wiping out their conscript armies, is consonant with Western values. Moreover, the United States made it clear that that it was targeting the individual as an enemy combatant in the context of "hot" war. Consequently the attack, regardless of whether or not it was successful, was justified on ethical and practical grounds.

Conclusion

War can be appallingly costly. It is not only contemporary wars such as the first and second World Wars, Vietnam, the first Persian Gulf War (Iraq vs. Iran), and the Rwandan genocide that exact a terrible toll on troops and civilians alike. Indeed, one can turn to any page in history and see the tragedy of war, be it the conquests of the Assyrians, the Mongols, or the Aztecs. In response, Just War theory and contemporary international law developed strictures limiting the conduct of war.

Unfortunately, the traditional Just War paradigm has changed little in centuries. Its principles were first elucidated when infantry actually walked, when cavalry was equine, and artillery was shot from a bow. Times have changed and it is appropriate to reconsider how decision makers and war fighters should prosecute conflict in the twenty-first century.

This chapter resonates a key theme of the larger work: Just War doctrine's past utility was its marriage of pragmatism and morality. Unfortunately, in recent years most Just War users, at least those featured in popular venues, have become quasi-pacifists insisting on perfectionism instead of dealing with the realities of this world. However, the argument of this chapter is that there are ways to apply just war thinking to war-fighting that are moral and practical.

A twenty-first century principle of proportionality retakes its position as the privileged concept of *jus in bello*. Proportionality, in the context of conflict, evaluates not only harm incurred but the gravity of threats. Consideration of and action against threats is the appropriate response in an era of weapons of mass destruction, non-state terrorist actors, suicide bombers, and outlaw regimes.

Similarly, discrimination must focus on active threats rather than on strict notions of non-combatant immunity or tired distinctions between "civilians" and "soldiers." None of the recent attacks on Western troops and civilians have been perpetrated by traditional military members in army uniforms. Instead, from African peacekeeping to NATO action in Afghanistan to the war in Iraq, threats come from individuals camouflaged by civilian attire in the local population. Likewise, discrimination means holding the right people accountable. In the Iraq case, it would have been best to hold Saddam Hussein and his circle of henchman accountable rather than bomb poorly trained Iraqi conscripts.

Of course, actual war-fighting is not all there is to war. Wars have causes and conclusions that are affected by how the battles are fought, and *jus in bello* is only one consideration. Surprisingly, traditional Just War theory has had little to say about what follows termination of actual hostilities. It is to this that we turn, applying just war thinking to war's end.

Notes

1. Michael Walzer has made similar assertions numerous times over the years, the most prominent being in his *Just and Unjust Wars*, third ed. (New York, Basic Books, 2001), chap. 2.

2. For this discussion, the alternatives of pacifism or non-violent resistance do not apply.

3. Carl von Clausewitz, *On War*, Michael Howard and Peter Paret, eds. and trans. (Princeton: Princeton University Press, 1976), 571.

4. Henry Shue disagrees. He calls for severe limits on jus in bello. Shue argues that rather than "never give up" and the utilization of whatever means necessary in cases of national emergency, the weaker party should give up, even if that means risking "terrible aggression" in the aftermath. See his "Liberalism: The Impossibility of Justifying Weapons of Mass Destruction" in *Ethics and Weapons of Mass Destruction: Religious and Secular Perspectives*, Sohail H. Hashmi and Steven P. Lee, eds. (Cambridge: Cambridge University Press, 2004), 153–154.

5. James Turner Johnson distinguishes between the Just War tradition and its offspring, international law, in his *The Just-War Tradition and the Restraint of War: A Moral and Historical Inquiry* (Princeton: Princeton University Press, 1981); Michael Walzer also discusses what he calls the "legalist paradigm," as distinct from Just War theory, in *Just and Unjust Wars* (2001).

6. This point is made in James Turner Johnson, "Just War, As it Was, and Is" in *First Things* 149 (February 2005): 14–24.

7. There are obviously other controversies attendant on dropping the atomic bombs on Japan; this is simply one that relates directly to proportionality rather than noncombatant immunity.

8. Oliver O'Donovan, *The Just War Revisited* (Cambridge: Cambridge University Press), 61.

9. The case has been made by numerous commentators that the "piracy" paradigm is the best approach for creating a legal framework for classifying and dealing with al Qaeda. One such example is by David B. Rivkin, Jr., Lee A. Casey, and Darin R Bartram. "Bringing Al-Qaeda to Justice: The Constitutionality of Trying Al-Qaeda Terrorists in the Military Justice System," Legal Memorandum #3, Policy Research and Analysis Series, Heritage Foundation, available at http://www.heritage.org/Research/LegalIssues /LM 3.cfm (accessed May 30, 2005); Joseph McMillan, "Apocalyptic Terrorism: The Case for Preventive Action," Institute for National Strategic Studies (November 2004).

10. One of the issues here is whether to consider terrorists such as al Qaeda members a law enforcement problem or the provenance of the armed forces. However, it need not be "either-or." A thoughtful case for a hybrid approach is Noah Feldman, "Choices of Law, Choices of War" in *Harvard Journal of Law and Public Policy* 25, no. 2 (Spring, 2002).

11. Thomas Friedman argued in an editorial that the war in Iraq is precisely this—a war for ideas between competing value systems in "Ardent Opposition in Backwards Regimes," *Orange County Register*, August 26, 2003. Joseph Nye has long been a proponent of "soft power," for instance in "US Power and Strategy After Iraq," *Foreign Affairs* 82, no. 1 (2003).

12. This is not a defense of the Iraq war. Although the international community obviously believed Iraq had weapons of mass destruction, they too were apparently wrong.

13. Michael Ignatieff, *The Lesser Evil: Political Ethics in an Age of Terror* (Princeton, NJ: Princeton University Press, 2004); Alan Dershowitz, *Why Terrorism Works* (New Haven, CT: Yale University Press, 2002).

14. For example, see O'Donovan, 59–61.

15. There is a literature applying Just War criteria to humanitarian intervention, but almost all of the work is about the decision to go to war rather than consideration of jus in bello during intervention. Examples include Kjell-Ake Nordquist, *From 'Just War' to Justified Intervention* (Uppsala: Department of Theology Publications, 1998); Dean K. Chatterjee and Don E. Scheid, eds., *Ethics and Foreign Intervention* (Cambridge: Cambridge University Press, 2003); Robert L. Philips and Duane L. Cady, *Humanitarian Intervention: Just War vs. Pacifism* (Lanham, MD: Rowman and Littlefield, 1996).

16. The year before, an identical conflict in neighboring Burundi caused the death of 50,000 with no international action.

17. Eric Patterson, "Rewinding Rwanda: What if?" *Journal of Political Science* 35 (2005).

18. For a critique of multi-ethnic states and the argument for forced resettlement based on ethnic homogeneity, see Chaim Kaufmann, "Possible and Impossible Solutions to Ethnic Wars" in *International Security* 20, no. 4 (Spring 1996): 136–175.

19. The closest example of such a robust intervention is the recent Australia-led effort in East Timor. It also seems that UN peacekeepers recent efforts to stem gang violence in Haiti goes beyond mere policing.

20. An introduction to the historical development of non-combatant immunity is James Turner Johnson, "Maintaining the Protection of Non-Combatants," *Journal of Peace Research* 37, no. 4 (July, 2000).

21. Jean Bethke Elshtain makes a similar point about the US action in Afghanistan in her *Just War Against Terror* (New York: Basic Books, 2002), chap. 2.

22. A.J. Coates, *The Ethics of War* (Manchester: Manchester University Press, 1997), 235.

23. Peter Warren Singer, *Children at War* (New York: Pantheon, 2005), 127.

24. This perspective is similar to that of Oliver O'Donovan who considers discrimination a term of justice. For O'Donovan discrimination distinguishes the guilty from the innocent. He defines guilt as "direct material cooperation in the doing of wrong." O'Donovan, 36.

25. For more details, see http://news.bbc.co.uk/1/hi/world/south_asia/1680506.stm (accessed May 1, 2005).

26. Carlotta Gall, "Witnesses Recount Taliban Dying While Held Captive," New York Times, December 11, 2001. A well-known hyperbolic critique of this is Stephen Gowans, "Truth Behind Afghan Fortress Massacre Gets Edited Out," in Middle East Times, December 7, 2001. Available at Global Policy Forum www.global policy.org/w tc/media /1207mazir.htm (accessed June 4, 2004)

27. The Bush Administration has struggled with some of these issues, including differentiation of POWs from "enemy combatants."

28. The Department of Defense report on the USS Cole disaster, including policy recommendations, is available at http://www.defenselink.mil/pubs/cole20010109.html (accessed May 1, 2005).

29. For a history, see William J. Crotty, *Assassinations and the Political Order* (Harper and Row: New York, 1971).

30. For a more complete discussion of targeted killing in the war on terrorism see Eric Patterson and Teresa Casale, "Targeted Killing and the War on Terror" in *International Journal of Intelligence and Counterintelligence* 18, no. 4 (Winter 2005).

31. A historical example of a legitimate targeted killing across borders occurred thirty years ago when Ehud Barak led a clandestine commando raid against Fatah terrorists living in Beirut. The attack successfully dispatched the terrorists and then the team returned to Israel.

32. The concept of killing a dictator or tyrant is defined as tyrannicide. Typically carried out by domestic citizens, tyrannicide is based on the premise that a leader abdicates his right to rule when he violates the most fundamental rights of his citizens, therefore rendering it morally justifiable to remove him from power by whatever means possible. For detailed accounts of the history and justification of tyrannicide see Franklin Ford, *Political Murder: From Tyrannicide To Terrorism* (Cambridge, MA: Harvard University Press, 1985).

33. Available: CNN.com, "Decapitation Strike was aimed at Saddam," March 20, 2003.

34. The horrors of Saddam Hussein's Baathist regime are well-documented. A terse introduction can be found in, "Life Under Saddam Hussein: Past Atrocities by Saddam Hussein's Regime" White House Press Secretary, Washington D.C., April 14, 2003. Also available at www.state.gov/p/nea/rls/19675.htm (accessed October 7, 2004).

35. A cogent expression of this argument is by Mikael F. Nabati, "Anticipatory Self-Defense: The Terrorism Exception," *Current History* (May 2003).

Chapter 5

Finishing Well: Security and Punishment at War's End (*jus post bellum*)

There are many reasons that World War II has been lauded as the "great war for civilization" and its protagonists as "the greatest generation." Historians garland Churchill, Roosevelt, and members of the Truman Administration as the leaders who prosecuted a war against barbarity and handed us a new world order in the aftermath. However, all of the post-war achievements—the Nuremberg and To-kyo trials, the Marshall Plan, the Truman Doctrine, the Bretton Woods System, the inauguration of the United Nations—were ad hoc. They were often experimental quick-fixes to the dilemmas of international politics in that day and time, and they were not tethered to a robust strategic and ethical analysis that provided a long-term future picture of what international relations might look like at war's end. Certainly some planning did occur on specific issues, but neither Churchill, Atlee, Roosevelt, Truman, Acheson, Marshall nor any other major figure as far as we know utilized a formal ethical framework to think ahead to the long-term issues of justice and security at war's end beyond immediate victory over the Axis powers, securing Europe and the Pacific, and prosecution of the enemy leadership.

Moreover, even had they turned to the Just War tradition for guidance, they would have found no *jus post bellum*—justice at war's end. Although Just War theory is the bedrock of Western ethics and law regarding the resort to force with almost two millennia of tireless consideration of the justice of going to war and the ethics of actual war-fighting, Just War theorists largely ignored *jus post bellum*. Augustine suggested that wars should end in ways that promote a "se-cure peace," but he was far more preoccupied with questions about the just re-sort to violence and whether the Christian, as an individual, could morally par-ticipate in war.[1] *Jus post bellum* is likewise undeveloped by the Scholastics; Aquinas focused on criteria for justly going to war, although he points out that punishment of evildoers is commensurate with just war.[2] Much the same can be said of Vitoria, Suarez, and the international jurists such as Hugo Grotius.[3]

Even the most influential contemporary just war works neglect a theory of *jus post bellum*. Michael Walzer's influential *Just and Unjust Wars* says little on the topic.[4] James Turner Johnson's multiple histories of the Just War tradition are virtually silent about *jus post bellum*, although he has recently suggested that part of the just resort to war (*jus ad bellum*) is the goal of a just post-conflict environment.[5]

Just war thinking must consider the period beyond the fighting's end. After analyzing the arguments against *jus post bellum* this chapter makes a pragmatic and ethical case for adopting a "justice in endings"[6] framework for war's end. *Jus post bellum* is multi-dimensional or layered, emphasizing Order first (stopping the killing), and then principles of Justice, including punishment, when appropriate. The chapter concludes with a consideration of Reconciliation in intra- and inter-state conflicts.

Arguments Against *Jus Post Bellum*

What is *jus post bellum*? Literally, it is the just end of war. *Jus post bellum* takes the past, present, and future into account: 1) What caused this war and can the causes be ameliorated, satisfied, and/or redressed? 2) How was this war fought, and are there legitimate claims for justice due to the conduct of the war? 3) How will the settlement create a just and lasting peace?

Although justice and reconciliation are superior values, they are often not possible at war's end. Instead, states must seek settlements that at the minimum establish a secure political arrangement that stops the killing and prevents further bloodshed. However, before consideration of the arguments for *jus post bellum*, it should be recognized from the outset that there are arguments against applying just war thinking to war's end.

First, some will say that an America (or "the West") trumpeting *jus post bellum* is really a thinly disguised *realpolitik*. The critique goes something like this: declaring principles of justice and reconciliation is simply a clever way of obscuring American power and interests via a kangaroo court. America will demand excessive security arrangements, inordinate military guarantees, and the like in its play for a "secure" peace. This is mere power politics by another name, disguised by virtuous phraseology.

This may be true. It is possible that victors will use the language of Just War to legitimize revisionist policies. However, such machinations do not weaken the ethical power of just war thinking, rather they pay tribute to the power of normative issues in war and at war's end. The very fact that most hard-core realists give lip service to morality is a testament to the value of morality. And in the real world of conflict settlement, it is likely that politics and ethics will usually restrain the U.S. and other victors from imposing onerous settlements on their opponents.

A second, though polar, critique is that *jus post bellum* authorizes idealistic crusades. In other words, a doctrine of *jus post bellum* might justify radical policies against the political and military leaders of opponents such as forced regime change, long occupation by foreign troops, the imposition of friendly governments, war guilt and massive reparations, and even (re)colonization—all in the name of justice.

This critique of *jus post bellum* is even weaker than the first. A thoughtful *jus post bellum* begins where all just war thinking begins, by emphasizing restraint. *Jus post bellum* is not a carte blanche for remaking the world in one's own image, it is the imperative to create conditions for state and human security in the aftermath of conflict.

The third critique is that of the moral relativists: *jus post bellum*, at least in its "justice" and "reconciliation" forms, employs a language of right and wrong that is inappropriate in the twenty-first century. This postmodern understanding of conflict asserts that "justice" is a problematic concept that is employed by the powerful at the expense of the weak. For most relativists all sides in conflict, as contributors to the conflict, are equally guilty. Thus, at worst *jus post bellum* is hypocrisy and power politics, at best *jus post bellum* should apply to both winners and losers as equals or not at all.

The relativist position is unsatisfying on many grounds. At the fundamental level, it is not true that politics is the absence of values. International politics prioritizes the security of states; domestic politics [should] privilege the security of society and of individuals. Thus, there is a hierarchy of values beginning with Order. In addition, it is simply not true that all sides engaged in a conflict are equally guilty. For instance, it is ridiculous and morally irresponsible to suggest that the Poles were as guilty as Hitler for the conflict in September 1939.[7] Even if we cannot employ universal values of justice in every situation, we can apply contextual notions of security, ethics, and even reconciliation on a case by case basis.

Practical and Moral Arguments for *Jus Post Bellum*

Only recently have scholars begun to consider *jus post bellum* as a distinct doctrine. The end of the Cold War and its accompanying maelstrom of small but deadly conflicts around the globe have created the conditions for a dialogue about ending wars well. But what should conflict termination look like? In a recent article Michael Walzer writes that a goal of war in the just war tradition is restoration, meaning restoration of the status quo ante bellum. Walzer recognizes that this is often not enough, and that some form of "restoration plus" is often appropriate.[8] Similarly, Brian Orend asserts that a just settlement "vindicates our basic rights of life liberty and property."[9] Orend provides a formula for *jus post bellum* emphasizing proportionality and discrimination in seeking justice, but suggests that his framework only applies to inter-state war. His criteria is essentially the usual Just War checklist applied to conflict cessation (right intent for ending war, just cause for ending war, etc.).[10] Elsewhere, Davida Kellogg wisely argues for a specific *jus post bellum* technique for punishing aggression—war crimes tribunals—but the article lacks a larger theory of *jus post bel-*

lum. Just as in *jus ad bellum* and *jus in bello*, there are practical and ethical reasons for striving for a just end to war.

The Practicality of *Jus Post Bellum*

For *jus post bellum* to have utility in the real world, it must deal with the past, present, and future issues surrounding the conflict. Michael Walzer writes that one characteristic of "justice in endings" is closure: is the cessation of hostilities part of a larger multidimensional termination of conflict?[11] A good end to conflict is one where the politics and economics that caused the war come to resolution, where the social and emotional energies of the conflict are dealt with or satisfied (through victory, compromise, or exhaustion), and where the military and geographical condition that led to war are explicitly dealt with. In short, a pragmatic approach to war's end seeks a durable peace based on resolving the causes of the war.

Another practical reason for ending war well is that it avoids stand-offs that perpetuate the conditions of insecurity. The end of some wars is simply stalemate: the stasis of two exhausted, yet surviving parties in a gladiatorial exchange. Stasis resolves nothing, but is extremely expensive as the decades of war between Britain and France in the eighteenth and nineteenth centuries demonstrate. Stalemate results in long-term, Hobbesian dispositions of military readiness and the potential for renewed hostilities which is generally in no one's immediate or future interest. The contemporary Kashmir and Cyprus situations are cases in point. No doubt cold war is better than hot war, but a negotiated settlement would be even better. *Jus post bellum* seeks a secure peace, not an intermission.

Jus post bellum is eminently practical because at times it calls for the restraint or removal of leaders who initiate conflict. In some wars there are obvious aggressor states whose policies are clearly identified with specific leaders. Slobodan Milosevic fits the bill. Milosevic was a warmonger—his policies initiated a decade of warfare and he was explicitly responsible for not just disrupting international peace but authorizing gross violations of *jus in bello*. A pragmatic step at the end of war is to remove the "bad" leaders who started it in the first place. Imagine how different the Kosovo crisis, not to mention tensions in Montenegro and Macedonia, would have been in the late 1990s had Milosevic not remained in power in 1995. In some instances disposing of bad leaders, via systems of international justice or even buying them off into exile, sets the stage for a present and future peace.[12]

Finally, a really useful peace settlement based on *jus post bellum* may move beyond the initial causes of war to chart a "fresh start" between the combatants. This was the basis for U.S.-Japanese rapprochement at the end of World War II. It is unlikely that raw U.S. force alone, nor the Soviet threat, could have created the environment of partnership that developed between these two countries in the 1950s and beyond. The United States imposed a victor's peace on Japan, but did so in a way that nurtured opportunity for many segments of Japanese society. In retrospect, what was more in the United States' interests in 1945? To obliterate or rehabilitate Japan? The U.S. chose the latter course and it has proven to be spectacularly successful.[13]

The Morality of *Jus Post Bellum*

A just and secure peace is extremely practical. It is in the interest of governments to practice restraint, seek security, and strive for closure at war's end. However, what is moral about *jus post bellum*? At the outset, we should return to the purpose of just war thinking: international security and the preservation of human life. Just war thinking is an approach calling for restraint: restraint in the decision to go to war and restraint in the prosecution of war. A twenty-first century *jus post bellum* extends this notion of restraint to war's end: post-conflict settlements should exhibit restraint in their terms and in the pursuit of justice and punishment. More specifically, many wars have ended with a victor's peace based on vengeance and destruction. In contrast, *jus post bellum* is moral in seeking punishment and restoration as well as focusing on a shared, secure future rather than on revenge for historic or imagined grievances.

Jus post bellum is multi-dimensional in that it is concerned with both *jus ad bellum* and *jus in bello*. *Jus post bellum* requires moral accountability for past actions, including the decisions by leaders which led to war. There should be accountability for those in power who are responsible for the advent of conflict, in fact, at times our military response is an act of justice. Suarez wrote, "The only reason for it [war] was that an act of punitive justice was indispensable to mankind. . ."[14] Generally, the breakdown of international peace is a complex set of circumstances, but in many cases war is directly attributable to the aggressive policies of a specific regime or cabal within the regime. Leaders are responsible for peace and security, and when they abrogate that obligation it may be appropriate to hold them accountable in post-conflict settlements.

The same is true for *jus in bello* violations. Soldiers and their leaders on both sides are responsible for their conduct during the fighting. A richer notion of just peace is one where steps are taken to hold those who willfully broke the laws of war in combat accountable for their misdeeds.

A related moral principle of *jus post bellum* is restitution. Michael Walzer notes that since World War II, and particularly in an era of military humanitarian intervention, "a more extensive understanding of restoration" is appropriate.[15] Of course, the destructive nature of war means that a complete return to the status quo ante bellum is impossible, and may not be desirable in cases of secession or civil war. Citizens, both in and out of uniform, have died. Vast sums have been expended. Natural resources and regions of land have been used up or destroyed. *Jus post bellum* takes the cost of war, particularly the cost in lives and material, into account and argues that when possible, aggressors should provide restitution to the victims. This principle applies both to inter- and intra-state conflict: at war's end, aggressors should remunerate, when appropriate and possible, the wronged.

An additional moral concern that *jus post bellum* addresses is that of punishment. Punishment is punitive action against a wrong-doer. It may mean loss of rank or position, fines, imprisonment, exile, or death. Thus, punishment is the consequence of responsibility and an important feature of post-conflict justice. Punishment is moral in that it moves beyond an abstract conception of accountability by employing sanctions against those responsible for initiating violence or transgressing the war convention and violating international law. As this chapter will later argue, punishment is a lost strand of Just War theory.

Finally, adding *jus post bellum* is moral in that its full realization will work toward reconciliation. The early Just War tradition was founded on the idea of "love thy neighbor," even in war. The principle of *jus post bellum* makes a normative commitment to viewing others as partners in a future peace. Such reconciliation is the ultimate step toward building a durable framework for domestic and international peace.

The Principles of *Jus Post Bellum*: Order, Justice, Reconciliation

Jus post bellum means ending wars well. However, the primary assumption of this chapter is that ending the war is usually more important than continued bloodshed in pursuit of better terms. This does not mean that one side should surrender simply to end the war. Rather, a negotiated settlement which ends the fighting and creates a stable post-conflict environment but which is short on justice and reconciliation is nonetheless a moral conclusion to conflict. Consequently in the real world of international politics, inter- and intra-state violence, and the numerous bloody wars our world is currently plagued with, we should think about *jus post bellum* on a case by case basis. *Jus post bellum* should be conceptualized as multi-dimensional, involving the goals of Order, Justice, and Reconciliation. Order is the fundamental goal of the just end of war. Some settlements will only feature Order, whereas others will add to Order features of Justice. On rare occasions comprehensive, deeper settlements will add Reconciliation to the principles of Order and Justice. Order is the necessary condition for *jus post bellum*, but in the twenty-first century we should look for opportunities to create peace settlements that utilize the deeper principles of Justice and Reconciliation.

Order

The first and fundamental principle of *jus post bellum* is Order. All wars should end in way that provides a minimal post-war order. Another way of saying this is that the end of war should be a situation of stability and security. This is a modest goal for it says little about justice, much less about reconciliation. Nevertheless, in the real world of bloody wars and dirty hands, a settlement that manages to provide for a post-war situation of security is a moral good.

Political order in the form of security for all parties is a moral good, for it is impossible for domestic politics to provide the conditions necessary for the good life without international security. Consequently, wars should be ended in ways that rehabilitate or create a political order that is durable. Such Order, at the minimum, is a security among states and thereby a security from outside attacks on their populations. The Korean Conflict is a case in point.

Order and the Korean Conflict

In June 1950, 75,000 North Korean troops attacked South Korea across the thirty-eighth parallel, the post-war boundary agreed to by the United States and Soviet Union. The blitzkrieg blasted across much of the Republic of Korea, catching the South Koreans and their U.S. allies completely off-guard. The ensuing war lasted for three years and brought the United Nations, the United States, and its allies into conflict with Communist China and the Soviet Union. At war's end more than four million people had died, including an estimated three million civilians.[16]

The armistice that arrested the conflict ended the fighting, demarcated a new boundary near the old border, and created a demilitarized zone between the Koreas. The agreement also led to a policy of allowing POWs a choice of remaining where they were or repatriation.[17]

Does this conflict meet any sort of *jus post bellum* considerations? If we take Orend's catalogue of *jus post bellum* requirements, the answer is no. The killing halted at an impasse, no wrongs were righted, and it is difficult to see how traditional notions of justice for *jus ad bellum* or *jus in bello* considerations were employed internationally. Although there was a clear aggressor, that regime remained in power without apology and without making reparations. Was this a just peace?

The Korean armistice falls short if our notion of *jus post bellum* is perfect justice. However, international politics is far from ideal. In the real world *jus post bellum* should privilege state security and protect individual human life. The armistice of 1953 did just that. It pulled major world powers, including the Chinese and nuclear-armed United States and Soviet Union, back from the brink of World War III. It de-escalated tensions not only in Korea, but in the greater Pacific and European theaters. It created a demilitarized zone and security guarantees for both sides that were superior to the situation in 1949.

Furthermore, the armistice preserved individual human life. On average, a million civilians died each of the three years of the conflict, as well as 250,000 troops of various nationalities. Many of those troops, both from the U.S. and Communist countries, were draftees. In 1954, however, no troops were killed in open combat. No civilians died as "collateral damage." Moreover, the peace held from 1954 through 2004.

Was it a "just" end? Yes. From the perspective of just war thinking the Korean armistice was a just ending because Order is a moral, and political, imperative.[18] Of course, conceptualizing *jus post bellum* as Order will have its critics. But consider the alternative. Should we continue prosecuting every war against aggressors until we can throw someone into prison (World War II) or force a defeated government to admit wrongdoing (World War I)? How long will that take and how costly will it be?[19] Should we refrain from entering into post-conflict settlements with aggressors because we refuse to recognize their existence (e.g. "Red" China)? This is hubris. In short, international politics is imperfect and justice is rarely attainable. Therefore, in complex and deadly conflicts we may have to be satisfied with a minimal *jus post bellum*: post-conflict settlements that promote international Order and the preservation of human life.

A Richer *Jus Post Bellum*: Justice

Order is a necessary condition for *jus post bellum*. Nonetheless, at the end of some conflicts, particularly since WWII, a richer dimension of *jus post bellum* has been employed—settlements with provisions for Justice. By Justice I mean that in addition to creating a situation of security, aggressors are held accountable in some way for their actions. Accountability is a moral principle based on the notion of responsibility—political and military leaders have a responsibility to their citizens and their neighbors to promote security. This is expected in domestic society, and when possible, we should employ the notion of Justice at the end of inter- and intra-state war. The same also applies for warriors and political leaders who, during the fighting, violate the war convention: they should be held, when possible, responsible.[20]

Most wars conclude with Order, not Justice. Indeed, Justice is not available at the end of every war. The reality of warfare is that ending the carnage soon is often preferable to prolonging the conflict in hopes of "ending with justice." Nevertheless, in those cases where Justice is possible, it should be pursued. Although in practice it is problematic, Justice may take the form of restitution, a payment of some sort to the aggrieved or the victim(s). A better mechanism for Justice in international politics is punishment—a penalty for employing violence in the first place or for how violence was perpetrated. In any event, Justice is desirable and may lead to a better peace that both sides can find acceptable.[21]

Restoration

In theory, a holistic notion of justice takes into account the losses of victims as well as the responsibility of the aggressors. In other words, there is a need for restitution to the victims and punishment of the aggressors. Both sides of the coin are necessary for a comprehensive justice to be achieved. The concept of restitution is that victims or their representatives are entitled to the restoration of something. Unfortunately, there are many flaws with employing reparations in international politics, not the least of which is that it is often impossible to return what was taken: personal property, a home filled with memories, or the life of a loved one.

Restitution is not punishment. There are critics who suggest that reparations are simply a "pound of flesh." Unfortunately, international relations usually conflates restoration and punishment, but real restitution has to do with providing for victims and is separable from punishing wrong-doers. Indeed, restoration cuts across the conflict—it is possible that both sides "owe" something to victims of *jus in bello* violations.[22] Although this issue is best considered on a case by case basis by studying the details of each situation, at a theoretical level reparations can provide an element of justice in attempting to restore some of the conditions of the status quo ante bellum. However, in practice reparations may result in more questions than answers.

Restoration may take many forms. For instance, the Romans forced the Carthaginians to pay an indemnity of 10,000 talents at the end of the second Punic War, as well as downsize their navy to a token force.[23] Similar draconian reparations were forced on Germany at the end of the First World War, including the expropriation of its navy and much of its merchant marine.[24] After World War II the Allies seized machinery and durable goods from the Axis powers as well as requiring reimbursement for the cost of war.[25] Vanquished Japan took "voluntary" restitution to an entirely new level beginning in the 1950s when it created an Overseas Development Assistance Program that provided "grants" to its Asian neighbors.[26] In the 1990s, the governments of some Latin American countries and South Africa awarded damages to citizens for the torture or death of loved ones under previous authoritarian regimes.[27] More recently, contemporary headlines have made much of the corrupt Iraqi oil-for-food program, of which thirty percent of the proceeds were earmarked for reparations to Kuwait and others.[28]

Restoration Policies in Theory

Michael Walzer suggests that a just war "should end with the restoration of the status quo ante bellum. The paradigm case is a war of aggression, which ends justly when the aggressor has been defeated, his attack repulsed, the old boundaries restored." Walzer goes on to note that this may not be enough—"a more extensive understanding of restoration" may be needed that includes reparations and "perhaps. . .new security arrangements, of a sort that did not exist before the war, so that the status quo will be more stable in the future."[29] Walzer notes that the punishments handed out at Nuremberg and the rise of military humanitarian interventions require innovations in how we think about restoration, but in his consideration of Rwanda he writes, "most states do not want to take on this kind of responsibility."[30]

Similarly, Brian Orend asserts three "propositions" for the "vindication of rights" at the end of a just war: the "roll-back" of aggression (restoration of the status quo), compensation to victims and punishment of aggressors, and deterrence of future aggression "perhaps through demobilization and the political rehabilitation of the aggressors."[31] Orend rightly distinguishes compensation and punishment as two separate but complementary components of justice. Orend problematizes the notion of compensation in two ways: "*how much* and *from whom* in the Aggressor [state] is the compensation to be paid out?"[32]

Orend's answer is thoughtful, although it may not be realistic in international relations. Orend asserts that the best course of action would be to utilize "the personal wealth of political and military elites in Aggressor who were most responsible for the crime of aggression." This makes sense because many aggressive dictators have amassed tremendous personal fortunes. However, Orend is concerned with vindictive treatment of the Aggressor's civilian population at the end of the war and argues for safeguarding them from overwhelming reparations payments. He suggests that if no "personal wealth of elites" is available, that a "token amount of purely symbolic significance" may be enough to demonstrate the principle of justice. If this is not enough, he suggests a "moderate, universal tax of some kind, for a pre-set period, designed to raise only the agreed-upon amount for just compensation."[33]

I agree with Orend that "from whom" should primarily be those elites responsible for the war effort. However, there are at least two further considerations necessary. First, the "how much" calculation is exceedingly difficult to nail down with confidence. Indeed, no amount of money will ever bring back lost homes or loved ones. Consequently, any notion of compensation must be intertwined with policies of punishment for those elite responsible for the war effort, and government agencies (such as the German SS) whose sole purpose was its promotion. Furthermore, the historical record has few examples of reparations policies that resulted in significantly enhanced security regimes.

Second, Orend's formula leaves out *to whom*. Like Walzer, Orend's model says little about flesh-and-blood victims. States are not the primary victims—actual human beings are. It is human beings who lose their fathers, sons, and daughters in war. This disjuncture between the loss and resulting need for justice for individuals and families on the one hand, in contrast to the formal mechanics of political reparative mechanisms which usually redistribute wealth from the losing government to the winning government on the other, is one of the critical dilemmas of compensation and punishment.

Problems with Restoration in Practice

The principle of restoration seems, at face value, to be straightforward: what is fair treatment for the victims of aggression? However, on deeper reflection restoration is a much more complicated issue. The questions raised by reparation are numerous. Most of them center on two obvious facts. First, people, not states, are the aggressors and victims. Second, restitution is not punishment.

How do reparations work in practice? In cases of interstate war, reparations are usually paid from one government to another government.[34] The Carthaginians paid the Romans, the French the Germans (1871–1873), and the Germans the French (1920s). In some ways, such damages are appropriate because it is governments who mobilize armies, pay for the war effort, and are left with many of the costs of rebuilding as well as veterans claims in the aftermath.

That being said, reparations are only a weak approximation of justice. The dilemma here is one that bedevils the study of war itself. Wars are fought and dictated by people acting as the representatives of states. States are the "legitimate authority," the seat of sovereignty, the primary actors of international life. However, it is individual people who violate *jus ad bellum* and *jus in bello*. Hence, the entire notion of restoration from a foreign government is problematic due to the conflation of the individual level of analysis with the domestic politics level of analysis.

Therefore, real justice would mean that actual people, not simply state coffers, would receive some compensation for their loss. In practice, this is rarely the case as creditor governments collect and spend the reparations. Granted, governments do pay for many of the costs of war from paying military salaries to major infrastructure rehabilitation. Nonetheless, such restoration would be entirely separate from the punishment handed out to aggressors for their behavior.

A second dilemma for the issue of restoration is that of time. Whereas punishment is temporal and must take place in the lifetime of the individual aggressor, demands for restitution know no such constraints. Because individual aggressors live and ultimately die, the fact that justice is never complete in this life is usually assuaged by the passage of time. In contrast, states endure. Thus, the descendants of victims would never ask for the execution of the aggressor's grandchildren but may make claims against a government in perpetuity. For instance, in Chile it is one thing for octogenarians like Pinochet to be punished, but an entirely different thing for the state, now in the hands of a Socialist president and former political dissident, to provide reparations for crimes which occurred decades ago under their political enemies.

A high-profile international case in point recently occurred in Europe. In 2003–2004 Poland and Germany issued counter-claims for reparations based on losses suffered during the second World War. [35] The Poles sought damages for the destruction of Warsaw at the same time as the Germans were requesting indemnities for the loss of property in East Silesia at the war's end. How should we untangle such a skein of claims? Is there no statute of limitations on restitution?

Similarly, what responsibility does a new regime, a representative one, have for the debts, both material and moral, of its authoritarian predecessor? Should the Iraqi government of 2007 compensate the foreign victims of a dictator they executed as a criminal? Did the German people of the 1960s owe something to the victims of the Gestapo? What many call the "Armenian genocide" of 1915 provides a case in point. Not only are the perpetrators of the terrible violence long dead, the government they represented, the Ottoman Empire, dissolved almost a century ago. However, there are some today who are calling for reparations. A more thoughtful approach to the issues of justice in war would focus more on punishing aggressors when possible, rather than trying to extract payments from successor governments. It is also unfortunately the case that in some situations there is nothing left to extract from the aggressor with which to compensate the victims.

What this all boils down to is the problem of responsibility in international politics. In few cases are actual individuals held accountable for their misdeeds. Instead, their state, via taxation of the populace, foots the bill. Often reparations are paid among states without any real punishment of the actual perpetrators. Individual victims are often sidelined from the process altogether.

Furthermore, in the battle governments fight against dangerous non-state actors, the principle of restoration seems almost ludicrous. In what way will the United States force al Qaeda to pay reparations to the victims of September 11? The same disjuncture is true for the victims of apocalyptic terrorism in Bali, Spain, Kenya, Tanzania, Israel, Iraq, and elsewhere. Twenty-first century conflicts between citizens represented by states versus groups committed to the overthrow of the state system will not conclude with indemnities paid by the perpetrators of terrorism. Similarly, it is hard to imagine an appropriate compensation program for victims of crimes against humanity. Instead, a *jus post bellum* for aggressors is punishment.

As observed earlier, restitution can be a component of a holistic framework for justice. Restitution may provide some damages to the victims but can never really repair or restore the ravages of war. Moreover, reparations fall short of justice because they are usually used as a substitute for punishment. The problematic nature of reparative policies should make us skeptical of restitutive mechanisms in peace settlements. Instead the focus should be on punishment— holding aggressors accountable for their actions, regardless of whether or not indemnities are paid to veterans and civilians. Reparations without punishment in many ways feels like "hush money:" pay off the claimants and maybe they will "shut up." Time and time again we have seen that victims and their families may be assisted by financial damages but really want the aggressor to face punishment and be forced to accept responsibility for the aggression. This is even more so the case in the war on terrorism. A robust *jus post bellum* will not substitute reparations for the punishment of aggression.

The Reviled Doctrine of Punishment

Punishment is an unpopular topic in international relations, as we have seen in debates following the U.S. response to 9/11. In contrast, early Just War theorists saw punishment of aggression as just. For instance, Augustine argued that just wars punish evildoers and right wrongs. Why is this? He recognized that politics could be the agent of restraint and moral judgment against lawbreakers.

Augustine and others extended the analogy to international politics: states can punish other governments for their lawless behavior.[36] This notion is also supported by the Old Testament. Augustine understood the early wars of Israel to be punishment on its neighbors for their violations of the moral law.[37]

In a recent superb application of the traditional Just War doctrine, Oliver O'Donovan criticizes Just War theory for dispensing with the frame of "justice" for one of "rights," thus making the sole legitimate motivation for war self-defense without punition and reparation. O'Donovan reminds his readers of the duty states have for punishing wrong and he cites Vitoria on this point: The victor must think of himself as a judge sitting in judgment between two commonwealths, one the injured party and the other the offender; he must not pass sentence as the prosecutor, but as the judge. He must give satisfaction to the injured, but as far as possible without causing the utter ruin of the guilty commonwealth."[38]

For O'Donovan, states act as judges in international life with a responsibility to promote what is right. I have suggested that a formal *jus post bellum* was neglected for centuries—a sin of omission. In contrast, in recent years the idea of punishment has been largely rejected in international politics, perhaps a sin of commission. This is probably the case because, as James Turner Johnson has written, the international legal paradigm distanced itself early on from the normative foundations of Just War theory. International jurists imagined international politics as a game played by sovereign equals governed by rules and custom rather than as a system of moral agents characterized by right and wrong. [39] The global norms of sovereignty and non-intervention made punishment for aggression, at least until Nuremberg, nearly impossible. Consequently, until well into the twentieth century the settlement of conflict, if not the rare occasion of absolute victory and unconditional surrender, was generally characterized as a settlement restoring some form of the status quo ante bellum.

This brings us back to the question: what is the goal of war? At war's end, what did we fight for? Certainly if one is attacked the goal is self-defense, first and foremost. But is that all? No, at the least we want to live in conditions of peace with security. Thus we want a post-war settlement which safeguards that peace and security. Furthermore, we want justice. We want to see aggressors pay a penalty for disrupting our lives, destroying property, and causing the loss of human life. Certainly not all wars end with an accounting for justice's sake, but certainly a principle of just war should be just ending.

In many wars, there is clear aggressor who instigated the conflict, usually in treacherous ways that resulted in deaths of many people. Moreover, many wars have obvious violations of the war convention and the moral restraint we expect in war. Some of those responsible are members of the military, others are political leaders. Some implemented unjust acts (e.g. rape, torture), others directed them. In any event, individuals worthy of punishment can usually be found but first must ask, "Why is punishment appropriate for some at the end of war?"

The Case for Punishment

Today when *jus post bellum* is considered we should ask, "How do we want to end this war? Is our goal a return to the pre-war order or do we want to see a new political order established and justice meted out to the aggressor?" Justice demands that there be consequences for unethical behavior. The consequences may be sanctions, occupation, loss of sovereignty, commitment to large-scale disarmament, or something else. Such accountability to the moral law, as well as domestic and international conventions, is personal and individual—we hold people accountable for their evil acts.

The arguments against punishment are based on the larger arguments against *jus post bellum* and will be discussed later. However, by punishing wrongdoers, we do a number of things. First, we limit the wrong-doer. Punishment in effect says, "You transgressed the boundaries of morality, therefore we are going to confine you within strict limits (e.g. imprisonment or even death). At the same time punishment reinforces the moral order and the durability of law by "calling a spade a spade" and acting against injustice.

Third, punishment may be a deterrent to other potential lawbreakers. Deterrence works for some crimes and restrains some criminals. The fear of getting caught, usually reinforced by a strong police reputation and various preventive mechanisms like surveillance cameras in obvious locations, will deter some criminal activity. *Ergo*, although deterrence is not a sufficient argument for punishment in *jus post bellum*, it may work in some cases. It is possible that the fear of punishment may restrain the behavior of combatants in battle (*jus in bello*), and that a track record of punishment in international relations may in the future help deter genocide and crimes against humanity in some contexts.

Finally, punishment avenges the suffering of victims. It is unlikely that retaliating against the aggressor will bring total, long-term peace of mind to victims, but, justice is often the first step towards healing. Punishment should occur as quickly as possible at war's end because when no requital is possible or offered the memory of wrong done by the aggressor will likely fester over time, often resulting in renewed hostilities.[40] It is perfectly reasonable to expect the aggressors to pay some price for the misdeed. We want that price to be discriminating (the right people paying) and proportionate (to the damage caused).[41] Punition is a principle of justice.

Justice in Action: The Nuremberg Trials

The London Agreement of August 8, 1945 chartered the International Military Tribunal (IMT) to prosecute leaders of the German war effort. Made up of four judges from each of the four victorious Allied powers, the Tribunal at Nuremberg and later Allied judgments ultimately passed 25 death sentences, 20 life sentences, 97 lesser prison terms, and acquitted an additional 35 individuals. However, the primary drama was the testimony in the first six months of the trial against the leaders of the German military and Nazi regime, and their sentencing at the end of September 1946.[42]

The defendants were charged on one or more of four counts: conspiracy to commit crimes, crimes against the peace (initiating aggressive war), war crimes (violating the laws of war), and crimes against humanity (genocide). The moral and legal logic of these counts is important. Most critically, Nuremberg symbolized the rule of law and morality, however imperfectly applied, at war's end. The IMT argued that war is not ethical anarchy, and that the laws of civilization and morality apply even in wartime. Robert Jackson, the lead Allied prosecutor and a member of the U.S. Supreme Court argued, "The wrongs which we seek to condemn and punish have been so calculated, so malignant and so devastating that civilization cannot tolerate their being ignored because it cannot survive their being repeated."[43]

Second, Nuremberg assigned individual responsibility for immoral and/or illegal behavior. Unlike the Versailles Treaty which condemned the entire German nation, the Nuremberg principle was that individuals were personally responsible for their behavior. This principle was applied in a limited fashion to senior leaders who had responsibility for the war effort and the Holocaust, and was applied to a lesser degree to lower-ranking members of the military and government who committed crimes while "under orders." The rationale was to avoid the collective guilt associated with Versailles and thereby reconcile the German nation to Europe.

Third, Nuremberg established the doctrine of "crimes against humanity." This is the idea that some crimes are not merely directed against individuals, but against collectives. The attempted extermination of European Jews, not to mention Gypsies, homosexuals, and other groups, was a mass murder policy, calling for accountability and punishment at war's end.

The Critique of Nuremberg

Andrew Rigby notes that there are many arguments against Nuremberg: it was implemented by force at the hands of the victors, it was selective in prosecuting only the defeated, it pursued only a small percentage of those who could have reasonably been indicted, it was not a trial by one's peers, and it held individuals responsible for acts normally attributed to governments.[44] These arguments can be made more generally against the doctrine of punishment in international affairs and are worthy of consideration.

The underlying argument against punishment is simply, "by what standard do you measure justice?" This critique is really the hidden claim that international politics is anarchy: the absence of overarching government and the lack of shared norms of moral behavior. Just war thinking disagrees. For Augustine and Aquinas the response was simple: there is a moral order based on God's commandments found in Scripture. Aggressors, in other words violators of "love thy neighbor," should be punished. Similarly, international law advocates such as

Grotius would argue that aggression violates customary law—it is the custom of nations to interact peacefully. Indeed, on a day to day basis most countries do interact peacefully with one another. Today, most of those states have signed numerous covenants articulating the quality of the peace. At the least, international law is a minimum standard by which to measure justice.

A related critique of punishment at war's end is the dirty hands argument: "We all have dirty hands, so, who are we to punish others?" In the Nuremberg case, the argument runs thus: "The British Empire was an evil world power. It and its allies were responsible for Dresden and Hiroshima. . .how dare we judge!" This view is morally immature. True, there are no perfectly "good" and "evil" sides in war. Nevertheless, the responsible individual or government can morally discriminate between lesser and greater evils.[45] When considering punishment, our own failings should make us humble in proposing sentences, but cannot emasculate our duty to justice. We should think of ourselves not as omnipotent magistrates handing down a victor's justice, but rather as peers initiating a trial by jury. In a real sense that is exactly what Nuremberg was—a trial of peers by peers: it was the trial of a state, as represented by its leaders, by the representatives of its peers—other states. Indeed, Nuremberg was a reaction to the failure of members of the international community to restrain their peers in Manchuria, Abyssinia, and Central Europe in the 1930s.

Third, critiques of punishment at war's end quote Herman Goering, "this is but a victor's justice." The implication is clear: the mechanism of justice, in this case the Nuremberg court, is merely a show trial, not a legitimate juridical proceeding. It is true that it is likely that the victors will be able to impose some terms on the vanquished. It is also likely that those terms may be harsh if the victor was the initial victim of aggression. Nevertheless, this argument is specious for two reasons. First, victors and victories do have limits. Even the unconditional surrender of the Germans and Japanese was not really unconditional because the Allied Powers operated within a realm of restrictions. Second, victors have a responsibility to law and to the international order. Certainly, they won, but their responsibility in the aftermath of war is to create conditions that will foster peace. Indeed, it is in their every interest to design and implement a settlement that is just and which makes the resumption of conflict unlikely.

Finally, critics of the punishment doctrine say that retribution leads to resentment and that resentment leads to future war. The obvious case is the German people at the end of the First World War. Hobbled by ruined industry and agriculture, humiliated by war guilt, and emasculated by reparations, the German people felt that the settlement of 1918 was anything but just. That resentment, in part, propelled Hitler to power and caused World War II.

However, World War I proves the point about justice. The settlement was not one of punishment for the sake of justice; it was a true case of the victor's unbridled vengeance. A just end to war punishes the right people discriminately such as political leaders and those in the military who violated the war convention. This is why most people feel that Nuremberg was just. In contrast, the Versailles Treaty humiliated and shattered the German people in ways that seemed unjust, at least to the German people. This also may explain why many people were skeptical about UN sanctions on Iraq in the 1990s. The Iraqi leadership continued to feast and swagger from palace to palace while the people slowly starved. A just punishment would have targeted leaders, not civilians.

Regardless of its shortcomings, Nuremberg (and the Tokyo trials) better approximate *jus post bellum* than merely ceasing battle. Nuremberg was a historic achievement—it had no antecedent and it established precedents which underlie contemporary international law. The victors pursued justice not only as victors, but as and on behalf of victims. In international anarchy there were no other obvious avenues for justice.

Finally, it should be noted that at least in the case of the United States, *jus in bello* considerations applied not only to the aggressor state, but also to the victim. Although it is unlikely that most violations of the war convention were brought to trial, it is telling that some American GIs were prosecuted for breaking the laws of war, mainly the killing or rape of civilians, in the European theater.[46]

In the end, 1945 approached justice—a comprehensive *jus post bellum*—in a way that went much further than the armistice of 1953. The terms not only ended the fighting, but also called to account the leadership responsible for initial aggression (*jus ad bellum*) as well as prosecuted *jus in bello* violations. In this way, Nuremberg "vindicates our rights" in a way somewhat like Orend's Kantian ethic.[47] Nevertheless, even the approximate justice of the Nuremberg and Tokyo variety fails to implement a richer notion of justice at war's end that can transcend past conflict and develop a partnership for peace among former belligerents: (re)conciliation.

Conciliation/Reconciliation

If Order is the attainable and Justice the possible, then (re)Conciliation is the desirable. Conciliation is future-focused in that it sees former enemies as partners in a shared future. Sometimes, particularly in intra-state conflict, it is *reconciliation*—building bridges between parties that have some shared past. In international conflict it is more likely that the goal is *conciliation*, the mutual effort of both sides to overcome past hostility and reframe the relationship as one of partnership. If the fundamental goals of just war thinking are to promote international security and to protect human life, then conciliation does this by ameliorating the conditions that can lead to new or renewed violence.

Christian Just War theory has a theological basis for reconciliation: love. *Caritas*, or love (charity), is the notion of brotherly regard. Love calls on individuals to protect their neighbors and may result in self-defensive war or intervention on behalf of allies or the weak. Love may motivate just punishment, the righting of wrongs, and restitution for the victim. Love calls into questions our motives, restrains our behavior, and foresees a better peace approximating the ideal: the City of God.[48]

Although I believe that reconciliation based on *caritas* is important in individual human relationships and can be called on in intra-state conflicts, it is a tricky notion for international affairs.[49] The international system is based primarily on national interests, and unless interests are engaged, conciliation is unlikely at war's end. In other words, *among states common interests are the basis for conciliation.* In most conflicts, enemies have a history of tension and competition, and have probably fought openly at numerous times in the past. In this scenario, a change in interests is the usual mechanism for conciliation to be possible.

Conciliation based on evolving interests is not a new idea. Rousseau and Kant both argued for a perpetual peace based, in part, on sovereigns realizing that war was not in their long-term interest.[50] However, in the real world, such relational changes usually takes a long period of time (e.g. U.S. and Canada) and/or may require a shared threat to provide a context for shared interests (e.g. Cold War France and Germany).

The Scandinavian countries provide a case in point. Formerly a region of competition and violence, today it is difficult to imagine a more pacific set of relationships than those among the Nordic countries. What caused the conciliation of these governments? The answer is not culture, language, religion, or some formal acts of forgiveness. Rather, the balance of power struggles of the nineteenth century, first the Napoleonic wars and later the Franco-Prussian wars, created a situation of shared interests. Moreover, this process of conciliation has weathered the tests of the World Wars, the Cold War (including Finnish alignment with the Soviet Union and Swedish neutrality), and the rise of the "New Europe" (European Union).

Of course, in international life, Justice might be a mechanism that helps change the socio-political context in such a way as to allow for a positive change in relationship. Certainly one outcome of Nuremberg was the effect the punishment of Third Reich leaders had on thawing relations between Germany and its neighbors. Acts of justice can provide vindication to the victims and provide the conditions wherein a change in the quality of relationship is possible.

However, it is more likely that the looming Soviet threat played a larger role in Germany and its former adversaries coming to a shared set of strategic interests. The development of Western European institutions, including the Coal and Steel Community, atomic cooperation, NATO, and the EEC all are rooted in mutual interests and shared threats, not forgiveness and reconciliation.

Idealists argue that forgiveness and mercy is the fulcrum for conciliation in international affairs. I am skeptical that this is the case. There are almost no examples in international life of heads of state asking for forgiveness from their neighbors, and resulting acts of conciliation among states. The reasons for this are numerous, but primary among them is the multi-causal nature of conflict and the recognition that states go to war because they feel that it is in their interest to do so. States are self-interested and it is folly to expect them, except under the most unique of circumstances, to plea, "We were wrong, won't you please forgive us?"[51] Consequently, the mercy/forgiveness path to conciliation among states is improbable at best, however, conciliation is possible based on the evolution or reinterpretation of national interests.[52]

Conclusion

In the past wars have simply ended. In general, wars end in stalemate or in a victor's peace. Although Augustine said that war was just if it was waged for self-defense, to right a wrong, or to punish evil, medieval and contemporary Just War theorists have largely focused on *jus ad bellum* and *jus in bello*, excluding consideration of the post-conflict environment.

Therefore, a natural area of consideration for contemporary scholarship is *jus post bellum*—justice at war's end. Such a discussion is particularly timely in light of the types of conflict we have seen in the past decade: ethnic and religious nationalisms, civil war, genocide enhanced with modern tools of warfare, international terrorism, and the possibility of weapons of mass destruction being employed against civilian population centers in any of these scenarios.

Jus post bellum begins with the concept of Order. Order is a moral principle in that it is the foundation for domestic and international security. Just War theory has historically privileged Order as the practical and necessary condition for more robust scenarios of Justice. As Table 1 below indicates, *jus post bellum* is built on the notion that Order and security come first. Therefore, a war is said to end justly if it establishes a secure framework for peace between the belligerents even if deeper issues of justice and reconciliation are not resolved. Such a peace promotes international security and preserves human life, which should be the fundamental goals of twenty-first century just war thinking.

Table 1. Elements of *jus post bellum*.

Reconciliation
Justice
Order

That being said, the goals at war's end should be richer than mere Order. When possible, the parties involved should seek post-conflict Justice. Such Justice should hold accountable both the leaders who incited the war as well as individuals who violated the war convention in the prosecution of war. Of course, a settlement that does not provide a secure framework (Order) for the peace will not be able to employ processes of Justice except against its own personnel who violated the laws of armed conflict. Nevertheless, intra- and inter-state post-conflict settlements are more likely to endure if they seek Justice.

Finally, it is possible that in some cases Conciliation is possible between those involved in the conflict. In international relations, Conciliation proceeds from an environment of security and is based on shared interests. In some rare cases, Justice provides a change in relationship that makes Conciliation possible. Reconciliation is more likely in cases of civil war or past strife where there is a shared past that can be built upon, and a future that must be shared. (Re)Conciliation should be the ultimate goal of *jus post bellum* because it changes the relationship of those involved in conflict from belligerents to partners in peace.

In sum, *jus post bellum* is essential to a comprehensive just war thinking. Durable post-war settlements that promote Order, Justice, and when possible, Conciliation, restrain future conflicts from breaking out over unresolved disputes and old grievances. Moreover, *jus post bellum* provides a new venue for scholarship by philosophers and practitioners of politics in elucidating specific mechanisms and structures for a just and lasting peace.

Notes

1. See Augustine's "Letter to Boniface" as well as *City of God* (i.e. Book XIX).

2. St. Thomas Aquinas, *The Summa Theologica* Part II, Question 40 (New York: Benziger Bros., 1947).

3. Interestingly, Suarez did point out the importance of war's end, but failed to develop a cogent jus post bellum. He wrote, "Three periods must be distinguished with respect to every war: its inception; its prosecution before victory is gained; and the period after victory." Quoted in Davida E. Kellogg, "Jus Post Bellum: The Importance of War Crimes Trials" in *Parameters* 32, no. 3 (Autumn, 2002): 87.

4. As a political philosopher, Walzer does not claim that Just and Just Wars elucidates a Christian or traditional Just War perspective. Although he references the tradition, his work is largely based on his own working out of justice-in-war claims within a Western worldview. He does not articulate a jus post bellum, but Part V of his book does deal with the issues of responsibility, war crimes, and military necessity. In his discussion of the Korean Conflict, he speaks of "justice in settlements."

5. James Turner Johnson, *Morality and Contemporary Warfare* (New Haven, CT: Yale University Press, 1999), 33.

6. Michael Walzer, "The Triumph of Just War Theory" in *Arguing About War* (New Haven, CT: Yale University Press, 2004), 18.

7. Perhaps the best statement of this is Reinhold Niebuhr's "To Prevent the Triumph of an Intolerable Tyranny" in *The Christian Century* December 18, 1940, reprinted in D.B. Robertson, ed. *Love and Justice: Selections from the Writings of Reinhold Niebuhr* (Louisville, KY: Westminster John Knox Press, 1957), 28–29.

8. Michael Walzer, *Arguing About War*, 18.

9. Brian Orend, "Justice After War," in *Ethics and International Affairs* 16, no. 1 (Spring 2002): 45.

10. Orend, "Justice After War." Also see Orend's book *War and International Justice: A Kantian Perspective* (Waterloo, Ontario, Canada: Wilfrid Laurier Press, 2000).

11. Walzer, *Arguing About War*, 18.

12. See Louis Sell, *Slobodan Milosevic and the Destruction of Yugoslavia* (Durham, NC: Duke University Press, 2002) and Laura Silber and Allan Little, *Yugoslavia: Death of a Nation* (New York: Penguin, 1997); on Kosovo see Leonard J. Cohen, *Serpent in the Bosom: The Rise and Fall of Slobodan Milosevic* (Boulder, CO: Westview Press, 2002).

13. A recent Pulitzer-prize winning account of this is John Dower's *Embracing Defeat: Japan in the Wake of World War II* (New York: W.W. Norton, 1999).

14. Quoted in O'Donovan, 18.

15. Walzer, *Arguing About War*, 18.

16. Paterson, Clifford and Hagan report 500,000 North Korean, 47,000 South Korean, 54,246 American, and 148,000 Chinese troops, as well as other UN forces, died in the Korean Conflict. *American Foreign Relations Since 1895: A History* (Boston, MA: Houghton Mifflin, 2000), 272.

17. See William Stueck, *Rethinking the Korean War : A New Diplomatic and Strategic History* (Princeton, NJ: Princeton University Press, 2004); Spencer C. Tucker et al, *Encyclopedia of the Korean War: A Political, Social, and Military History* (New York: Facts on File, 2002).

18. Michael Walzer has an interesting account of the Korean War. His purpose is to discuss the "inflation of ends" (the goal of the war, at least for MacArthur, went from defending South Korea to punishing and liberating North Korea). His conclusion is that "just wars are conservative in character" and should generally seek "a better peace," not a revised international system. Michael Walzer, *Just and Unjust Wars*, 3rd edition (New York: Basic Books, 2000), 121.

19. In addition, most just war theorists are extremely uncomfortable with the "unconditional surrender" policies which make war crimes tribunals and international judgments possible. Brian Orend argues that proportionality and discrimination make unconditional surrender impossible. Orend, *War and International Justice*, 228–230.

20. Moreover, the codification of the Geneva protocols, as well as the American Uniform Code of Military Justice, became the basis for numerous trials of American GIs during the Vietnam conflict.

21. There is a burgeoning literature on related topics. See Rami Mani, *Beyond Retribution: Seeking Justice in the Shadows of War* (Cambridge: Polity Press, 2002); Michael Walzer, "Just and Unjust Occupations" in *Dissent* 51 (Winter 2004).

22. Western discussions of reparations usually occur in the context of twentieth-century Allied victories in the World Wars. One rarely reads scholarship on "reparations" demanded by a victorious aggressor against its victims. Again, the notion of restoration needs conceptual clarity.

23. See Adrian Goldsworthy, *The Fall of Carthage: The Punic Wars 265–146 BC* (London: Cassell, 2004), chap. 6.

24. There is a long list of references on this topic, one of the most interesting being Robert E. Bunselmeyer, *Cost of the War 1914–1919: British Economic War Aims and the Origins of Reparation* (London: Archon, 1975). For a post hoc (revised) look at his country's own policies, see David Lloyd George's *Truth About Reparations and War Debts* (London: Howard Fertig, 1970).

25. Ian Dear, M.R.D. Foot, and I.C.B. Dear, eds. *The Oxford Companion to World War II* (Oxford: Oxford University Press, 2001), 591–593, 1006–1008.

26. Micheline Beaudry-Somcynsky and Chris M. Cook, *Japan's System of Official Development Assistance: Profiles in Partnership* (New York: International Development Research Center, 2001). One apologist for Japan's post-war commitment to "reparations" can be found at http://www.jiyuu-shikan.org/e/db4a.html (accessed July 20, 2005).

27. One such example in the literature is Richard Wilson's *The Politics of Truth and Reconciliation in South Africa: Legitimizing the Post-Apartheid State* (Cambridge Studies in Law and Society) (Cambridge: Cambridge University Press, 2001). An important volume on Latin America cases is *Democracy and Human Rights in Latin America*, Richard S. Hillman, John A. Peeler, and Elsa Cardozo da Silva, eds. (New York: Praeger, 2001).

28. Critiques of the use of sanctions as a blunt tool for punishment include T. Clifton Morgan and Valerie L. Schwebach, "Fools Suffer Gladly: The Use of Economic Sanctions in International Crises" in *International Studies Quarterly* 41, no. 1 (March, 1997); Kim Richard Nossal, "International Sanctions as International Punishment" in *International Organization* 43, no. 2 (Spring, 1998).

29. Walzer, *Arguing About War*, 18–19.

30. Walzer, 19.

31. Brian Orend, *War and International Justice: A Kantian Perspective*, 226.

32. Orend, 227.

33. Orend, 227.

34. In cases of domestic regime change (e.g. South Africa), the new government may redress past wrongs with financial compensation and perhaps even a direct public apology. As noted above, such acts are well-documented elsewhere and are not the focus of this study because they are not clearly the immediate consequence of war.

35. "Poland, Germany, appoint coordinators to improve ties" in eubusiness.com, April 11, 2004, available at http://www.eubusiness.com/Germany/041104140603.uzdnf9 jh (accessed June 25, 2005).

36. For those who do not want to trudge through Augustine's various writings on war, Paul Ramsey provides a comprehensive overview in *War and the Christian Conscience* (Durham, NC: Duke University Press, 1961), chapter 2.

37. Johnson, *The Just War Tradition and the Restraint of War*, xxix.

38. Francisco de Vitoria, *Political Writings*. Anthony Pagden and Jeremy Lawrence, eds. and trans. (Cambridge-New York: Cambridge University Press, 1991), 327.

39. James Turner Johnson, *Ideology, Reason, and the Limitation of War: Religious and Secular Concepts* (Princeton, NJ: Princeton University Press, 1974), especially chapters 3-4.

40. Oliver O'Donovan argues that timeliness is one of several features of an ideal tribunal for war's end. *The Just War Revisited*, 112–113.

41. Orend, *War and International Justice*, 227.

42. See Eugene Davidson, *The Trial of the Germans: An Account of the Twenty-Two Defendants Before the International Military Tribunal at Nuremberg* (Columbia, MO: University of Missouri Press, 1997); Joseph E. Persico, *Nuremberg: Infamy on Trial* (New York: Penguin, 1995); Drexel A. Sprecher, *Inside the Nuremberg Trial* (Lanham, MD: University of America Press, 1999). It should be noted that in addition to the trial of the twenty-two top Nazi leaders at Nuremberg, the Allies continued to try Nazis through 1949 under the Control Council 10 law; these numbers account for both.

43. Sprecher, 103.

44. Rigby, *Justice and Reconciliation*, 4–5.

45. Reinhold Niebuhr termed this "discerning the signs of the times," and called for us to evaluate the moral character not only of the actions of others, but our own actions and motives as well. Niebuhr, *Discerning the Signs of the Times: Sermons for Today and Tomorrow* (London: SCM Press, 1946). A similar argument from the Christian realist perspective underlies Jean Bethke Elshtain's *Just War Against Terror: The Burden of American Power in a Violent World* (New York: Basic Books, 2003). A secular "lesser evil" argument can be found in Michael Ignatieff's *The Lesser Evil: Politics in an Age of Terror* (Princeton, NJ: Princeton University Press, 2004).

46. J. Robert Lilly and J. Michael Thompson "Death Penalty Cases in World War II Military Courts: Lessons Learned from North Africa and Italy." Paper presented at the 41st meeting of the Academy of Criminal Justice Sciences, March 10-13, 2004, Las Vegas, NV. Available at http://www.nku.edu/~thomson/ACJS04.pdf (accessed May 5, 2005).

47. Orend, *War and International Justice*, 222.

48. Paul Ramsey, War *and the Christian Conscience*, chapter 2; Augustine, *The City of God* (Cambridge: Cambridge University Press, 1994).

49. There is a growing literature on domestic reconciliation, forgiveness, and intra-state change. For examples see A. Boraine et al, *Dealing with the Past: Truth and Reconciliation in South Africa* (Cape Town: IDASA, 1994); Brian Frost, *The Politics of Peace* (London: Darton, Longman, and Todd, Ltd., 1991); James L. Gibson and Amanda Gouws, "Truth and Reconciliation in South Africa: Attributions of Blame and the Struggle over Apartheid" in *American Political Science Review* 93, no. 3 (September, 1999); Neil J. Kritz, ed., *Transitional Justice: How Emerging Democracies Reckon with Former Regimes*, vol. 2 (Washington, DC: US Institute of Peace, 1995); Dan Markel, "The Justice of Amnesty? Towards a Theory of Retributivism in Recovering States" in *The University of Toronto Law Journal* 49, no. 3 (Summer, 1999); Martha Minow, *Between Vengeance and Forgiveness* (Boston, Beacon Press, 1998); Andrew Rigby, *Justice and Reconciliation* (Boulder, CO: Lynne Rienner, 2001); "Accommodating Individual Criminal Responsibility and National Reconciliation: The UN Truth Commission for East Timor" in *American Journal of International Law* 95, no. 4 (October, 2001); Barbara F. Walter, "The Critical Barrier to Civil War Settlement" in *International Organization* 51, no. 3 (Summer, 1997).

50. Immanuel Kant, *Perpetual Peace and Other Essays*, T. Humphrey, trans. (Indianapolis, IN: Hackett, 1983); Jean Jacques Rousseau, *"The Social Contract" and Other Later Political Writings*, Victor Gourevitch, ed. (Cambridge: Cambridge University Press, 1997).

51. Interestingly, we can observe countries which experience significant regime change (e.g. Latin America and Eastern Europe in the early 1990s) make public statements breaking with the past, but we do not see these countries ask for forgiveness or offer restitution to neighbors they have threatened or harmed.

52. There is a relatively new literature championed by Glen Stassen and others called "Just Peacemaking." Although most of its proponents are from the pacifist tradition, nonetheless the efforts of Stassen and his colleagues are to address the real-world dilemmas the bedevil areas of intractable conflict. For an introduction, see Glen Stassen, "New Paradigm: Just Peacemaking Theory" in *Council of the Societies for the Study of Religion Bulletin* (Spring, 1997).

Chapter 6

Public Opinion, Postmodernism, and Supranational Governance: Challenges for New Thinking on Just War

War has been present with us since the dawn of recorded history. On the one hand warfare is evolutionary. Tactics, weapons, and strategy change over time, as opponents adapt to the conditions under which previous wars were fought. Thus the French learned the "lesson" of quick offense from the Franco-Prussian wars only to learn a new "lesson" about defensive emplacements from World War I. France continued to try to evolve its military in tandem with the developments of its competitors, such as the epic struggle to build its navy in the 1930s, the fortification of the almost useless Maginot Line prior to Second World War, and the challenge of terrorism and insurgent campaigns in Algeria and Indochina. France's struggle to adapt in the twentieth century to innovations in the use of military force illustrates the complexity and transience of some tactics and strategies.

On the other hand, many aspects of violent conflict are constant, among which the most obvious are fear, suffering, and bloodshed. It is safe to say that the experience of warriors enduring bombardment, be it Persians facing coordinated archery and "Greek fire," artillery cannonade at Jenna or Gettysburg, or carpet bombing in Rolling Thunder, has been a shared feeling of dread over the centuries.

Fortunately, an important legacy of the Western tradition is the consideration of normative aspects of warfare from sacred and secular perspectives. Although warfare itself changes, our concern for the values implicit in our choice of whether or not to do battle as well as how wars are fought and concluded is an important reflection of the nature of our individual humanity as well as our civilization. This book has argued that the essential notions of just war thinking—moral consideration in the decision to go to war, just war-fighting, and resolution of conflict—should be thoughtfully applied to twenty-first century conflicts. However, it is also the argument of this book that reifying outdated concepts is not the best way to approach the novel threats states face from weapons of mass destruction, non-state terrorist actors, and failed states.

This chapter recapitulates the primary arguments of the work and suggests two areas for new scholarship on justice and war. The first is the problematic relationship between democratic governance and just wars. Democratic theorists often hold that democracy is a normatively superior form of governance and thus its policies are more likely to be moral. However, even friends of democracy have long recognized that the representative form of governance has its own particular failings. Such vices are most likely to come out in war, and when it comes to war democracies are guilty of both sins of omission and commission. What of democracy and just war? And what of the democratization, or better pluralism, of moral systems in Western societies—how does this effect the normative context of war?

The second question regards changes to the international system, in particular the rise of various transnational and supranational agencies. How does just war thinking apply to the novelty of force employed by international "committees" like the African Union, UN, and NATO? How does the principle of responsibility, as well as ideas of authority, legitimacy, sovereignty, and justice, pertain to international collectives?

Just War Thinking in the Twenty-First Century

This book does not assert the demise of just war thinking. Concern about justice in war predates Christianity and is not simply a Western construct—it is a concern in many societies. Moreover, the purpose of this work is not to denigrate traditional Just War doctrine. Indeed, the opposite is true. Historic Just War scholarship was not a catechism nor was debating it a heresy. Ambrose, Augustine, Aquinas, Vitoria, and Suarez all applied their concerns for justice to the real world conflicts of their day. Ambrose and Augustine wrote in the context of declining *Pax Romana* whereas Vitoria and Suarez considered the expansion of the early Spanish Empire in the New World. Aquinas wrote not only about the battlefield but also took into account the chivalric tournaments of his day. More recently some, but not enough, thinkers have struggled with the innovations of the twentieth century: Michael Walzer on military humanitarian intervention, Paul Ramsey on nuclear weapons, and Jean Bethke Elshtain on terrorism.

None of these later thinkers regurgitated the extended Just War dogma in all of its components. Rather, they have applied the basic notions of justice in the decision to go to war and justice in war-fighting to the conflicts of their day.

Such is the effort of this work. The threats of the twenty-first century demand a reemphasis on the priority of a strong state and the state's responsibility to the security of its population's life, livelihood, and way of life. Moreover, a political ethic of responsibility provides a starting point for consideration of the decision to fight, decisions about how to fight, as well as decisions about an adequate post-conflict environment in light of the innovations of the era: dirty bombs, suicide bombers, apocalyptic terrorism, failed states, genocide, economic and electronic warfare, and military humanitarian intervention.

Jus Ad Bellum

In 1983 the (American) National Council of Catholic Bishops issued the declaration *The Challenge of Peace*. In it they redefined the parameters of Just War theory in at least two ways. First, they elucidated a long list of *jus ad bellum* tenets: just cause, right authority, right intent, likelihood of success, last resort, proportionality, and comparative justice. The list is important because the bishops say that the decision to go to war is "governed" by these criteria. The bishops do not articulate a hierarchy among the criteria, and a reading of the entire document makes it clear that the decision to go to war must meet all of these criteria simultaneously to be considered just. In practice, it is difficult to justify even the "good wars" like those fought by Lincoln or Franklin D. Roosevelt based on the bishops' standard.

Second, the document alleges that Just War theory is founded upon a "presumption against war." Again, this is a mutation which vastly constricts the state's prerogatives. Indeed, the bishops' missive conflates "peace" with the absence of direct inter-state conflict.[1] *The Challenge of Peace* seems short-sighted because the dilemmas of international politics include the period of hostilities prior to actual military engagement, the issues of preemptive and preventive action against terrorist cells, considerations of post-war justice, punishment, restitution, and the like. In short, the pastoral letter lacks complexity in conceptualizing peace and war in light of the dilemmas of world politics.

In short, thinking about justice and war has largely given way to moralizing against war, both in religious settings and the academy, without considering the realities of politics, threats, and contemporary violence. Twenty-first century just war thinking needs to reconceptualize *jus ad bellum*.

The argument of this book is that it is just for the state to act in accordance with its responsibility to security. Security, or Order, is the cardinal virtue of domestic and international life. Rather than arguing for a halcyon notion of peace, a minimal notion of order in political life is an appropriate starting point for just war thinking. States are the legitimate authorities in international life and it is their responsibility to maintain the security of their populace and the international system. Procuring security should be the first cause and intent of the state. Therefore, the first consideration of whether it is moral for the state to go to war is whether it is necessary for defense of that security.

What of "likelihood of success," "last resort," and the rest of the Just War checklist? Such tenets are helpful in thinking about specific cases, but they are more pragmatic calculations than moral imperatives. More importantly, it is incumbent to carefully consider the practical application of concern for security and human life in the context of contemporary threats.

For example, leaders in the United States and throughout the Western world should consider what international threats have the greatest potential to disrupt the lives, livelihoods, and way of life of their populaces. States acting on behalf of their security and the security of the international system against malignant electronic terrorism, nuclear weapons, rogue states, and terrorist groups are acting morally. This is not to say that every act is moral, but that the decision to refuse appeasement and passivity in favor of thoughtful and creative action meets the requirements of a twenty-first century *jus ad bellum*.

A twenty-first century concern for justice in the decision to utilize force recognizes that there are some things worse than war and that "self-defense" is not the only sufficient criteria for considering employing the military instrument.[2] The victory of tyranny, the enslavement of human beings, torture, the systematic incarceration and extra-judicial killing of people based on race or creed, long-term environmental degradation—these are horrors worth fighting against. There is no one-size-fits-all approach for *jus ad bellum*, each threat must be carefully appraised and when appropriate, action must be taken to deter, dissuade, prevent, and/or preempt enemy attack.[3] In short, a doctrine of *jus ad bellum* based on a political ethic of responsibility behooves states to act.

Jus in Bello

The second component of just war thinking concerns justice in the fighting of war. *Jus in bello* is usually thought of as having two primary dimensions. The first is proportionality. In its traditional form proportionality means that the amount of force used should be in proportion to our military objectives and no greater. For example, the actions of Marines targeting and fighting against armed insurgents in Fallujah are more ethically appropriate than simply carpet bombing the entire city. The other is discrimination or non-combatant immunity. This is the idea that there are those against whom war should not be prosecuted, including civilians, prisoners, and the wounded.

One development in recent Just War writing is that proportionality has lost its privileged place in *jus in bello* and that position has been taken over by non-combatant immunity.[4] Reflection on bombing cities in World War II, atomic and nuclear devices, and Vietnam has privileged non-combatant immunity over proportionality. The effect of such reflection is a crescendo of interest in military humanitarian intervention since the end of the Cold War where the welfare of non-combatants is seriously threatened such as in Bosnia and Sierra Leone.

However, hyper-privileging non-combatant immunity is as problematic today as it always has been. In many parts of the world non-uniformed soldiers (i.e. guerrillas, insurgents, rebels) are at the command of local warlords and violate their state's sovereignty every day (e.g. Colombia, Somalia). We have also witnessed the rise of "corporate warriors"—professional security firms, or better private armies, such as the Steele Foundation and Executive Outcomes who are more than individual mercenaries—they are armies for hire. However, it is not clear how international law and the war convention apply to them. Moreover, terrorism challenges non-combatant immunity in many ways. For instance, why is it that rigid adherence to non-combatant immunity protects the supply lines and support networks of terrorists from deterrence and destruction by legitimate military forces?

This book argues for returning to primacy the old principle of discrimination rather than the idealistic and unrealistic standard of non-combatant immunity. Discrimination is the idea that leaders and soldiers discriminate against the real-world threats that they face. Discrimination means containing, deterring, or destroying active threats.

Discrimination means that not all soldiers or armies are a threat. Some are, some are not. Discrimination also means that not everyone in civilian attire is a non-combatant. A contemporary doctrine of discrimination calls for engaging active threats. Thus, it is appropriately discriminatory to attack the supply lines and support networks of terrorists, including monitoring and perhaps incarceration of associates and family members. Discrimination means that active threats, such as Osama Bin Laden, are fair targets even when they are among their wives and children. Western soldiers in the war on terrorism are always targets for the enemy; the same should be true for terrorists and rogues. Likewise, discrimination means acting against the source of threats when possible. It may be practical as well as certainly moral to decapitate the leadership of an outlaw regime or organization, such as Kim Jong Il or Saddam Hussein, rather than kill thousands of their conscripts on the battlefield.

A contemporary principle of discrimination locates it in right relationship to proportionality. Proportionality should be the preeminent *jus in bello* criterion within which discrimination is considered. Most importantly, proportionality needs to be rethought not in terms of means, but in terms of threats. The old doctrine of proportionality worried over achieving the right proportion of throw weight. A thoughtful and useful proportionality for the war on terrorism asks what is an appropriate response to the active threat posed by weapons of mass destruction in the hands of al Qaeda or a rogue regime like North Korea? What actions, be they diplomatic, economic, or military, are in proportion to the threat states face to their populace, their livelihood, and their way of life?

A reconceptualized doctrine of proportionality based on threat is useful not only when considering weapons of mass destruction in the hands of terrorists and outlaw regimes. It is also useful in considering the appropriate level of force in military humanitarian intervention. If political and military leaders define proportionality in terms of the possible loss of life due to genocide, say in Yugoslavia or Rwanda, perhaps the level of response would be commensurate with those threats. Such was the case in the UN intervention in Congo in the early 1960s—over 20,000 peacekeepers arrived, the first troops hitting the ground within days of the UN resolution. Contrast that with the example of Rwanda in 1994 where the UN pulled out ninety percent of its forces, drawing down to a token presence of about 250 peacekeepers without appropriate equipment and without a mandate to stop the killing. Even had a theoretical early intervention not saved all the lives of local Hutus and Tutsis who died, it may have prevented the war from spilling over into its neighbors which resulted in the loss of over three million Africans over the next several years.

Jus Post Bellum

Surprisingly, traditional Just War theory articulates no framework for justice at war's end. It is true that churchmen from Augustine to Martin Luther that the objective of war is a "better state of peace," but this is more a *jus ad bellum* consideration than one of *jus post bellum.*[5] It is only recently that a handful of scholars have begun exploring the characteristics of *jus post bellum*.

Why the neglect of justice at war's end? This is a difficult question. *Jus post bellum* may have been ignored because Just War doctrine was about restraining the advent and prosecution of war, not governing its aftermath. Indeed, scholars and statesmen alike may have despaired that justice other than that delivered by the sword was possible at battle's end. It may have been overlooked due to the limited nature of medieval and early modern warfare in Europe. Such warfare was often, although not always, "politics by other means" and did not result in the widespread devastation characteristic of twentieth century total wars. Similarly, *jus post bellum* might have been neglected because wars tended to end in negotiated settlements between governments whereas early Just War theory was about the moral disposition of the individual, soldier or sovereign, in deciding when and how to fight war. The medievals absolved the troops of sin *prior* to battle and at war's end, what was done was done. Just War doctrine ended at war's end.

In any event, a comprehensive just war approach for the twenty-first century needs *jus post bellum*. Thinking about justice at war's end makes sense both practically and morally. States should do the hard work of planning and security forecasting with the pragmatic goal of eliminating threats, deterring future aggression, and establishing a robust Order. They must also engage in the hard ethical work of considering the claims of justice at war's end because of their commitment to serve humanity, with the goal in mind of remediating some of the causes and conditions of the conflict.

One way to develop *jus post bellum* criteria is to borrow them from existing Just War tenets. As discussed in chapter five, a philosopher has recently done this in a thoughtful way.[6] However, I am not convinced that the move from no *jus post bellum* criteria to an expansive list taken from *ad bellum* and *in bello* is appropriate. It seems to be stretching the issue to the point of breaking to try to say that a just settlement includes all of the traditional criteria such as "just cause to quit," "right intention for quitting," "last resort," and "reasonable hope of success."

Instead, this work proffers a three-dimensional conception of justice at war's end. A minimal *jus post bellum* focuses on Order: creating an enduring framework that secures the states and peoples affected by the conflict. Order is a moral concept—without security there is no opportunity for the good life in domestic society and international politics is a Hobbesian nightmare. Without Order there is no opportunity for punishing wrongdoers or making restitution to victims.

Some would suggest that calling a durable armistice, such as that which ended the Korean Conflict, a "just" peace is oxymoronic. . .or just plain moronic. However, if the priority is the implementation of a security regime in the international system and the preservation of the lives of our citizens, then it meets the minimal criteria for justice. Consider the evidence: the Korean War cost the lives of over a million people in 1951, another million in 1952, a third million in 1953, but there were no battle casualties in 1954. Although such a peace may not satisfy all of our political and moral aspirations such as the liberation of the North Korean citizenry, the armistice is superior on both counts to the hot war that preceded it.

Fortunately, at times we can seek a better justice, one that is founded on security and approximates justice by punishment and restitution. It is important to point out that the claims of justice at war's end are predicated on security and not vice versa. In other words, to institute reparations, criminal trials, or other instruments of justice there must be a condition of order. Unfortunately however, real accomplishments of justice are few and far between.

One way to implement justice is through restitution to the victims. However, meaningful remuneration is extremely difficult at war's end because it is impossible to restore many of the things, especially human beings that were lost in the fighting. Reparations may cause more havoc than they solve, as occurred in Germany and its neighbors during the 1920s. Instead, a focus on punishment is appropriate for approximating justice.

As observed in chapter five, punishment has fallen out of vogue in the past half century. In truth, punishment of individuals responsible for aggression at the beginning of war or during its conduct is a rare thing historically. Many felt that Nuremberg and the Tokyo war crimes trials inaugurated a new era in international life, when those in positions of responsibility were held accountable for their actions. However, for fifty years no similar actions were taken on the international stage, although there were certainly enough grievances to justify such action. In the past decade, criminal cases against the leaders of violence in the former Yugoslavia and Rwanda have made the headlines, although at present barely a handful of leaders from either country are behind bars.

Does this mean that we should not punish aggressors or those guilty of violating the war convention? Certainly not. It means, however, that we should employ such measures on a case by case basis, seeking the punishment of those responsible at the highest levels and not seeking war guilt for the entire country. Of course, such punishment is often simply not practicable. For instance, in many cases the only faction that can guarantee and maintain a ceasefire is exactly the most murderous of the enemy. Treating with them is simply a necessity. One author observes regarding the former Yugoslavia,

"More embarrassing still has it been to find that the ethnic chieftains in former Yugoslavia who were prematurely denounced as war criminals and orderers
of genocide now have to be negotiated with as the only persons capable of delivering ceasefires and even peace settlements."[7]

Those "chieftains" and "criminals" usually seek a secure peace just as we do,
and their participation may be necessary for the implementation of order. A
more comprehensive justice may be impossible to seek, at least in the short-
term.

Interestingly, one aspect of punishment that has received little attention in
the scholarly literature is how *jus in bello* principles permeate the military codes
of Western societies in courts martial and other forms of punishment of service
members who violate the laws of war. This is a significant success story for just
war thinking that calls for further scholarship. Although we are horrified by My
Lai and Abu Ghraib, these are just two examples of hundreds of investigations
by Australian, British, American, and other Western militaries into violations of
proportionality and discrimination. Such mechanisms are imperfect, but far better than the ethical void characteristic of some military behavior in other parts of
the globe.

This view of *jus post bellum* focuses primarily on the past. It builds a secure
peace on ameliorating past conditions which led to the violence and seeks reparations and punishment for past activities. A robust justice-at-war's-end goes
further; it seeks the conditions for Conciliation that could transform past enemies into partners for peace.

There is a burgeoning literature on reconciliation in politics, but almost all of
it deals with intra-state conflict. In most examples the cases are not even civil
wars but rather instances of government repression of sectors of the population.
The best known examples are post-apartheid's South African Truth and Reconciliation Commission, the efforts to bring Latin American military dictators such
as Augusto Pinochet and their cronies to justice in the 1990s, and legislation and
judicial proceedings to deal with the old Communist apparatus in Eastern
Europe with the raising of the Iron Curtain.

In contrast there is almost no literature on states and their populations seeking conciliation with other countries with whom they have warred in the past
century. Indeed, I am skeptical that we can import into international politics the
transcendent qualities necessary for real conciliation to occur in the hearts of
individual human beings. That being said, I am cognizant of how changes in
perceived interests, over time, can change the relationship of governments. As
discussed in chapter five, it is entirely possible that former adversaries will grow
closer and conciliate to one another as their security situation changes. Thus,
Germany and France have allied for most of the past century when they fought
for the previous three. The same is true of numerous other cases. The question is
what changed? The answer seems simple—a reevaluation of their interests over
time brought them into new relationships of harmony that were impossible in the
past. Moreover such relationships can become enduring patterns of behavior that

outlast the initial conditions that caused the relationship to develop in the first place.

In conclusion, in rare cases political leaders may be ideational entrepreneurs and lead their countries in acts of conciliation that will transform international relationships. This may not change the hearts of the individual publics, but it can radically alter the status quo and the institutionalization of shared security may become something more over time. In the end, however, we have come full circle—security is the fulcrum for advancing conciliatory initiatives.

Just War and Democracy

Just war thinking predates contemporary forms of representative government by centuries. The political milieu of the original Roman and later scholastic Just War theorists was hierarchical and monarchical. Thus, *jus ad bellum* considerations were the domain of a single sovereign, in practice a king and his advisors. *Jus in bello* norms were also the domain of an exclusive group in the feudal and early modern eras. In the age of chivalry knights had a code of fair play to which they subscribed in battle. Often the average foot soldier was in actuality a tenant farmer or townsman recruited for a short time to battle on behalf of his lord or to protect the village. They had no training on the laws of war or the chivalric code. In sum, *jus ad bellum* and *jus in bello* considerations were largely the writ of elites for centuries.

The past two centuries have seen numerous innovations in the structure and behavior of Western polities. Perhaps the most important developments that effect this discussion are the rise of the mass army and the accompanying mobilization of the entire nation for total war as well as the simultaneous introduction of mass politics in the form of parliamentary and presidential forms of republican government.[8] The question is simply this: can democracy be relied upon to wage just war?

"Democracy" is used here to mean forms of contemporary representative government such as those we have in the West. There are no true direct democracies where all citizens have a say on all issues, rather the complexity of modern societies has resulted in republican forms of governance. At the minimum democracy in practice today is characterized by two things. The first is free, fair, and contested *elections* which provide the opportunity for citizens to have a voice in the direction of their country and the circulation of elites. The second is the rule of law, most notably the enshrinement of individual *civil liberties* including freedoms of speech, press, assembly, worship, and so forth. No country meets the minimum qualifications of democracy without some form of elections and the protection of individual civil liberties by law.

There are dozens of real-world examples of democracy in various guises from every inhabited continent. What they share is representative government that is at least somewhat responsive to its public. Nonetheless, democracy is a recent innovation in world politics. True, tiny Greek city-states and Swiss cantons, what would today be called "towns," practiced governance by representation and public opinion in the past, but it is only in recent history that democracy at the national level has taken root in world politics. Thus, one should ask how just war thinking—a doctrine from another historic era—interacts with representative government.

The Dark Side of Democracy

Is democracy equipped to handle the reflective nature of just war thinking? The answer may be "no." Democracy-in-practice today has several shortcomings which may weaken its ability to engage in the moral discourse necessary for just war thinking. The first and most obvious failing is the nature of public opinion itself. Oliver O'Donovan suggests, "The opinionated public constitutes a positive obstacle to deliberation about the praxis of judgment." [9] Republics are structured so that politicians must respond to public opinion in some measure or they will no longer have a job. Recent history provides us with many examples of politicians who charted a course that they felt was dictated by public opinion but was not necessarily in the national interest nor attune to justice. For example, Neville Chamberlain's appeasement of Hitler was dictated by the public's unwillingness to confront the Nazi threat. The reluctance of the Roosevelt Administration to engage the wars in Europe and Asia was likewise caused by over reliance on public opinion. [10]

Unfortunately, popular democratic theory trumpets "majority rule" without appreciating how often majorities, or mobs, get it wrong. In other words, public opinion is not necessarily virtuous simply because it represents the will of the majority. Although public opinion may be wise and moral, when it comes to foreign and military policy it is just as likely to be misinformed, uninformed, or wrong...not to mention cowardly or malicious. As de Tocqueville noted almost two centuries ago, it is possible that public opinion represents something far from the best in the citizenry because it may reflect the lowest common denominator—what we can all agree upon or what the polls say a plurality can live with. [11]

Public opinion is complex and often not the best guide to policy but it is the very heart of contemporary representative government. Public opinion in the American South goaded the country to civil war, war "fever" was responsible in large part for the early revolutionary wars of France, the Spanish-American War, and World War I. Public opinion has supported questionable means such as the internment of Japanese-Americans and supported the war effort in Vietnam well into the early 1970s, but the American public was against helping the Poles, British, and French in 1939–1940 and opposed intervention in Korea a decade later. More often than not it seems that a characteristic of democracy is deliberate stupor when confronted with legitimate opportunities for the use of force.

Democratic Peace theorists argue that the reluctance of democracies to go to war is a good thing and exactly why the spread of democracy around the globe is imperative. The expansive form of Democratic Peace Theory (DPT) suggests that democracies are more pacific than other types of regimes. In its more limited form, DPT asserts that democracies are unlikely to go to war against one another and therefore herald an era of democratic peace.[12] Why is this the case? DPT advocates suggest two major lines of reasoning. The first has to do with political structure. The structure of democratic government is slow and conflictual. It takes time for citizens and public officials to debate the merits of using force, and the structure of democratic governments often means that it takes considerable effort for the government to be in the position to act. Consequently, the friction of debating war, the influence of partisanship, public opinion, and the press, and the procedures of passing legislation through various houses or assemblies tempers a mad rush by the executive into violence.

A second school of DPT suggests that democratic culture deserves the credit for the absence of war between democracies in the twentieth century. Democracies are characterized by openness, tolerance, the opportunity for debate, and peaceful conflict resolution. DPT argues that these traits characterize not only domestic politics but also the interactions between democratic governments. In other words, it is the nature of democracy to resolve conflict peacefully, both at home and abroad.

The point is that DPT suggests that democracies are less likely to go to war due to institutional or societal constraints. In fact, in times of real conflict or emergency the demos may be too pacific. It may have limited or inaccurate knowledge of events and therefore not provide a wise or just referent to its leaders. It may struggle to act due to its Madisonian institutions or public opinion may simply be self-absorbed to the point of sloth. In any event, it is often the case that the West has chosen inaction in deference to public opinion.[13] For instance, Europe and the U.S. took several years before really engaging the brutality of Slobodan Milosevic in Bosnia and many have calumniated the United States in particular for not intervening against the genocide in Rwanda (1994) and the bloodbath in neighboring DRC (1996–2002).[14] However, the political leaders in Washington and Europe were convinced that their primary duties lay with their own citizens and that their publics would not countenance the death of their own sons and daughters to stall what was apparently a hopeless situation. Indeed, in the U.S. case the "Blackhawk Down" affair had occurred just months before the Rwanda genocide in nearby Somalia, pitting public opinion against African peacekeeping (and nation building) efforts. Whether the public was right or wrong about the utility of peacekeeping in Africa, the simple fact is that American officials—in 1914, 1940, and 1994—felt constrained by public opinion from engaging in war.

At times the unwillingness to act is a direct contravention of the principle of responsibility adumbrated earlier in this work. This is not to say that the United States should or should not have engaged its military in specific instances like

Bosnia, Somalia, Rwanda, or elsewhere. Rather, the question is a more subtle one—was the decision to use force (Haiti, Iraq) or not use force (Rwanda, North Korea) based on clear considerations of the responsibilities of the U.S. government to defend and enhance the security of its public and the international system? Can uninterested public opinion be counted on to provide ethical guidance about the appropriate means to counter insecurity and genocide, even if it means a massive introduction of foreign troops, martial law, and robust rules of engagement including "shoot to kill" authorization? A real discussion of responsibility is where contemporary just war thinking should begin, and such analysis should be applied on a case by case basis to the real conflicts of the world today. The decision might be to employ force, it might be to not engage the military. Regardless of the ultimate decision, the obvious dilemma of public opinion-based foreign policies is that they may result in inaction that is detrimental to promoting security and preserving human life.

In sum, public opinion can be too militaristic, dragging its leaders into total wars without regard for the wisdom or virtue of conflict. Or, public opinion can drag its feet resulting in temerity and inaction. What makes the moral content of applying public opinion to such questions even more problematic is that contemporary publics are increasingly unlikely to share a common moral basis, making it a doubly problematic foundation from which to derive policies about life and death.

Moral Pluralism

The increasing import of public opinion is not simply a structural component of representative governance nor is it just a political reality in the calculus of those campaigning for public office. There is a deeper philosophical trend, a democratization of values, apparent in Western society as well. One author pointed to some of the symptoms which he calls "radical individualism" ("Don't tell me what to do!") and "radical egalitarianism" ("No one is better than me!").[15] This results in a loss of hierarchies, of shared meaning, and of collective truth because no ones ideas are superior to my own. The Left has noticed this and criticized the lack of moral restraint of individuals in the marketplace; the Right has likewise observed this trend and condemns the lack of moral restraint in Hollywood.

This heterodoxy of values is symptomatic of the normative pluralism associated with ethical relativism and postmodernity. The key feature of these trends is moral pluralism: the loss of or emancipation from, depending on one's point of view, a single, shared basis for morality within Western culture. Postmodernity is the notion that the rationalist and universalistic paradigm associated with the Enlightenment and its antecedents is best understood as simply one narrative of human experience among many. The postmodern project is to strip all meta-narratives—the accepted ways of viewing the world—of their emperor's clothing and reveal how such discourses are really myths designed to protect the power of some and disenfranchise others. Consequently, any statement of universal morality, such as that associated with Christianity, the natural law tradition, and Western civilization is anathema to postmodern intelligentsia.

It is possible that there are positive features to the postmodern critique. For instance, it may shine a light on past abuses and lack of toleration in Western society. It may also help us develop a sense of humility with regards to the contributions and values of non-Western civilizations.

That being said, humility and introspection are not a sufficient basis for developing a political ethic of responsibility or for evaluating the just application of military force. In theory, the moral pluralism of postmodernity asserts that the values of each tribe may be useful within their context, but that there are no universal moral norms. Furthermore, in practice postmodernism advocates an ethical relativism which robs society of the moral tools necessary for reflection, restraint, and the pursuit of security and justice.

How can a postmodern public debate *jus ad bellum*? Is there a moral basis for a postmodern *jus in bello*? It is beyond the scope of this work to offer an in-depth critique of the ethical relativism explicit in postmodernism, but suffice it to say that such a view is diametrically opposed to the value system of traditional and contemporary just war thinking. Historical Just War theory was tied to a religious understanding of the structure of the world order: the value of politics, the need for political authorities to fight evil and punish evil-doers, the right of self-defense, the legitimate justice of some causes, and a useful moral order that could distinguish between unfortunate but lawful warfare and cold-blooded murder.

Contemporary just war thinking in any of its forms, sacred or secular, has an explicit moral position—it values human life and international security. The tenets of just war thinking privilege human life and the conditions which make for moral living in society.

In contrast, the postmodern relativism popular in the academy and some of the press for the past thirty years provides no basis, other than perhaps mob rule or elite guidance, for a comprehensive understanding of justice and consistent policies dedicated to the preservation of human life and international security. Unfortunately, as Western civilization succumbs to the meaninglessness of postmodern philosophy, it erodes the foundations for thinking about justice and war.

Just war thinking's progeny, international law and the war convention, are entirely secular in nature. Nonetheless, postmodernism challenges even the secular legal paradigm regarding justice and war. First, international law is based in part on a set of historical and philosophical assumptions that predate contemporary postmodernity. The state system and legal authority, the notion of sovereignty and non-intervention, the war convention which grants or observes legal rights to enemy combatants even when they are from a different civilization—these are ideas based on Western philosophical notions of the rule of law, authority, and the value of individual human life. One has to wonder how postmodernism's project to deconstruct political life, theoretically and practically, complements the existing state system. Indeed, the deconstructionist project may be a threat to the norms of Western international politics.

Of course, one could make the positivist case that contemporary international law is simply the sum of agreements signed among states such as laws, treaties, and conventions. This strips the law of nations of its normative and historical context and allows us to entertain the postmodern project of deconstructing such covenants in order to display the power relations inherent in them. It is unclear what practical political value such efforts would achieve, and even then the question remains: on what basis is law created? What should be the philosophical foundation for considerations of human life, conflict, and war? Indeed, what is the postmodern rationale for protecting individual human life anyway?

Postmodernism renders a potent challenge to just war thinking. Postmodernism is skeptical of ethical norms, is ambivalent about a philosophical basis for right and wrong, and disdains the claims of universal morality. Postmodernism lacks any rationale for restraint in war—it does not have a moral organizing center like Augustine's *caritas*, Aquinas' justice, Grotius' customary law, Elshtain's "equal regard," or this work's focus on responsibility and security. Moreover, without universal values of some sort the normative content of the American Declaration of Independence, the French Declaration of the Rights of Man, and the Universal Declaration of Human Rights are meaningless, as are all attempts at mitigating war for moral reasons based on distaste of destruction and regard for human life.

In sum, proponents of just war thinking must engage the postmodern challenge in the twenty-first century. Just war thinking must demonstrate not only its utility in real-world politics, but also the superiority of its philosophical foundations in comparison with the deconstructionist and relativistic claims of postmodernism. This is a debate that is happening at a practical level in international politics. Before his death, the trial of Slobodan Milosevic before the International Criminal Tribunal for Yugoslavia was such an exercise. Milosevic represented the postmodern position: he challenged the very existence and authority of the court as well as any universal standards of accountability to which he is responsible. It was not surprising that same charges of victor's justice and ethical relativism were made in the trial of Iraqi dictator Saddam Hussein.

However, the other arena of conflict between the claims of justice and postmodernism is in the academy. Just war thinkers must assert their case for just war thinking before the university elites of the Western world and persuade future generations that the philosophy which sees claims of Order and Justice as universal is superior to the relativism of postmodernism.

Just War Thinking and the Changing International System

One of just war thinking's greatest achievements is to be adaptable enough to weather the changes in international life. This flexibility is challenged today by the evolution of domestic and international political systems. The issue of *right authority* in traditional Just War theory is the most problematic criterion as forms of governance change. This work's emphasis on *responsibility* shares many of the features of right authority and is likewise affected by changes in the structure of international politics.

Historic Just War doctrine located authority in a single person. That person was sovereign in his or her realm and made the ultimate decisions about war and peace. During the medieval period that person existed in the web of social obligations characteristic of feudalism, but nonetheless was the final authority when it came to decisions about the use of force. With the rise of the "new monarchies" in the early modern period the sovereign individual became inextricably linked to the state, hence Louis XIV's famous "l'etat c'est moi."[16] In the nineteenth century the state began to de-link itself from an individual monarch by instituting constitutional provisions and national parliaments, but again the seat of sovereignty remained in the state. Interestingly, the doctrine of democracy is a radical departure from such views of sovereignty, because in its classic form sovereignty rests in the people and is delegated to the state. Nevertheless, in the practice of twentieth century international politics states remained the preeminent sovereign actors in world politics.

We may be at a new crossroads in international affairs that problematizes the notions of authority and responsibility when it comes to war. The "democratization" of firepower to non-state actors, the rise of military humanitarian intervention in failing states, and the increasing respect accorded supranational institutions, notably the United Nations, bespeak a changing world. In this world the notion of political responsibility at the heart of any discussion of justice and war is fluid.

On the one hand, international life now has units smaller than states utilizing the weapons once reserved for government arsenals in their assault on states. This is true of guerrilla and insurgent campaigns, drug cartels, private security firms, as well as legitimate revolutionary movements. When it comes to the question of authority there is little disagreement that in general these types of movements are illegitimate and have no proper authority. In other words, the perpetrators of violence via terrorism or insurgency such as Colombia's drug cartels, Afghanistan's rural warlords, Iraqi Sunni suicide bombers, or the shock troops of al Qaeda and Hezbollah have no legitimacy, no real political authority, and no responsibility for or to their intended constituencies. Hence their reliance on terror rather than the voting booth.

Although many developing states find their sovereignty challenged by substate movements, just war thinking's larger focus on state responsibility faces little challenge from sub-state movements because the illegitimacy of such groups and their methods actually reify the sovereign state system. On the other hand, it is the augmentation of authority at the supranational level that most challenges just war thinking today. Numerous dilemmas suggest themselves, such as: when states fail and other states intervene via supranational agencies, who is morally responsible? When states fail and their neighbors refuse to intervene, who is morally responsible? When states turn to international agencies, notably the UN, NATO, or the African Union (AU) to act where individual states have refused to act, who is morally responsible?

The UN is the most interesting case because it is not a politico-military alliance like NATO or the Warsaw Pact. In theory it is an agency at the mercy of states because in theory it derives its authority from the authority delegated to it by states. But the UN is more than the sum of its parts. It has established programs such as UNICEF and UNESCO and thousands of employees spread around the world. The UN is an enduring institution that has outlived many countries (e.g. Zaire, the Soviet Union, Yugoslavia, Rhodesia) and has taken on a life of its own. Many states cannot challenge its power, at least not if they are poor, backward, and not members of the Security Council.

Numerous contemporary Just War quasi-pacifists no longer trust individual states to make the decision to go to war. The most famous recent case, that of the U.S. invasion of Iraq, is telling in the Just War debates that surrounded the six months of controversy leading to armed conflict in March 2003. As reported in chapter three, many (mis)used the Just War tenet of *right authority* by claiming that only the UN has the authority to declare war in the twenty-first century.

This argument is novel. It claims that states no longer are ultimately responsible for international security and that such authority resides in the UN. This is not simply a practical political argument, it is one with moral content. The idea that a supranational entity, the harbinger of a world government, should be the guarantor of world peace is not new—plans for "perpetual peace" and world government are old hat. But, it foreshadows a radical shift in sovereignty away from states to centralized governance.

The questions multiply. If the UN is the only legitimate forum for deciding to utilize force, then is it the sole sovereign authority in international relations? How does one implement the *jus ad bellum* at the Security Council, or worse, at the General Assembly? Should UN constituents have voted on each criterion to determine whether or not to halt Saddam Hussein's advance into Kuwait? What of the *jus in bello* criteria? Who is responsible for the behavior of UN blue helmets? Currently it is up to individual states to train their troops and loan them to the UN. Is the UN morally accountable for the misdeeds of its peacekeepers, such as the rapes of African women by African "blue-helmets" under UN auspices? UN Secretariats are notorious for dodging any question of responsibility for the actions of their functionaries and family members. Can we realistically expect more in the context of war?

Just war by committee is likely to achieve little that is just or effective in fighting wars, punishing evil-doers, and halting aggression. Indeed, a problem shared by the EU, the African Union, and the UN is the tendency for inaction when action is called for. The hallmark of such collectives is dithering when responsible action is required. Why is this the case? Supranational organizations, especially the UN, tend to require consensus among members to act. Because the UN is not a unified whole with a single set of interests, it is often paralyzed because its constituents cannot agree on action. This is certainly the case for any of the murderous wars of the 1990s in Europe, Asia, and Africa. If military humanitarian intervention did finally occur, it was generally undermanned and poorly supported. This begs the question of whether states can pawn their responsibility for security off on international organizations.

A second, deeper flaw of supranational organizations serving as the twenty-first century locus of responsibility for international security is their inability to make right distinctions. This is especially true of the UN. The first rule of the UN is that all states are equal and except in extreme cases, sovereignty and non-intervention are inviolable rights. It certainly seems absurd that tiny Equatorial Guinea has a vote in the General Assembly but that the world's seventh largest economy, California, does not. It is absurd that murderous regimes like Sudan sat on the UN Human Rights Commission. In short, the UN is simply not representative of the realities of global politics today due to its very constitution.

This moral confusion results in the UN refusing to take sides in a given conflict. This has been a boon to dictators, thugs, and murderers particularly in the age of genocide. The UN's position consistently is to not take sides in an interstate war but to treat with the "legitimate" representatives of all sides in the conflict. This effort at neutral arbitration emasculates the UN as a real force for security and justice. Moreover, the statist nature of the UN often predisposes it to value the reigning government in intra-state conflicts, regardless of its actual legitimacy or the cruelty of its policies, rather than the popular representatives of challengers. If the UN does engage both sides in peace talks to end a long-term civil war, or deals with multiple governments in an interstate war, the UN's policy is to deal with each equally, not casting blame or aspersions on any party.

This is utterly irresponsible. If the UN wants to serve as a mediator, so be it. But if the mediating role is what it seeks, then it cannot be a guarantor of security. In a world of warfare, terrorism, and failing political systems one must ask what good is a mediator in stopping a suicide bomber or deterring a drug kingpin? Those Just War users who wish to turn responsibility for international security over to the UN are either naïve or truly wish the end of the state system as we know it. In short, just war thinking emphasizes the responsibility of states to protect their populaces first and then promote international security outside their borders. In contrast, exponents of world government or supranational organizations promoting international security fail to understand the fundamental nature of political responsibility and the moral calculus necessary to pursue security in international affairs.

Conclusion

Just war thinking has been useful in calling leaders and strategists to consider their ideals when confronted with the necessity of violence. The purpose of this book is to remind us that just war thinking must engage the real world of domestic and international politics with creative, thoughtful, and ethical measures to preserve and promote the lives, livelihoods, and way of life of our populace. Unlike moral perfectionists who reject all war as sinful, and unlike those jihadis who believe their highest good is obtained in the fight, just war thinking takes a different position, recognizing that war is destructive but that at times it is a moral obligation. Just war thinking seeks to restrain the ravages of war. Just war thinking takes responsibility for fighting in self-defense of one's own citizens as well as acting on behalf of one's global neighbors in some cases. Nevertheless, just war principles do not absolve the leader or soldier for the destructive nature of war, but force us to come to terms with our motives and actions during and after conflict. It is this realistic yet moral assessment of human conscience and the injuriousness of war which is the essential fabric of just war thinking, and it is this which will induce future generations to continue to study and debate the justice of our actions in the context of conflict. The duty of this generation, a democratic generation with the ability to influence domestic policy and international relations, is to preserve and promote the values and way of life that we hold dear against the acknowledged threats to its future.

Notes

1. One writer who disagrees with my assessment that the Catholic bishops' position is "just war pacifism" is Richard B. Miller, who argues that the bishops do allow for the use of force in cases such as military humanitarian intervention. "Aquinas and the Presumption Against Killing and War" in *The Journal of Religion* 82, no. 2 (April, 2002).

2. It is common to drain the rich jus ad bellum discussions of early Just War theory of all causes of war other than self-defense (i.e. intervention to save weak) in contemporary applications of Just War thinking. "The Challenge of Peace" certainly focuses almost exclusively on post-attack self defense response. A more recent article that assumes that "self-defense is the only legitimate cause of war" is Neta C. Crawford's "Just War Theory and the US Counterterror War" in *Perspectives on Politics* 1, no. 1 (March 2003).

3. The argument for preventive and preemptive action is made by Eric A. Posner and Alan O. Sykes, "Optimal War and Jus ad Bellum," University of Chicago Law & Economics, Olin Working Paper No. 211/University of Chicago, Public Law Working Paper No. 63 (April 2004). Available at: http://ssrn.com/abstract=546104 (Accessed September 15, 2005).

4. James Turner Johnson, *Morality and Contemporary Warfare* (New Haven, CT: Yale University Press, 1999), chap. 4.

5. This point is made by James Turner Johnson in *Morality and Contemporary Warfare*, 28–29.

6. Brian Orend, "Justice After War," in *Ethics and International Affairs* 16, no. 1 (Spring 2002): 45.

7. This is a tragic dilemma of real world politics that Geoffrey Best points out in "Justice, International Relations, and Human Rights," the 21st Martin Wight Memorial Lecture, London School of Economics and Political Science (March 9, 1995), printed in *International Affairs* 71, no. 4, 785.

8. An interesting introduction to norms of civilized warfare among the first standing armies of modern Europe is Robert A. Kann, "The Law of Nations and the Conduct of War in the Early Times of the Standing Army" in *Journal of Politics* 6, no. 1 (February, 1944).

9. Oliver O'Donovan, *The Just War Revisited* (Cambridge, Cambridge University Press, 2003), 17.

10. Kathleen M. McGraw provides a very different analysis—politicians use moral justifications to shape public perception and opinion on some issues. The dilemma is the near impossibility of discerning veritable versus deceitful moral justifications by leaders. "Manipulating Public Opinion with Moral Justification" in *Annals of the American Academy of Political and Social Science* 560, "The Future of Fact," (November, 1998).

11. Reinhold Niebuhr understood the difference between the morality of individuals and the character of collectives. In his famous Moral Man and Immoral Society he asserted that individuals may choose altruistic behavior at times in accord with the best aspirations of the human race. Individuals may act selflessly to provide services and benefits to others even if it is not in the benefactor's best "interest." However, Niebuhr observed that this was generally not true of collectives. Instead, he argued that societies, whether democratic or not, usually fail to live up to idealistic expectations because they act on the collective impulses of the majority in ways that protect and promote the interests of what sociologists would call the "in-group" in competition with other societies. *Moral Man and Immoral Society* (Chicago: Scribners, 1934).

12. The best book on this topic is Sean Lynn Jones et al, eds. *Debating the Democratic Peace* (Cambridge, MA: MIT Press, 1996), especially the articles by Michael Doyle "Kant, Liberal Legacies, and Foreign Affairs" and Bruce Russett "The Fact of the Democratic Peace." There are critics of DPT, such as Raymond Cohen, "Pacific Unions: A Reappraisal of the Theory that 'Democracies do not go to War with Each Other'" in *Review of International Studies* 20, no. 3 (1994) and Kenneth Waltz, "Structural Realism After the Cold War" in *International Security* 25, no. 1 (2000).

13. Peter Viggo Jakobsen analyzed what caused UN peace enforcement operations to be activated and found that the so-called CNN effect on public opinion was an important determinant. "National Interest, Humanitarianism, or CNN: What Triggers UN peace Enforcement after the Cold War" in *Journal of Peace Research* 33, no. 2 (May, 1996).

14. See Samantha Powers' *A Problem from Hell: America in the Age of Genocide* (New York: Basic Books, 2002).

15. Robert Bork, *Slouching Toward Gomorrah: Modern Liberalism and American Decline* (New York: Reganbooks, 1996).

16. "I am the state," or better, "the state is me."

Selected Bibliography

Aquinas, Thomas. *Summa Theologica*. New York: Benziger Bros., 1947.

Augustine. *The City of God*. Marcus Dods, trans. New York: The Modern Library, 1950.

Bainton, Roland. *Christian Attitudes Toward War and Peace*. New York: Abingdon, 1960.

Best, Geoffrey. "Justice, International Relations, and Human Rights," the 21st Martin Wight Memorial Lecture, London School of Economics and Political Science (March 9, 1995), printed in *International Affairs* 71, no. 4.

Chaney, Jonathan I. "The Use of Force Against Terrorism and International Law." *The American Journal of International Law* 95, no. 4 (October, 2001).

Charles, J. Darryl. *Between Pacifism and Jihad: The Christian and the Just War*. Colorado Springs, CO: Intervarsity Press, 2005.

———. "Presumption Against War or Presumption Against Injustice? The Just War Tradition Reconsidered." *Journal of Church and State* 48, no. 3 (Fall 2005).

Chartier, Gary. "Just War Theory and the Resort to Force in Iraq." Paper presented as part of Global Issues Forum, February 2, 2003 at Vanguard University, Costa Mesa, California.

Chatterjee, Dean K. and Don E. Scheid, eds. *Ethics and Foreign Intervention*. Cambridge: Cambridge University Press, 2003.

Chesterton, Simon. *Just War or Just Peace? Humanitarian Intervention and International Justice*. Oxford: Oxford University Press, 2003.

Childress, James F. "Just-War Criteria." In *War or Peace? The Search for New Answers*, Thomas A. Shannon, ed. Maryknoll, New York: Orbis Books, 1980.

Coates, A.J. *The Ethics of War*. Manchester: Manchester University Press, 1997.

Crawford, Neta, C. "Just War Theory and the U.S. Counterterror War." *Perspectives on Politics* 1, no. 1 (March 2003).

Crowl, Philip A. "The Strategist's Short Catechism: Six Questions Without an Answer." In M. Reichart and E. Sturm, eds. *American Defense Policy*, fifth edition. Baltimore, MD: Johns Hopkins University Press, 1982.

Elshtain, Jean Bethke. *Just War Against Terror*. New York: Basic Books, 2003.

———, ed. *Just War Theory*. New York: New York University Press, 1992.

Epp, Roger. "The Augustinian Moment in International Politics." International Politics Research Papers, No. 10 Aberystwyth, UK: Department of International Politics, University College of Wales, 1991.

Ford, Franklin. *Political Murder: From Tyrannicide to Terrorism*. Cambridge, MA: Harvard University Press, 1985.

Hartigan, Richard Shelly. "Francesco de Vitoria and Civilian Immunity." *Political Theory* 1, no. 1 (1973).

Ignatieff, Michael. *The Lesser Evil: Political Ethics in an Age of Terror.* Princeton: Princeton University Press, 2004.

Johnson, James Turner. *Ideology, Reason, and the Limitation of War: Religious and Secular Concepts, 1200-1740.* Princeton: Princeton University Press, 1975.

———. "Just War, As it Was and Is." *First Things* 149 (January 2005).

———. *The Just War Tradition.* Princeton: Princeton University Press, 1981.

———. *Morality and Contemporary Warfare.* New Haven, CT: Yale Univerity Press, 1999.

Kann, Robert A. "The Law of Nations and the Conduct of War in the Early Times of the Standing Army." *The Journal of Politics* 6, no. 1 (February, 1944).

Kellogg, Davida E. "Jus Post Bellum: The Importance of War Crimes Trials." *Parameters* 32, no. 3 (Autumn, 2002).

Langan, John. "Just War Theory After the Gulf War." *Theological Studies* 53 (1992).

Lango, John, et al. *Rethinking the Just War Tradition.* New York: SUNY Press, 2006.

McMillan, Joseph. *Apocalyptic Terrorism: The Case for Preventive Action.* Institute for National Strategic Studies (November 2004).

Miller, Richard B. "Aquinas and the Presumption Against Killing and War." *The Journal of Religion* 82, no. 2 (April, 2002).

———. *Interpretations of Conflict: Ethics, Pacifism, and the Just War Tradition.* Chicago: University of Chicago Press, 1991.

Nabati, Mikael F. "Anticipatory Self-Defense: The Terrorism Exception." *Current History* (May 2003).

Nardin, Terry. "The Moral Basis of Humanitarian Intervention." *Ethics and International Affairs* 14, no. 1 (2002).

Niebuhr, Reinhold. *Discerning the Signs of the Times: Sermons for Today and Tomorrow.* London: SCM Press, 1946.

———. *Moral Man and Immoral Society.* Chicago: Scribners, 1934.

Nordquist, Kjell-Ake. *From 'Just War' to Justified Intervention.* Uppsala: Department of Theology Publications, 1998.

O'Brien, William V. "The Challenge of War: A Christian Realist Perspective." In *The Catholic Bishops and Nuclear War.* Judith A. Dwyer, ed. Washington, D.C.: Georgetown University Press, 1984.

O'Donovan, Oliver. *The Just War Revisited.* Cambridge: Cambridge University Press, 2003.

Orend, Brian. "Justice After War." *Ethics and International Affairs* 16, no. 1 (Spring 2002).

———. *War and International Justice: A Kantian Perspective.* Waterloo, Ontario, Canada: Wilfrid Laurier Press, 2000.

Patterson, Eric, ed. *The Christian Realists: Reassessing the Contribution of Niebuhr and His Contemporaries.* Lanham, MD: University of America Press, 2003.

———. "Just War in the 21st Century: Reconceptualizing Just War Theory after September 11." *International Politics* 42 (Spring 2005).

——— and Kendra Puryear. "Outlaws and Barbarians: The Bush Administration's Revolution in Sovereignty." *Journal of Diplomacy and International Affairs* 7, no. 1 (Spring 2006).

———. "Rewinding Rwanda: What If? (A Counterfactual Approach)." *Journal of Political Science* 33 (2005).

——— and Teresa Casale. "Targeted Killing and the War on Terror." *International Journal of Intelligence and Counterintelligence* 18, no. 4 (Winter 2005).

Pfaff, Tony. *Peacekeeping and the Just War Tradition.* Carlisle Barracks, PA: Strategic Studies Institute, U. S. Army War College, 2000.

Philips, Robert L. and Duane L. Cady. *Humanitarian Intervention: Just War vs. Pacifism.* Lanham, MD: Rowman and Littlefield, 1996.

Pierce, Albert G. "Just War Principles and Economic Sanctions." *Ethics and International Affairs* 10 (1996).

Pollard, Neal A. "Globalization's Bastards: Illegitimate Non-State Actors in International Law." *Low Intensity Conflict and Law Enforcement* 11, no. 2 (Winter 2002).

Ramsey, Paul. *The Just War: Force and Political Responsibility*, rev. edition. Lanham, MD: Rowman and Littlefield, 2002.

——. *War and the Christian Conscience: How Shall Modern War Be Conducted Justly?* Durham, NC: Duke University Press, 1961, 1985.

Regan, Richard J. *Just War: Principles and Cases.* Washington, D.C.: Catholic Institute of America Press, 1996.

Russell, Frederick H. *The Just War in the Middle Ages.* Cambridge: Cambridge University Press, 1976.

Smith, Dan. "Just War, Clausewitz, and Sarajevo." *Journal of Peace Research* 31, no. 2 (1994).

Stassen, Glen. "New Paradigm: Just Peacemaking Theory." *Council of the Societies for the Study of Religion Bulletin* (Spring, 1997).

Temes, Peter. *The Just War: An American Reflection on Morality in Our Time.* New York: Ivan R. Dees, 2004.

Vitoria, Francesco de. *De Indis et de Iure Belli Reflectiones.* Ernest Nys, ed., J.P. Bate, trans. New York: Oceana/Wildy and Sons, 1964.

Walzer, Michael. *Arguing About War.* New Haven, CT: Yale University Press, 2004.

——. *Just and Unjust Wars,* third ed. New York: Basic Books, 2000.

Index

About the Author

Eric Patterson is Assistant Director of the Berkley Center for Religion and World Affairs at Georgetown University. Prior to this he was Assistant Professor of Political Science at Vanguard University in California. Prior to that he was awarded a William C. Foster Fellowship at the U.S. State Department's Bureau of Political-Military Affairs (2005–2007) where he was a visiting scholar on the issue of the illicit international trade in small arms and light weapons. His teaching and scholarly work focuses on religion and politics, just war theory, and international affairs. He is the author or editor of five books, including *The Christian Realists: Reassessing the Contribution of Niebuhr and His Contemporaries, Latin America's Neo-Reformation: Religion's Influence on Politics*, and *Christianity and Power Politics Today* as well as a dozen articles in academic journals such as *Journal of Diplomacy and International Affairs, International Journal of Intelligence and Counterintelligence, Journal of Political Science, Latin American Politics and Society, International Politics, Journal for the Scientific Study of Religion, Security Studies*, and *International Relations*. His degrees include a Ph.D. from U.C. Santa Barbara, a MS from the University of Wales at Aberystwyth, and baccalaureate degrees from Evangel University. Among his awards are the Calihan Fellowship and the Rotary International Ambassadorial Scholarship.

FROM THE LIBRARY OF

Harry Therwanger

7/87

Luther on Ministerial Office and Congregational Function

GERT HAENDLER

Luther on Ministerial Office and Congregational Function

Translated by Ruth C. Gritsch
Edited by Eric W. Gritsch

FORTRESS PRESS   PHILADELPHIA

Library of Congress Cataloging in Publication Data

Haendler, Gert.
    Luther on ministerial office and congregational function.

    Translation of: Amt und Gemeinde bei Luther im Kontext der Kirchengeschichte.
    Bibliography: p.
    1. Pastoral theology—History of doctrines—16th century—Addresses, essays, lectures. 2. Church—History of doctrines—16th century—Addresses, essays, lectures. 3. Luther, Martin, 1483–1546—Addresses, essays, lectures. I. Gritsch, Eric W. II. Title.
BR333.5.P32H3313   253   81–43075
ISBN 0–8006–0665–5

9007C81   Printed in the United States of America   1–665

Contents

Abbreviations

ANF   Alexander Roberts and James Donaldson, eds., *The Ante-Nicene Fathers* (Buffalo and New York, 1885–96; American reprint of the Edinburgh edition).

BS   *Die Bekenntnisschriften der evangelisch-lutherischen Kirche,* 3d ed. rev. (Göttingen, 1930).

BC   Theodore G. Tappert, trans. and ed., *The Book of Concord: The Confessions of the Evangelical Lutheran Church* (Philadelphia: Fortress Press, 1959).

CR   *Philippi Melanchthonii Opera,* vols. 1–28 of the *Corpus Reformatorum,* ed. Carl G. Bretschneider and H. E. Bindseil (Halle, 1834–60).

LW   *Luther's Works,* American Edition (Philadelphia: Fortress Press; St. Louis: Concordia Publishing House; 1955–).

MPG   J. P. Migne, ed., *Patrologia, Series Graeca,* 161 vols. (Paris, 1857–66).

MPL   J. P. Migne, ed., *Patrologia, Series Latina,* 221 vols. in 222 (Paris, 1844–1904).

WA   *D. Martin Luthers Werke,* Kritische Gesamtausgabe (Weimar: Hermann Böhlau, 1883–).

WA Br   *D. Martin Luthers Werke: Briefwechsel* (Weimar: Hermann Böhlau, 1930–48).

Introduction

A SATIRICAL BOOK entitled *Little Journeys with Martin Luther* appeared in 1916. It was subtitled, "A real book wherein are printed diverse sayings of Dr. Luther in these latter days when he applied for synodical membership in the United States. Carefully set down in writing at that time by Brother John of the Order of Poor Brethren commonly known as Lutheran Pastors." Brother John was W. N. Harley of Columbus, Ohio, who dedicated the book "to the pieces of the church of today for the sake of the peace of the church tomorrow." A chapter entitled "Brethren Bland and Otherwise" depicts the General Synod's colloquy with a Martin Luther requesting admission to the ministry somewhere in southeastern Pennsylvania. After asking Luther about a variety of subjects ranging from millennialism to membership in secret societies, the examiners turned to the doctrine of the ministry. When it became obvious that there were radical differences of opinion between Luther and the examiners, as well as among the examiners themselves, the chairman of the colloquy adjourned the meeting.

"I say this, Brother Martin, that you may lose no sleep over these differences."

"You take the most diligent care on every occasion to be slippery and pliant of speech," Luther retorted angrily. "Is that to act the part of a faithful theologian? My resolution is taken!" Then he left.

"Nothing lost," declared one of the examiners. "We couldn't have consistently received him, anyhow. He's got heretical views on the office of the ministry. Saves us an unpleasant task. That's all."[1]

Luther's view of the ordained ministry, and its relationship to the ministerial function of the congregation, has been the subject of considerable research and debate. Some Luther scholars find Luther stressing the ordained ministry, the clergy, to such a degree that the laity appear to be completely subordinated to clerical authority. Other scholars claim the opposite for Luther. Some argue that Luther emphasized the "common ministry" of the laity before 1525, in the context of his attack on medieval clericalism, and stressed "special ministry" of the clergy after 1525, when he discovered the spiritual poverty and intellectual weakness of the medieval laity.[2]

Gert Haendler, who is professor in the Theological Faculty of the University of Rostock in East Germany, tackles Luther's views of the relationship between ordained and unordained ministry in the context of three questions: (1) To what extent was Luther's thought shaped by his pastoral dealings with certain congregations which faced problems of transition from medieval Roman Catholicism to the Reformation? (2) How do Luther's views fare when compared with dominant views in the history of the church, especially in the early church and in post-Reformation Germany? (3) Are Luther's views a help or a hindrance to contemporary Lutherans who wrestle with the question of the relationship between the ordained and unordained ministry of Christians? While the greater part of this study con-

1. W. N. Harley, *Little Journeys with Martin Luther* (Columbus, Ohio, 1916), pp. 133–62. Quotations, pp. 161–62.
2. Two recent German works illustrate the state of scholarship on this issue: Wilhelm Brunotte, in *Das Geistliche Amt bei Luther* (Berlin, 1959), stresses the "special ministry"; Hellmut Lieberg, in *Amt und Ordination bei Luther und Melanchthon,* Forschungen zur Kirchen- und Dogmengeschichte, no. 11 (Göttingen, 1962), emphasizes the "common ministry." Brian A. Gerrish, in "Priesthood and Ministry in the Theology of Luther," *Church History* 34 (1965): 404–22, summarizes the debate in English and offers a critical evaluation of the evidence. Lowell C. Green, in "Change in Luther's Doctrine of the Ministry," *Lutheran Quarterly* 18 (1966): 173–83, argues for a change in Luther's view after 1526. Robert H. Fischer, in "Another Look at Luther's Doctrine of the Ministry," *Lutheran Quarterly* 18 (1966): 260–71, attacks both Gerrish and Green, arguing against a change of view.

sists of a rather detailed analysis of Luther's writings, extending from the young to the old Luther, chapters 2 and 8 home in on the evidence from the early church and post-Reformation German Lutheranism. Chapter 8 tells the story of a small rural congregation's resistance to church authorities in league with Hitler's National Socialist government. The story illustrates the theses of this study—that Luther consistently argued for active congregations as guardians of the freedom of the gospel.

Although English readers of this study may not be familiar with sixteenth-century Saxony or twentieth-century Mecklenburg, they will gain insights into Luther's work as a leader and pastor of that reform movement within the church catholic now known as the Reformation. Germany never had a constitutional amendment to guarantee religious freedom. After the Peace of Augsburg in 1555, the Lutheran church throughout Germany took the institutional form of a cluster of territorial churches under the authority of territorial rulers. After Hitler came to power in 1933, a number of Protestant church officials formed a church of "German Christians" *(Deutsche Christen)* that would identify Christianity with racist National Socialism. When a slim minority calling itself the "Confessing Church" *(Bekennende Kirche)* opposed such a move in 1934, a Church Conflict *(Kirchenkampf)* began. Though never successful against the state, the Confessing Church did survive until the end of World War II in 1945 and later shaped German postwar Lutheranism.[3] Haendler shows how, in the name of Luther, a Mecklenburg congregation did resist a tyranny of church and state.

Readers should be aware of the origins and meaning of *Amt,* which is translated "the office of the ministry," a designation used for the ordained ministry in ecumenical discussions. Originally, *Amt* was a Celtic term for vassal *(ambactus* in Latin), a person who was granted land by a feudal landlord and who in return paid homage and served the landlord. Teutonic tribes used the term to describe someone who offered services within

---

3. For a comprehensive account of the *Kirchenkampf* see Ernst C. Helmreich, *The German Churches Under Hitler: Background, Struggle, and Epilogue* (Detroit: Wayne State University Press, 1979).

the feudal system of servant and master. Luther used *Amt* for both the "secular" public work of princes and the "spiritual" public work of priests. If both are Christian, as Luther assumed in the sixteenth-century world, they are of the "spiritual estate" *(geistlicher Stand)* by virtue of their baptism.

> For whoever comes out of the water of baptism can boast that he is already a consecrated priest, bishop, and pope, although of course it is not seemly that just anybody should exercise such an office [*Amt*]. . . . There is no true difference between laity and priests, princes and bishops, between the religious and the secular, except for the sake of office and work, but not for the sake of status [*Stand*]. They are all of the spiritual estate. . . . Therefore, just as those who are now called "spiritual" [*geistlich*], that is, priests, bishops, or popes, are neither different from other Christians nor superior to them, except that they are charged with the administration of the Word of God and the sacraments, which is their work and office, so it is with temporal authorities.[4]

According to Luther, the congregation *(Gemeinde)*, as the gathering of the people of God created and maintained by Word and sacraments, shares in the work of ministry. There is no ordination without a "call" *(Berufung)*. Ordination is the call to function in the ministry as one Christian who has been chosen by other Christians to serve in public. The holder of the office of the ministry does not receive a special charism, an "indelible character" *(character indelebilis)*, as medieval canon law taught. Thus the power of ordination ceases when there is no longer a call to work in the ministry of Word and sacraments. That is why Luther insisted on an active ministry on the part of both "officeholders" *(Amtsträger)* and congregations.

References to sources in the footnotes include English titles, either listing an English translation of the primary work cited by the author, or supplementing the references with treatments of the same subject in English. Except where noted, translations of quotations from primary and secondary sources and from the Bible are the translator's. In general, Luther quotations have

---

4. "To the Christian Nobility of the German Nation Concerning the Reform of the Christian Estate," 1520, *WA* 6:407; *LW* 44:129–30. Cf. the alternate translation below, p. 32.

been translated according to the author's rendering of them, with references then supplied to the American Edition of *Luther's Works* (the English titles of which have been used for easy reference). In some cases the translation has been taken over almost completely from the American Edition of *Luther's Works;* such cases can usually be identified by the presence of a footnote citing the American Edition anew at that point in the text (in addition to the general footnote giving references with inclusive page numbers for the American Edition, which appears when the work by Luther to be discussed is first mentioned). The Bibliography lists the English titles for the works of Luther and supplies as well a selection of additional works in English on the topic of this study.

Eric W. Gritsch

Preface

THE PRESENT STUDY had its origins in a lecture I delivered to Wittenberg congregations in the autumn of 1973. The framework was a theological workshop on Reformation research in the German Democratic Republic, which commemorated the four hundred fiftieth anniversary of Luther's 1523 treatise "That a Christian Assembly or Congregation Has the Right and Power to Judge All Teaching and to Call, Appoint, and Dismiss Teachers, Established and Proven by Scripture." Then, during the fall semester of 1975, I taught a seminar in Rostock on the subject of Luther on ministerial office and congregational function. Finally, the Theological Faculty of the University of Copenhagen invited me to deliver a series of lectures on this topic in the fall of 1976. This book is a slightly expanded version of the Copenhagen lectures.

One could say more on this subject, and one could certainly change the emphases. This study, however, is meant to be a historical view which calls attention to sources.

I would like to dedicate this work to the teacher who most especially introduced me to Luther's thought: Dr. Rudolf Hermann. Thirty years ago—in the fall semester of 1947—I, as a student in Greifswald, for the first time attended the seminar in systematic theology in which, under the direction of Hermann, we studied Luther's 1520 treatise "The Babylonian Captivity of the Church." On 3 October 1977 Rudolf Hermann would have been ninety years old. He is not forgotten.

Rostock, Autumn 1977   GERT HAENDLER

1

The State of Research and the Approach to the Task

THE TOPIC "Luther on ministerial office and congregational function" is not a new one. Thus it is necessary to explain why, and for what purpose, it should be dealt with again. First, the subject is of interest to historical research. In 1952 Holsten Fagerberg wrote the book *Confession, Church, and the Office of the Ministry in the German Confessional Theology of the Nineteenth Century*,[1] which deals with a wealth of material. In 1959, Wilhelm Brunotte prefaced his book *The Spiritual Office According to Luther* with an instructive research report entitled "Luther's Conception of the Spiritual Office in Luther Research Since the Middle of the Nineteenth Century."[2] Such surveys of the varied researches on this topic are a sign of the existence of a problem deserving attention.

Second, there is a confessional aspect to the topic. In 1967, at the Wittenberg celebration of the four hundred fiftieth anniversary of the posting of the Ninety-five Theses, Erdmann Schott lectured on "The Office of the Ministry and Charism from the Perspective of the Reformation."[3] Four chapters deal

1. Holsten Fagerberg, *Bekenntnis, Kirche und Amt in der deutschen konfessionellen Theologie des 19. Jahrhunderts*, Uppsala Universitets Årsskrift, no. 9 (Uppsala, 1952). On the office of the ministry, see pp. 101–20, 271–312. The congregation is only cursorily dealt with (pp. 225–39).
2. Wilhelm Brunotte, "Die Auffassung Luthers vom geistlichen Amt in der Lutherforschung seit der Mitte des 19. Jahrhunderts," in *Das geistliche Amt bei Luther* (Berlin 1959), pp. 9–32.
3. Erdmann Schott, "Amt und Charisma in reformatorischer Sicht," in *Reformation 1517–1967*, Wittenberger Vorträge (Berlin, 1968), pp. 127–44.

with the duties of the office, the qualifications for the office, the conferring of the office, and the authority of the office. Schott contrasted Catholic and Protestant teaching in each chapter. In 1972, the Catholic theologian Jan Aarts presented to the Theological Faculty of the University of Helsinki a comprehensive study of *Martin Luther's Teaching Regarding the Office of the Church*.[4] This is not a polemico-confessional work; rather, it is typical of the cooperation in Luther research that is possible between the two communions.

Confessional differences in the evaluation of the office of the ministry have played an important role in the dialogues between the Roman Catholic Church and the Lutheran World Federation. The concluding "Malta Report"[5] lists questions on the office of the ministry in section I E, and especially in section III, "The Gospel and the Office of the Ministry in the Church." There were divergences of recommendations on this section in particular. The Catholic theologian Heinz Schürmann (Erfurt) expressed the wish that "the Lutheran churches would achieve a more binding common understanding on the doctrine of the ministry."[6]

Finally, the confessional aspect produces a third group of writings on our topic. Lutheran theologians have often set themselves the goal of formulating a Lutheran doctrine of the office of the ministry. Luther expressed quite a diversity of views on ministerial office and congregational function, and repeated efforts have been made to harmonize Luther's divergent statements. Regin Prenter formulated the problem very clearly in the title of a 1961 essay, "The Divine Institution of the Preaching Office and the Universal Priesthood According to Luther." Using a large number of Luther quotations, he arrived at the concept of a functional partnership between preaching office and universal priesthood. "The office of the ministry was instituted so that the boundary between preaching office and gen-

---

4. Jan Aarts, *Die Lehre Martin Luthers über das Amt der Kirche*, Schriften der Luther-Agricola Gesellschaft, no. A 15 (Helsinki, 1972).

5. Joint Lutheran/Roman Catholic Study Commission, "Report on 'The Gospel and the Church,'" *Lutheran World* 19, no. 3 (1972), pp. 1–15.

6. Ibid., p. 14.

eral priesthood would be eliminated through the functioning of the office of the ministry. But only in Christ is the boundary eliminated; it is retained in the world until Judgment Day for the sake of the gospel." He then described the functional partnership more closely: "The general priesthood can survive only through the work of the office of the ministry; only the gospel, which is given to the general priesthood, can proclaim the office of the ministry."[7] If one wishes to harmonize Luther's different statements, one can hardly improve on this formulation.

The following study is not intended either to contribute to the history of research or to further confessional dialogue. Nor do I have any new proposals to offer for a systematic determination of how Luther's doctrine on the office of the ministry should be defined. The task I have set myself was otherwise motivated. My unfortunate experience has been that young theologians have very little interest in Luther. Our theology students are focused on present-day congregations, and they want only to be trained for service in a congregation. Dutifully, they also spend some time on Luther, but they expect very little practical help from him for their service in a congregation. And if I am correctly informed, this attitude toward Luther is shared by theologians in Scandinavian countries. To this must be added a second viewpoint in our situation: only the first three centuries of church history concern us directly. After that came the "Constantinian age,"[8] which lasted until the twentieth century, and which is usually written off with the negative judgment that the church was allied to whoever ruled. But since Luther belongs right in the middle of this Constantinian age, he drives us to the question of how he could possibly help us in our situation.

This is the experience that has led me to my concern with this topic. I want to show that interest in the congregation does indeed have very much to do with Luther. In his study "The Congregation and Its Office of the Ministry" (1973), Eberhard

7. Regin Prenter, "Die göttliche Einsetzung des Predigtamtes und das allgemeine Priestertum bei Luther," *Theologische Literaturzeitung* 86, no. 5 (1961): 329.

8. See Gert Haendler, "Das neue Bild Kaiser Konstantins und der sogenannte Konstantinismus," in *Theologische Versuche* (Berlin, 1972), 4:71–88; on Luther, pp. 85ff.

Winkler touched upon this connection when he stated that "Luther, with all his knowledge of the dismal realities of the congregation, counted on a Spirit-guided adulthood. . . . Thus the congregation becomes, in principle, responsible for the order of its life."[9] In 1962, in his book *The Office of the Ministry and Ordination in Luther and Melanchthon,* Hellmut Lieberg looked at the role of the congregation.[10] A section of chapter 2, "Universal Priesthood as the Embodiment of the Office of the Ministry," carries the heading, "The Congregation as Possessor of All Rights and Powers." Chapter 3, "The Establishment of the Concrete Office of the Ministry on the Basis of the Universal Priesthood," contains the heading, "The Delegation (of the Office of the Ministry) by [*durch*] the Congregation." Unfortunately, Lieberg does not work historically, but instead substantiates his investigations with Luther quotations taken from the most diverse chronological periods. In contrast, I would like to present and explain Luther's statements in their historical context. The following study also contains many Luther quotations, but these will always be interpreted in light of their context in the pertinent Luther treatise. In this way I intend to demonstrate how Luther took specific positions derived from very particular situations.

In the formulation "Luther on ministerial office and congregational function," the second concept, the congregation, is intended to assume overwhelming importance. The high point comes in chapter 5, "Luther's Encouragement of Congregations to Be Active, 1522–24." Yet Luther's attitude toward the congregation is to be shown as a development within church history—from his first allusions to the problem in 1517, to his late writings. The context of church history, of course, should be extended much further: it spans the time from the New Testament to our twentieth century.

9. Eberhard Winkler, *Die Gemeinde und ihr Amt,* Aufsätze und Vorträge zur Theologie und Religionswissenschaft, no. 59 (Berlin, 1973), p. 10.

10. Hellmut Lieberg, *Amt und Ordination bei Luther und Melanchthon,* Forschungen zur Kirchen- und Dogmengeschichte, no. 11 (Göttingen, 1962), pp. 65–68, 82–89.

2

Ministerial Office and Congregational Function in the History of the Church Before Luther

THE RELATIONSHIP between the office of the ministry and the congregation in the New Testament has been examined many times. Every reader of the Bible has noticed the varied picture that emerges. This is especially true of the two congregations about which most is reported: Jerusalem and Corinth. The Acts of the Apostles tells the story of the first congregation in Jerusalem: the elders very soon take their place next to the apostles as the leaders of the congregation, which is made especially clear in the depiction of the Apostolic Council (Acts 15). The story is quite different in the congregation of about which Paul wrote in his First Letter to the Corinthians: here, prophets and teachers take their place next to the apostles, followed by miracle workers, those with the gift of healing, assistants, administrators, speakers in tongues (1 Cor. 12:28). Thus there were many offices in Corinth, although there was probably no officeholder whom Paul could have charged with collecting the offerings. The common meals were probably so disorganized because there was no officeholder charged with keeping order.

These short allusions to the differences between the congregations of Corinth and Jerusalem may afford us some insight. Eduard Schweizer began his book *Church Order in the New Testament* with the unequivocal statement, "There is no such thing as *the* New Testament church order."[1] Adolf-Martin Ritter, in the anthology *Who Is the Church? The Office of the Ministry and the Congregation in the New Testament, in Church History, and Today,* came to very similar conclusions. He stated quite clearly that "a uniform understanding of service and functions, and their coordination within the congregation of the New Testament, is out of the question."[2] The most recent studies on this subject, by Gottfried Schille,[3] Heinz Kraft,[4] and Joachim Rohde,[5] also point out the diversity in early Christianity.

The development of the early church can be summed up thus: The office of the ministry gained importance; the congregation lost significance. The First Letter of Clement, sent by the Roman congregation to the congregation in Corinth in A.D. 96, is a particularly informative and well-investigated source.[6] Thus one congregation was writing to another, but the letter's most important thesis was that a congregation did not have the right to dismiss a minister. Sometimes the letter indicates that only a minority of the congregation had conspired against the ministers, but other passages clearly show that the Corinthian congregation had dismissed ministers. First Clement 40 gives the reason for the new theory regarding the nondeposability of ministers:

> Those, therefore, who now present their offerings at the appointed times are acceptable and blessed; for they obey the laws of the Lord, and do not sin. For the high priest has been given his own

---

1. Eduard Schweizer, *Church Order in the New Testament,* trans. Frank Clarke, Studies in Biblical Theology, no. 32 (Naperville, Ill.: Alec R. Allenson, 1961), p. 13.
2. Adolf-Martin Ritter and G. Leich, *Wer ist die Kirche? Amt und Gemeinde im Neuen Testament, in der Kirchengeschichte und heute* (Göttingen, 1968), p. 53.
3. Gottfried Schille, *Anfänge der Kirche* (Munich, 1966); idem, *Die urchristliche Kollegialmission* (Stuttgart and Zurich, 1967).
4. Heinz Kraft, "Die Anfänge des geistlichen Amtes," *Theologische Literaturzeitung* 104 (1975): 81–98.
5. Joachim Rohde, *Urchristliche und frühkatholische Ämter,* Theologische Arbeiten, no. 33 (Berlin, 1976).
6. G. Leder, "Studien zum 1. Clemensbrief" (Th.D. diss., University of Greifswald, 1975), gives a thorough account of past research. Original 1 Clement text in *MPG* 1:287–90, 295–99. English text of 1 Clement in *ANF* 1:5–21. Quotations, 16–17 (*ANF* translation, altered).

office, and their own proper place is prescribed to the priests, and the Levites have been assigned their own duties. But the layman is bound by the laws that pertain to laymen.

The Latin translation uses *homo plebeius* for the word "layman." Cultic service thus distinguishes the minister from the congregation, and the Old Testament ideals of priesthood are taken over. Chapter 44 contains the sentence, "It will not be a small sin if we eject from the episcopate those who have blamelessly and piously made their offerings." The minister's superordination over the congregation was thus assumed, although this special status was at that time still applied to a wider circle: First Clement speaks of bishops and elders in the plural, and does not yet differentiate between these two offices.

The development toward a superordination of ministerial office over the congregation did not proceed all that smoothly. About A.D. 200 Tertullian wrote:

> Come now, you who would indulge your curiosity usefully, if you would apply it to the business of your salvation, run over to the apostolic congregations, in which the very chairs of the apostles are still in place, in which their own authentic epistles are still being read, uttering the voice and representing the face of each. If you are close to Achaja, you'll have Corinth; if you are not far from Macedonia, you have Philippi and Thessalonia; if you get as far as Asia, you will have Ephesus. But if you live close to Italy, you have Rome, where authority waits also for us. How happy is such a congregation . . .[7]

Tertullian did not write that one should rely on the bishops. He demanded that one rely on the congregations which had been founded by apostles and which had received the tradition from the apostles. But this viewpoint had few aftereffects; Tertullian himself became a sectarian in his old age. Nevertheless, his writings are included in every official collection of the church fathers.

The tendency toward an ever-growing emphasis on the office of the ministry is particularly clear in the church father Cyprian

---

7. Tertullian, from the opening speech, "On the Prescription Against Heretics," chap. 36, *MPL* 2:58–59; *ANF* 3:260 (*ANF* translation, altered).

of Carthage (around A.D. 250). This can be documented by quotations from two of his letters. In letter 26 Cyprian wrote:

> Our Lord, whose precepts we must note and obey, orders the honor of the bishop and the polity of his church when he speaks to Peter: "I say to you, you are Peter, and on this rock will I build my church, and the gates of hell shall not overpower it. I shall give you the keys to the kingdom of heaven; whatever you shall bind on earth shall also be bound in heaven, and whatever you loose on earth shall also be loosed in heaven" (Matt. 16:18). Ever since then, throughout the ages and in the change of bishops succeeding one another, the order and structure of the church is such that it is founded on bishops. All ecclesiastical life is regulated by them as the leaders of the church.

In letter 68 Cyprian expressed in even more extreme terms the primacy of one bishop over the congregation: "You must know that the bishop is in the church, and the church is in the bishop. He who is not with the bishop is not in the church."[8] In his book *Cyprian and Novatian,* Henneke Gülzow described how unwaveringly Cyprian strove to achieve primacy over his congregation. This is precisely how he regained the trust of the Roman clergy, which he had lost at the start of the persecution under Emperor Decius in A.D. 250.[9]

The trend toward clericalism finally resulted in the consolidation of the papal office. A letter written in A.D. 492 by Pope Gelasius to the emperor in Byzantium is typical. It deals with the relationship between secular and spiritual power.

> Of the two, the burden on priests is the heavier, since they must render account before God's tribunal even for the kings of men. For you know, most gracious son, that even though you tower over all mankind in honor, you nevertheless bend your head before the administrators of divine matters and expect from them the means of salvation. So also do you realize that at the reception of the heavenly sacraments, if they are properly distributed, you, according to sanctified order, are more the humble receiver, and certainly not the one who gives orders.

8. *MPL* 4:305–6 (Ep. 27); *ANF* 5:305 (*ANF* translation, altered). *MPL* 4:411 (Ep. 69); *ANF* 5:374–75 (*ANF* translation, altered).
9. Henneke Gülzow, *Cyprian und Novatian,* Beiträge zur historischen Theologie, no. 48 (Tübingen, 1975).

After Gelasius first demonstrated the superiority of priests in general, he elaborated the special superiority of the pope:

> If the hearts of believers must humbly devote themselves to all priests, in so far as they administer holy things worthily, how much greater tribute must be paid to the bishop of that see which the Godhead chose to tower over all bishops, and which the whole church has always honored in a childlike way ever since? Therefore, your pious majesty, draw the insightful conclusion that no one may, for any reason or under any pretext, proudly put himself above the unique office of the man who, by the command of Christ himself, has been set as head over all, and whom the holy, honorable church has always piously confessed and still today humbly acknowledges as its supreme head.[10]

Around A.D. 1200 Pope Innocent III reached a new high point in clerical conceptions of the office of the ministry. In his sermon on the occasion of his inauguration in 1198 he said, "For the prophet told me, 'I have set you over nations and over kingdoms to pluck up and to break down, to destroy and to overthrow, to build and to plant' [Jer. 1:10]. The apostle also told me, 'I will give you the keys of the kingdom of heaven. Whatever you bind on earth shall be bound in heaven . . .'" (Matt. 16:18). Innocent declared himself to be the representative of Christ and explained that he was "placed in the middle between God and man, under God but above man, less than God but more than man, judging all but judged by none."[11] The consciousness of the office of the ministry reached a new high point with this statement, while at the same time the congregation was increasingly regulated: Innocent III decreed that every parishioner must make confession to his pastor at least once a year. According to Ritter, in the Middle Ages the relationship between the office of the ministry and the congregation increasingly came to be one "described as in essence that between givers and receivers, between leaders and followers."[12]

---

10. Latin text in *MPL* 59:41–47 (Ep. 8). For a different English translation, see Sidney Z. Ehler and John B. Morrall, eds. and trans., *Church and State Through the Centuries* (Westminster, Md.: Newman Press, 1954), p. 11.

11. Latin and German text in *Quellenheft Die Weltmacht des Papsttums im hohen Mittelalter*, ed. Gert Haendler (Berlin, 1965), pp. 116–19; *MPL* 217:658.

12. Ritter and Leich, p. 90.

There was some opposition. Mystical movements sought a direct approach to God, which would have reduced the importance of priestly mediation. In the essay "The Defender of the Peace" *(defensor pacis)* of 1326, Marsilius of Padua raised doubts regarding the papal understanding of the office of the ministry. Papal power was opposed by conciliarists in Constance (1414–18) and Basel (1431–49). John Wycliffe and John Huss led their territorial churches of England and Bohemia into open opposition. Luther was to have many precedents on which to draw.

3

Luther's Criticism
of the Church's
Hierarchical Structure, 1517–21

LUTHER MADE a very cautious debut with his Ninety-five Theses. Although the Wittenberg congregation's situation was of decisive significance for him, Luther did not call the congregation to active resistance; since he did advise against buying letters of indulgence, one could cautiously use the term *passive resistance*. But he wrote his Ninety-five Theses in Latin and intended to address only his ecclesiastical superiors and professional theologians.

Some time ago there was a controversy over whether or not the public posting of the Ninety-five Theses had really occurred on 31 October 1517. The posting of the theses proved to have much less historical foundation than had been supposed; in any case, the image of a hammer-swinging Luther was problematical to begin with. Yet as late as 1957, at the Fourth Plenary Assembly of the Lutheran World Federation in Minneapolis, a float carrying a Luther constantly hammering the Ninety-five Theses to a door was paraded through the streets.[1] Many people's enthusiasm for a hammer-swinging Luther could have some connection with the residual mythical image of the hammer-swinging Teutonic God Asathor, even though Luther bears little resemblance to him. Luther probably did affix the Ninety-five

1. Franz Lau, "The Posting of Luther's Theses—Legend or Fact?" *Concordia Theological Monthly* 38, no. 11 (1967): 691–703.

Theses—but how seldom do public notices get read! Can one really imagine that many members of the Wittenberg congregation stopped in front of the Castle Church to read ninety-five theses in Latin? Perhaps not even Luther's colleagues noticed them; in any case, there is no record of any disputation about them. Moreover, a perusal of the theses shows that no case can be made for a call to active resistance. A hint relevant to our subject can be recognized in thesis 37, "Any true Christian . . . participates in all the blessings of Christ and the church."[2] But that is a very general formulation. Thus, in view of our topic, we can say that the beginning of the Reformation in 1517 occurred because of the situation existing in the Wittenberg congregation, but that the congregation was not asked to help itself actively.

Luther was driven on against his will. In 1519 he debated against Eck in Leipzig. Eck pressed for a debate of the primacy of the pope. Luther wished to avoid the subject. Eck succeeded in getting Luther to say that popes and councils could err. This was quite an achievement for Eck, who had intended to expose Luther as a heretic. Thus Luther was forced along a path he had not chosen. But as late as 1520 Luther still had no thought of a congregation helping itself. In his "Treatise on Good Works"[3] Luther declared, "Therefore, we must not despise those of little faith who cling to their ceremonies and perform them as though they were lost in their faith without them. They would gladly do right and learn better, but they are as yet unable to grasp it all. Instead, one should blame their ignorant, blind teachers, who have never taught them what faith is, and have led them so deeply into works." The responsibility for these abuses is therefore that of the ministers rather than the congregation. Luther drew the following pastoral conclusion: "One should gently lead them back to faith in their good time, as one would treat a sick person." Thus parishioners are compared to sick people who must be treated with consideration. Some of

2. *WA* 1:235. *LW* 31:29.
3. *WA* 6:202–76; quotations, 214–215, 259. *LW* 44:17–114; quotations, 36–37, 92–93.

the arguments that followed were used again in Luther's Invocavit sermons of 1522.[4] He permitted "that they cling for a while to some good works for the sake of their conscience and as necessary for salvation, so long as they do not yet really understand faith, so that they may not totally shatter and confuse their weak consciences, thus losing both faith and works when we tear them away too quickly." Luther did not expect much from the congregation. He recognized the primacy of the office of the ministry and soberly expressed himself on the matter as follows: "For the poor people believe and behave just as they see and hear the spiritual authority believe and behave. If they see and hear nothing, they believe and do nothing, because the only intention with which the spiritual authority was instituted was to lead the poor people to faith in God." Luther therefore assessed the situation very realistically and did not expect to achieve anything by activating congregations.

This viewpoint is also expressed in the title of his programmatic treatise, written in the summer of 1520, "To the Christian Nobility of the German Nation Concerning the Reform of the Christian Estate."[5] Luther turned to the authorities in the hope that a reform of the church and of society could be achieved through a council. The treatise begins with a description of the three walls the papacy has erected to protect itself against all attempts at reform. Luther said, "They have a horrible fear of a really free council"; and whoever has studied the historical development of the reform councils must agree with him. The new portrayal of the—until recently little-known—Council of Pavia-Siena in 1423–24 shows that although the pope had respected the Council of Constance's decision regarding the summoning of councils, he had already at that time, one hundred years before Luther, employed every means to limit and if necessary to suppress the convening of a council.[6]

Our topic, the office of ministry and the congregation, already

---

4. See below, pp. 47–54.
5. *WA* 6:404–69; quotations, 406–14. *LW* 44:123–217; quotations, 127–38.
6. Walter Brandmüller, *Das Konzil von Pavia-Siena 1423/24*, 2 vols., Vorreformatorische Forschungen, no. 16 (Münster, 1968–74).

comes into view in the treatment of the first wall. Luther said, "It has been an invention that pope, bishops, priests and the monastic people are called the spiritual estate, and nobles, masters, artisans, and farmers are called the secular estate." He then revealed his contrary position, which he would later state repeatedly: "All Christians are truly of the spiritual estate [*Standes*], with no difference among them but that of office [*Amtes*]. Paul says in 1 Cor. 12:12 that we are all one body, but every member has its own work by which it serves others. This is because we all have one baptism, one Gospel, one faith and are all Christians alike; for baptism, Gospel, and faith alone make a spiritual Christian people." Next to Paul, Peter is called upon as chief witness: "We are all consecrated priests through baptism; as St. Peter says in 1 Pet. 2:9, 'You are a royal priesthood and a priestly nation.'" The relationship between a minister and his congregation is described with an analogy. "It is like ten brothers, all king's sons and equal heirs, choosing one of themselves to rule the inheritance in the interests of all. In one sense they are all kings and of equal power, and yet one of them is charged with the responsibility of ruling."[7] Here the congregation is compared to royal children, whereas only a few months earlier it was likened to sick people!

Soon afterward, Luther presented another analogy:

> Suppose a group of earnest Christian laymen were taken prisoner and set down in a desert without an episcopally ordained priest among them. And suppose they were to come to a common mind there and then in the desert and elect one of their number, whether he were married or not, and charge him to baptize, say mass, pronounce absolution, and preach the Gospel. Such a man would be as truly a priest as though he had been ordained by all the bishops and popes in the world. That is why in cases of emergency anyone can baptize and give absolution. This would be impossible if we were not all priests.[8]

This allusion to emergency recurred in Luther. He pointed to examples in the history of the church: "In times gone by

7. *LW* 44:128.
8. Ibid.

Christians used to choose their bishops and priests in this way from among their own number, and they were confirmed in their office by other bishops without all the fuss that goes on nowadays. St. Augustine, Ambrose, and Cyprian each became [a bishop in this way]."[9]

This new definition of the relation of the office of the ministry to the congregation leads to far-reaching consequences. Luther demanded that the possessors of secular authority, insofar as they were baptized Christians, be considered priests and bishops, "and count their office as one belonging to and useful to the Christian congregation." This "Enlightenment" aspect of Luther is startling: usefulness to the congregation was important to him. He underlined the significance of the congregation: "Because we are all priests of equal standing, no one must push himself forward and take it upon himself, without our consent and election, to do that for which we all have equal authority. For no one dare take upon himself what is common to all without the authority and consent of the community."[10] On the basis of this presupposition Luther made the oft-quoted statements regarding the congregation's right to dismiss a minister. We should also keep tradition in mind: as early as the first century I Clement claimed that a minister could not be dismissed by the congregation! But Luther argued: "And should it happen that a person chosen for such [ministerial] office were deposed for abuse of trust, he would then be exactly what he was before. Therefore, a priest in Christendom is nothing else but an officeholder. As long as he holds office he takes precedence; where he is deposed, he is a peasant or a townsman like anybody else. Indeed, a priest is never a priest when he is deposed."[11] Luther did not elaborate in any way on the circumstances in which a priest may be dismissed. Dismissability need not be proven; it is self-evident. He expressed his opinion quite clearly: "But now the Romanists have invented *characteres indelebiles,* and say that a deposed priest is nevertheless something different

9. Ibid.
10. *LW* 44:129.
11. Ibid.

from a mere layman. They hold the illusion that a priest can never be anything other than a priest, or ever become a layman. All this is just contrived talk, and human regulation."[12]

Luther's further train of thought is marked by the fact that he often linked the words *office* and *work*. In this way the concept of ministerial office is whittled down even more. Luther explained "that laymen, priests, princes, bishops, and as they say, spiritual and secular ones basically differ in no way but in that of office and works. They do not differ in estate, for they are all in the spiritual estate." A few lines further on, we find the same combination: "Those who are now called 'spiritual'—or priests, bishops, or popes—are no further or more worthily separated from other Christians than that they are to deal in the Word of God and the sacraments. That is their work and office. In the same way, the secular authorities bear sword and rod to punish the wicked and protect the pious." Luther's formulation of work and office acquires an even sharper outline in the following sentences: "A cobbler, a smith, a peasant, each has his own trade's office and work, yet all are equally consecrated priests and bishops. Each should be useful to the other and serve him with his office and work, so that a variety of works are done for one congregation." An important argument is once again usefulness to the congregation. But even more important is the concept of the office of the ministry visible here, for Luther spoke quite naturally of the office of the cobbler, the smith, and the peasant.

Of course, Luther addressed the Christian nobility in this treatise; his main concern was the office of the authorities:

> . . . since the temporal power is ordained of God to punish the wicked and protect the good, it should be left free to perform its office in the whole body of Christendom without restriction and without respect to persons, whether it affects pope, bishops, priests, monks, nuns, or anyone else. If it were right to say that the temporal power is inferior to all the spiritual estates (preacher, confessor, or any spiritual office), and so prevent the temporal power from doing its proper work, then the tailors, cobblers, stone-

12. Ibid.

masons, carpenters, cooks, innkeepers, farmers, and all the temporal craftsmen should be prevented from providing pope, bishops, priests, and monks with shoes, clothes, house, meat, and drink, as well as from paying them any tribute.[13]

To tear down the first wall claiming superiority of the spiritual over the secular, Luther used scripture passages, specifically those passages demanding subjugation to secular authorities. "Thus St. Paul says to all Christians, 'Let every soul (I maintain the pope's too) be subject to authorities; for they do not bear the sword in vain, but to serve God with it to punish the wicked and to praise the pious' [Rom. 13:1, 4]. St. Peter too says, 'Be subject to all human regulations for the sake of God who desires it [1 Pet. 2:13, 15].'" Then Luther touched once more on the deposability of an ecclesiastical officeholder. At issue was the theory that a pope could not be judged by anyone. This theory had gained solid shape around A.D. 500 and was thus about a thousand years old.[14] Luther commented: "That is why the chief devil himself must have said what is written in the canon law: if the pope were so destructive as to lead a large crowd of souls to the devil, he could still not be deposed. In Rome, they build upon this cursed and satanic foundation and think that the whole world should go to the devil before their knavery is opposed."

The second wall concerns the opinion that only the pope is charged with the interpretation of Holy Scripture, so that no one else can appeal to it independently. Luther's refutation is significant. He referred to the apostle Paul's advice to the Corinthians, "If a better revelation is made to someone, even though he is already sitting and listening to someone else speaking God's Word, then the first, who is speaking, should be silent and give way" (1 Cor. 14:30). Luther interpreted, "Of what use would this command be if only the speaker sitting at the head is to be believed?" The office of the ministry and the congregation collide in sentences like these: on the one hand the papal

13. *LW* 44:130–31.
14. The theory was often circumvented. See Harald Zimmermann, *Papstabsetzungen des Mittelalters* (Vienna, 1968).

office in its medieval culmination, and on the other hand Paul's free congregation in Corinth. But Luther's preference is quite clear. "Thus it might indeed happen that the pope and his cohorts were wicked and were neither good Christians nor taught by God, and that they were without understanding, whereas an obscure person did have the correct understanding. Why should that person not be obeyed? Has not the pope erred many times? Who would help Christendom when the pope erred if there were not someone else who had Holy Scripture on his side and was believed more?"

Luther confronted the conviction, held to be valid for centuries, that only the pope, as the successor to Peter, had received the power of the keys; and again Luther assumed a clear stance of opposition which has relevance to our question regarding the congregation. It is "clear enough the keys were given not to St. Peter alone, but to the whole congregation." So once again there is a clear appeal to the congregation! Luther spoke of pious Christians who have the correct faith, spirit, understanding, word, and opinion of Christ. These Christians should be obeyed rather than the pope. This is substantiated by the words of the creed, "I believe in the holy Christian church" ("Ich glaube an die heilige christliche Kirche"). It does not say, "I believe in the pope in Rome." In the final analysis, our question regarding the relationship of the office of the ministry and the congregation is at stake, even in this kind of juxtaposition.

Luther once more recurred to the common priesthood of all believers. "Moreover, we are all priests, as has just been said; we have one faith, one Gospel, and the same sacrament. How could we not also have the power to taste and to judge what is right and wrong in faith? Where then is Paul's word in 1 Cor. 2:15, 'The spiritual man judges all things and is himself judged by no one'? as well as 2 Cor. 4:13, 'We all have the same spirit of faith'? How should we not feel, just as well as an unbelieving pope, what to faith is even and uneven?" So once again Luther took his arguments from Paul's Epistles to the Corinthians; once again the ideal of the early Christian free congregation is contrasted to an inflated concept of the office of the ministry. Luther added three examples of how famous men of God had to be instructed: "So, long ago, Abraham was forced to heed his Sarah, who was in much greater submission to him than we are to anyone on earth [Gen. 21:12]. So too was Balaam's donkey much wiser than the prophet himself [Num. 22:21–35]. Since God spoke against a prophet through a donkey, why should he not be able to speak against the pope through a pious person? In the same way St. Paul opposed St. Peter as a man in error in Gal. 2:11–12. That is why it is proper for every Christian to concern himself with faith, to understand it, to fight for it, and to condemn all errors."

Luther then attacked the third wall, the pope's right to convene a council. He again took his arguments from the Bible, naming two particular passages. The first is Matt. 18:15–17: "If your brother sins against you, go and tell him his fault, between you and him alone. . . . if he does not listen, take one or two others along with you. . . . If he refuses to listen to them, tell it to the congregation; and if he refuses to listen even to the congregation, let him be to you as a heathen." Luther interpreted this passage as, "Here every member is commanded to take care of every other. How much more must we do this when a governing member, common to us all, deals evilly and thereby harms and offends the others greatly! If I am to accuse him before the congregation, then I must first call them together." Thus Luther considered the congregation the highest court before which the highest officeholder of the church must defend himself.

The second passage is Acts 15, where the Apostle Peter did not hold a position of leadership at the Apostolic Council. Starting with this passage, Luther drew a parallel in the history of the church, explaining, "If St. Peter alone had been in charge, it would not have been a Christian council but rather a heretical council. Even the famous Nicene Council was convened and confirmed not by the bishop of Rome but by the Emperor Constantine. Following him, many emperors did the same, and these were the most Christian councils. But if the sole power rests with the pope, they must all have been heretical." Luther pointed to the emergency in the church that required a council: "That is why, when need requires it, and when the pope is offensive to Christendom, whoever can do so first—as a loyal member of the whole body—should see to it that a true, free council is convened. No one can do this as well as the secular sword, especially since they are now also fellow Christians, fellow priests, equally spiritual, equally powerful in all things, and must give free rein to their office and work—which they have from God over everyone—to go wherever it is needful and useful to go." We have here the same thought we have had before: office and work must be useful. Luther made it even plainer with an analogy.

> Would it not be unnatural if a fire broke out in a city and everybody were to stand by and let it burn on and on and consume everything that could burn because nobody had the authority of the mayor, or because, perhaps, the fire broke out in the mayor's house? In such a situation is it not the duty of every citizen to arouse and summon the rest? How much more should this be done in the spiritual city of Christ if a fire of offense breaks out, whether in the papal government, or anywhere else![15]

The thought of an active role for the congregation is becoming apparent here, although Luther was certainly thinking only of the council at the moment. He added one more point: "There is no power in the church except for improvement. That is why, when the pope intends to use his power to defend himself against convening a free council, so that the improvement of the church is obstructed, then we should ignore him and his power." The Letters to the Corinthians provided him with one more item of corroboration: "For Paul says, in 2 Cor. 10 [:8], 'God gave us authority not to ruin but to improve Christendom.' Who wants to skip this saying?" The premises behind Luther's thoughts on improving the Christian estate are obvious.

In June 1520, shortly before the publication of "To the Christian Nobility of the German Nation Concerning the Reform of the Christian Estate," a lesser-known Luther treatise appeared, "On the Papacy in Rome, Against the Most Celebrated Romanist

15. *LW* 44:137.

in Leipzig."[16] Clearly this essay is also significant for our topic. Luther outlined his theme with the words,

> This then is the matter in question: whether the papacy in Rome, insofar as it possesses actual power over all of Christendom, as they say, is derived from divine or human order. And if so, whether it would be a Christian statement to say that all other Christians in the whole world are heretics and schismatics—even though they adhere to the same baptism, sacrament, Gospel, and all articles of faith in harmony with us—if they do not have their priests and bishops confirmed by Rome.

Here Luther carried on a tradition of criticism which had been widespread in the Middle Ages, especially after the papal schism in the fourteenth century. But Luther did not criticize just the papacy; he questioned the whole hierarchical structure of the church. He spoke of an external Christianity and called it

> an assembly in a house or a parish, a bishopric, an archbishopric, a papacy. Externals at such assemblies consist of singing, reading, and the vestments of the mass. Here, above all, one calls bishops, priests, and monastics "spiritual estate" not because of their faith, which they may not have, but because they have been anointed with external ointments, wear crowns, wear particular clothes, say particular prayers, do particular works, hold mass, go to choir, and seem to do more of this kind of external worship.

Thus the issue is not just the papacy. Luther listed a number of offices again: "To these belong all popes, cardinals, bishops, prelates, priests, monks, nuns, and all those who can be taken for Christians by external characteristics, whether or not they are really thorough Christians." Through this process, Luther arrived at the conclusion that officeholders are by no means necessarily good Christians simply on account of their office. On the other hand, there may be good Christians who are not officeholders. Luther's devaluation of the office of the ministry is expressed in this argument as well, and every congregation is of course also affected by this formulation of the question.

Luther's "Babylonian Captivity of the Church," which was

---

16. *WA* 6:285–324; quotations, 286–87, 296–97. *LW* 39:51–104; quotations, 57–58, 69–70.

published in October 1520, is of decisive importance, since it questions the whole medieval doctrine of sacraments and deals with the necessary consequences of Luther's reformulations.[17] Luther wrote the treatise in Latin. Obviously, as with the Ninety-five Theses he had no intention of driving members of congregations to the barricades. Rather, he wished to challenge his theological colleagues to a discussion. We know about the sharp rejection this treatise called forth, but we also know how deep an impression it made on John Bugenhagen [since 1523 the pastor of Wittenberg's Town Church].

At the very beginning, Luther judged the papal office with bitterness: "I am sure that the papacy is the kingdom[*regnum*] of Babylon." But it must be remembered that this image did not originate with Luther. The idea of the pope as antichrist had appeared as early as the twelfth century and was reiterated often during the thirteenth and fourteenth centuries.

Luther dealt with the mass at length. He realized clearly that he was touching on difficult problems which also affected the financial foundations of the church. He wrote:

> I am here attacking something difficult, which may be impossible to tear down, for it is reinforced through centuries of usage, has been accepted unanimously, and has therefore dug itself in so deeply that one would have to change or abolish the majority of today's textbooks and almost the whole external structure of the church, and one would have to introduce, or rather reinstitute, a completely different structure of ceremonies. But my Christ lives, and one should heed God's Word more carefully than the thoughts of all human beings or angels. I shall exercise my office.

We shall encounter Luther's application of the word *office* to his own activities again many times.

Luther's statements regarding the sacrament of ordination of priests are of particular importance to our topic of the office of the ministry and the congregation. Luther sought the biblical foundation for this sacrament, as he did for all other sacraments. Is there a promise of grace for such a sacrament? The

17. *WA* 6:497–573; quotations, 498, 512, 560, 563, 564, 566. *LW* 36:5–126; quotations, 12, 36, 107, 112–13, 116–17.

answer is clear: the New Testament does not have a single word to say about it. There is an ancient custom in the church, but Luther wished to differentiate clearly between a sacrament instituted by God and church customs established at some point in history. He therefore wrote, "Nor does the church have any authority to establish new promises of grace, as many people foolishly say when they say that everything commanded by the church is no less important than what God has commanded." Luther returned to his basic assertion: "The Word of God is incomparably superior to the church." The consecration of priests signifies a devaluation of baptismal grace and encroaches on the rights of the evangelical community. "That loathsome tyranny of clerics over the laity" began with the ordination of priests. Luther very logically contrasted this medieval sacrament to his thoughts on the general priesthood of all the baptized, referring to 1 Pet. 2:9: "But you are a chosen race, a royal priesthood, and a priestly kingdom." Luther interpreted, "That is why we are all priests as much as we are Christians. But those we call priests are servants, chosen from among us, who do everything in our name; their priesthood is only a service." This passage states quite clearly that the office of the ministry grows out of the priesthood of all the baptized and that the minister serves in the name of the congregation. Once again Luther appealed to 1 Corinthians: "This is how one should regard us, as servants of Christ and stewards of the mysteries of God" (1 Cor. 4:1 RSV). Luther interpreted the significance of the consecration of priests positively: it is "a particular [*gewisse*] form of electing a preacher in the congregation." Once more the linking of the office of the ministry to the congregation is clearly expressed.

A little further on, Luther spoke of the duties of a priest: "The priest's office is to preach; and if he does not do so, he is a priest exactly as much as a painting of a person is a person." Once more he said, "we are all priests in the same way," which means "equal power in Word and sacrament." But Luther followed this with the demand "that no one should make use of this power unless permitted to do so by the community, or unless called to do so by a superior. For no one may usurp something that belongs to all until called to do so." For our modern understanding, the difference between being called by "everyone"—therefore by the local congregation, after all—or by an ecclesiastical superior is important. Luther on the other hand tended to give both possibilities equal weight, due to his polemics against ordination to priesthood; thus he anticipated present practice: a call to a parish originates at one time "above" with a church agency, at another time "below" by means of congregational election. Occasionally the way in which a pastor can carry on ministry is influenced by the pastor's ability to appeal to the fact of his or her election by the congregation. Luther himself, when undergoing personal troubles, consoled himself with the opposite, that he had been called to his office by the magistrate. He wanted to brandish this call, like a spear, before the devil.[18] But the question did not interest him much at this point.

The decisive factor for Luther was the task of the office of the ministry. "The priestly office is really nothing but service to the Word—to the Word, I say, not of law but of Gospel."[19] At this point Luther became upset and stated, "He who does not know the Gospel or does not preach it is not only not a priest or bishop, he is a plague in the church who, under the false title of priest or bishop, suppresses the Gospel by playing the wolf in sheep's clothing in the church." Luther once again mentioned in this connection the possibility of dismissing an officeholder:

> Therefore, insofar as we learn from scripture that what we call priesthood is a service, I do not see at all why someone who once became a priest could not become a layman again, since he distinguishes himself from a layman only through his service. But the likelihood of being dismissed from service is so great that it is even now the usual punishment meted out to a guilty priest.

At the conclusion of his statements on the ordination of priests, Luther spoke of already being at work on a new treatise.

18. *WA* 10³:3. See the first of the "Eight Sermons at Wittenberg," 1522, *LW* 51:73.
19. *LW* 36:116. This definition is reiterated in the strongest terms in the Latin text; see *WA* 6:566.

He hoped that the sacrament of the ordination of priests would one day collapse, and here elaborated on this hope. "Then the joyous freedom will return to us, we shall recognize our equality in the law; and, when the yoke of tyranny has been shaken off, we shall know that whoever is a Christian has Christ, and whoever has Christ has all things that are Christ's, and is a lord of all things. I shall write more, and more strongly, about this matter."

Two short months later, in November 1520, the above-mentioned treatise appeared, "The Freedom of a Christian."[20] Luther dedicated it to the then-ruling Pope Leo X, but it is extremely doubtful that the pope ever read it. At all events this version of "The Freedom of a Christian" can scarcely have evoked much papal enthusiasm. To summarize: the freedom of a Christian does not depend on a pope or on any other church official. The freedom of a Christian is a matter of the personal faith of individual Christians. Only faith attains for the soul what cannot be attained by external means, justification before God and therefore freedom. A decisive factor is the Word of God, Christ's consoling promise—the concept which underlay Luther's critical examination of the whole doctrine on sacraments in "The Babylonian Captivity." The freedom of a Christian is attained when the soul believes the Word and comes into agreement with God. In this way a mystical union between the soul and Christ can take place, and sinful humanity is freed through such a union. The contents of this first half of the treatise already demonstrate that the freedom of a Christian is completely independent of any ecclesiastical office. The second part delineates the ethical consequences. Here again Luther finds no place for a discussion of ecclesiastical office. Luther's main concern was rather that free Christians know they are committed to good works in order to tame their own bodies and serve their neighbors.

This short summary demonstrates that there can be no place in the treatise for the ecclesiastical office. Let me reinforce this

---

20. *WA* 7:20–38; quotations, 27–29. *LW* 31:329–77; quotations, 354–56.

view with a few quotations. Luther said that Christ was King and Priest, and elaborated on this traditional teaching: "Thus his priesthood does not consist of external demeanor and clothes, as we see it in people; rather, it is invisibly in the spirit, in the way in which he unceasingly intercedes for his own before God, sacrifices himself, and does everything a pious priest should do." Shortly after this Luther quoted the often-mentioned passage, "You are a priestly kingdom and a royal priesthood" (1 Pet. 2:9). His interpretation was, "And what therefore happens is that Christians are elevated so far above all things that spiritually they become lords of all; for nothing can impair their salvation." He continued, "That is a very great, honest honor, and a really omnipotent rule, a spiritual kingdom, since nothing is so good or so bad but that it must serve me to my good, as I believe; and yet I do not need it, for my faith is sufficient for me. See what precious freedom and power this is for Christians!" He elaborated on the priesthood of believers.

> Moreover, we are priests. That is much better than being king, because priesthood renders us worthy to appear before God and to plead for others. For to appear before the eyes of God and to plead is improper for anyone but priests. Thus Christ won us so that we may spiritually defend and plead for each other, as a priest bodily defends and pleads for the people.

It is quite clear that Luther did not think of officeholders specifically; they could be included, insofar as they possess this freedom of a Christian. But according to Luther, this freedom applies to all Christians, who are thus all called to the priesthood. Every Christian is urged to intercede for others. Every Christian thus fulfills a priestly service.

A little later, Luther addressed the difference between officeholder and lay person. He stated:

> Now if you ask, What then is the difference between priests and laity in Christianity, if all are priests? then I answer: The little words *priest, parson, spiritual* were treated unjustly when they were separated from the larger group of words and applied to the small group which is nowadays called "spiritual estate." Holy Scripture makes only the differentiation of calling the educated or consecrated *ministros, servos, oeconomos,* which mean "servants," "serfs,"

"stewards," who are to preach Christ, faith, and Christian freedom to others. Although we are all priests, we cannot all serve or work or preach. Paul, 1 Cor. 4[:1], said, "We want to be regarded only as servants of Christ and stewards of the Gospel."

Luther again took his arguments from Paul's Letters to the Corinthians; the difference between the first Christian congregation of Corinth and the papal church of the late Middle Ages is again pointed out. Luther continued:

> But now stewardship [*Schaffnerei*] has been turned into such a secular, external, magnificent, horrible rule and authority that the lawful secular power can in no way equal it, just as though laity were not Christian people. Thus our whole understanding of Christian grace, freedom, and faith has been abolished, as well as everything we have received from Christ, and Christ himself. Even though we have overcome much of human law and human works, we have become the absolute serfs of the most incompetent people on earth.

The wealth of ideas Luther developed in 1520 can be illustrated with one final example: in Wittenberg, in front of the Elster gate, he threw into the fire the papal bull condemning him. Other books were also burned, books of canon law. Given Luther's views on ecclesiastical office, this burning was logically a consistent act. Luther in his statements on the structure of the church delved deeply into canon law. In April 1521 he appeared before the Diet of Worms, where a recantation had been demanded from him.[21] Luther refused and thus adhered to all his previous statements. At the Wartburg he had time to think and was tempted by the thought that he might have erred, but he remained loyal to his cause. He also expressed himself again on the subject of the office of the ministry and the congregation. On 1 August 1521 he wrote to Melanchthon, "I never want to celebrate private mass again until eternity."[22] In his treatise "The Misuse of the Mass"[23] he also said that a congregation is necessary for the correct celebration of the mass. The Word

---

21. See Joachim Rogge, ed., *1521–1971 Luther in Worms* (Berlin, 1971); "Luther at the Diet of Worms, 1521," *LW* 32:103–31; De Lamar Jensen, *Confrontation at Worms* (Provo, Utah: Brigham Young University Press, 1973).
22. *WA Br* 2:372–73. *LW* 48:281.
23. *WA* 8:482–563. *LW* 36:129–230.

must be communicated to others, and the sacrament must be distributed to others. There cannot be such a thing as a private mass, a "corner mass" *(Winkelmesse)* which the officeholder celebrates by himself. The problem of the office of the ministry and the functioning of the congregation *(das Problem Amt und Gemeinde)* is not just a question of law; it has a vital connection with worship.

4

The Conflicts
in Wittenberg, 1521–22

Reforms were begun in Wittenberg under the decisive influence exerted by the newly appointed provost of the All Saints' Chapter Justus Jonas, who acted entirely according to Luther's ideas. The Augustinian Friars, Luther's fellow monks, were active partisans of Luther; and Gabriel Zwilling, especially, worked perseveringly for the abolition of the mass as hitherto celebrated. On 21 September 1521 Melanchthon distributed the Lord's Supper in both kinds; he did it in a rather small circle which had probably had some previous experience with this form of celebration.

But the most important man we have to deal with, one who strongly influenced the Reformation in Wittenberg, is Andreas Bodenstein, known as Karlstadt. Alfred Otto Schwede popularized this interesting personality in his novel *The Opponent (Der Widersacher)*. Karlstadt had come to Wittenberg in 1505, only three years after the founding of the university. His lectures were popular, his textbooks successful, and he could look forward to good opportunities for advancement. He was an important pillar of the new university. Karlstadt was dean of the Theological Faculty in 1512, when Luther received his doctorate. Luther's appearance on the scene undoubtedly pushed Karlstadt somewhat into the background. There were some strong theological differences between the two men despite their many agreements.[1] In 1521, when Luther moved to Worms and was later carried off to the Wartburg, Karlstadt received a prestigious call to Copenhagen but soon returned home to Wittenberg.

It was Karlstadt's turn to celebrate the Christmas service in 1521. He appeared without liturgical vestments and during the sermon explained that participation in the Lord's Supper without previous confession was possible. The Latin form of the mass was shortened considerably, and all phrases mentioning a sacrifice in the Eucharist were dropped. The words of institution were spoken in German, and the Lord's Supper was distributed in both kinds. Two thousand people supposedly took part in this celebration; the whole congregation was now involved. It must be remembered that these changes could find support in Luther, for Luther was convinced that his demands must also be converted into practice. On 12 December 1521 he had written to Spalatin that one could not confine oneself forever to debating; one must also act.[2] He also liked Karlstadt, welcoming the latter's marriage enthusiastically.[3]

Outbreaks of violence started in Wittenberg, mostly involving students. Karlstadt called for the removal of images. Two laymen from Zwickau claiming to be prophets appeared with the intent of speeding up the Reformation. They claimed to have the direct inspiration of the Holy Spirit, and they made a deep impression on the people. Melanchthon in particular was not sure how to evaluate these Zwickau prophets. He expressed his doubts in a letter: "I cannot tell you how deeply moved I am. . . . We must be very careful not to resist the Spirit of God; but we must also be sure not to fall into the devil's trap."[4] The elector was worried and wanted to preserve peace and order. On 14 January 1522 a formal complaint regarding the events in Wit-

1. See Leif Grane, *Modus loquendi theologicus,* Acta theologica Danica, no. 12 (Leiden, 1975), pp. 130–46; Ronald J. Sider, *Andreas Bodenstein von Karlstadt,* Studies in Medieval and Reformation Theology, no. 11 (Leiden: E. J. Brill, 1974); James S. Preus, *Carlstadt's Ordinaciones and Luther's Liberty* (Cambridge, Mass.: Harvard University Press, 1974).
2. *WA Br* 2:412. *LW* 48:353–55.
3. To Nicholas von Amsdorf, 13 January 1522. *WA Br* 2:423. *LW* 48:363.
4. To Elector Frederick, 27 December 1521, *CR* 1:514.

tenberg was presented before the imperial council of regency in Nuremberg; and on January 20 it was demanded in Nuremberg that the innovations be revoked.

This was the situation facing Luther when he returned home. He had returned secretly once, in December 1521, but now on March 6 he returned openly, against the wishes of his elector, who would have liked to keep him at the Wartburg a while longer. On March 9, Invocavit Sunday, he preached his first sermon after the enforced interim and preached every day for several successive days, restoring peace to Wittenberg.

Our topic, the office of the ministry and the function of the congregation, is touched upon several times in these "Invocavit sermons" of 1522.[5] He startled every hearer at the very beginning of the first sermon: "We are all summoned to die, and no one can die for the other. Everyone must individually be armored and armed to fight against the devil and death. We can shout into each other's ears, console each other, and urge patience, fight, and battle. But each one of us must be prepared for the time of his own death . . ." Luther wanted to sharpen the conscience of every single Christian. It is a matter of questions for which Luther too must bear responsibility at the hour of his death. The congregation is an assembly of believers among whom Luther counted himself. He could even say, "Some of you have a stronger faith than I." He did not wish to command others; rather, he was ready to hear others and to follow others. Again and again he defended the weak members in the congregation, who ought to be shown some consideration. Luther demanded "that we treat the divine Word with fear and humility, and help, advise, and do good to each other in all our needs, and accept the other's misfortune, fear, misery, and offensiveness as though they were our own." This is where the congregation's predicament is given expression: fear, misery, offensiveness!

Although the Wittenberg congregation had participated in the new form of worship service, there were probably many

5. *WA* 10³:1–64; quotations, 1, 6, 8–11, 15, 17, 21–22, 28, 30, 42, 45, 56–57, 59, 63. "Eight Sermons at Wittenberg," 1522, *LW* 51:69–100; quotations, 70–72, 74, 76–77, 79, 81–83, 89–90, 96–99.

reservations afterwards. Luther took these reservations seriously and pointed to the responsibility all Christians bear for themselves. He had no intention of deciding authoritatively and refused to absolve the congregation from its responsibility. Luther himself only wanted to be a believer among other believers and could say in his first sermon, "If there is someone who has something better, and to whom more was revealed, then I will subjugate my reason and understanding to his and not insist on my meaning but instead follow him." This once again refers to the early Christian congregation in Corinth, to whom Paul had given such directions in 1 Cor. 14:30. Luther had often used this passage to refute papal demands; now he was being consistent in applying the passage to himself as officeholder in Wittenberg. This readiness to accept correction did not, however, hinder Luther from telling his congregation what he thought. "That is why all those who helped or condoned the abolition of the mass have erred." Luther was the officeholder, and for him the office took on the character of a duty, an overriding obligation: "I know, and am certain, that I did not volunteer for the preaching office, nor did I put myself forward; instead, I was summoned into it and was chosen to preach here against my will." He saw that the Wittenberg congregation has strayed onto a path he considered wrong. He did not wish to revoke the congregation's responsibility, but he told them clearly that as their authorized minister he disagreed with them, and that they should have asked him. "That is why you did wrong to start such a game without my advice or consent, or without even asking me beforehand. I was not that far away from you; you could have reached me by writing, whereas not the slightest communication was sent to me." The situation in Wittenberg at the beginning of 1522 was complicated: the city council, the university, and the monastery disagreed among themselves; the elector had made his wishes plain; and Luther's attitude was also controversial. But from the viewpoint of our topic a certain logic cannot be denied: Luther did not wish to decide authoritatively, but he did speak his mind clearly. His criticism of the congregation also meant that he considered them responsible.

The second Invocavit sermon describes the situation in the Wittenberg congregation. "There are many who have to go along, but still don't know what to think, whether it is right or wrong. So they say, 'I do not know what to think; I had to follow the congregation, the crowd and its power.'" We see once again that Luther assigned a major role to the congregation. But he also recognized a danger, namely, that the congregation can become a prison for individual Christians. Helmar Junghans wrote in reference to Luther's Invocavit sermons: "A new order, rather than evangelical freedom, took the place of the papal order. This is what Luther opposed."[6] In his second Invocavit sermon Luther did in fact proclaim a principle of individualism which would leave the decision up to every individual. "But I did not wish to make a statute for them or press for a uniform order. Whoever wanted to obeyed, and whoever did not want to stayed out." He counted on some being won over sooner, others later. He warned, "But wherever total head and heart are not involved, let God handle it, I beg you, for you would not do any good." Luther the pastor knew that the congregation as such also carried its own weight. Thus he explained a little later in the sermon: "You will not accomplish anything with such storminess and violence. You will see. And if you get stubborn and refuse to be guided, then know that I won't be on your side. I will bluntly deny you!" At this point, Luther the officeholder threatened his congregation; and yet one can also see how highly he rated the importance of the congregation. Then comes the famous passage in which Luther explained that the Reformation had occurred only through the Word of God, that he himself had contributed nothing but had instead been drinking Wittenberg beer with his friends.[7] Luther had again returned to his basic premise, the Word of God; and he derived

6. Helmar Junghans, "Freiheit und Ordnung bei Luther während der Wittenberger Bewegung und der Visitationen," *Theologische Literaturzeitung* 97 (1972):98.

7. On this passage, see Kurt-Victor Selge, "Der Weg zur Leipziger Disputation zwischen Luther und Eck im Jahr 1519," in *Bleibendes im Wandel der Kirchengeschichte*, ed. Bernd Moeller and Gerhard Ruhbach, (Tübingen, 1973), pp. 170–71; *LW* 51:77.

from this the point that violence must not be used, not even by a congregation which forces its members to participate in new forms of worship services despite the fact that many members are not yet ready to do so.

Luther pursued this thought in the third Invocavit sermon. He explained that there are many things "left free by God, which one can do or not, such as getting married, eliminating images, becoming a monk or a nun, monks or nuns leaving the cloister, eating or not eating meat on Fridays, and whatever else there may be." Again he warned against letting the Wittenberg congregation decide for the individual. "It is not enough to say, 'This one or that one did it'; 'My neighbor eats meat on Fridays; that is why I eat it too'; 'Everyone is doing it now; that is why I am doing it too'; 'I went along with the crowd'; and whatever other senseless words may be used. . . . In this case every person must stand up for himself and be armed to the fullest." Thus Luther not only advocated greater independence for individual congregations; he also foresaw dangers.

Luther also dealt comprehensively with the problem of images,[8] which would come up again later. He knew about the possible misuse of images, but for him that was no reason to eliminate them entirely. "Why do you condemn something one could very well use?" He emphasized the freedom of a Christian and included himself. "It is quite true, dear friends, that we are free and masters of all food, be it meat, fish, or butter; that we may eat them all and use them when we wish. No one can deny that, for God has given us this freedom." But Luther warned against the congregation's abuse of such freedom. "We must know how to use our freedom correctly, and behave differently in this matter with the weak, and still differently with the obstinate." We must learn "that we should use our freedom at the right time."

Then, on the question of the sacrament, Luther again spoke as an officeholder, because things had happened that truly upset

---

8. See Hans von Campenhausen, "Die Bilderfrage in der Reformation," in idem, *Tradition und Leben* (Tübingen, 1960), pp. 361–407.

him. "You think it is necessary to grab the sacrament with your hands and want thus to be good Christians. In this matter you have made a crude mistake. . . . God could have borne all the other things, but to handle this thing so outrageously, that he cannot and will not bear." Luther scolded his congregation because they "wished to touch the body and blood of Christ with their own hands, greedily and insolently, without any timidity or fear." Thus in the fifth sermon he repeated the threat he had already made in the second sermon: "If you do not stop this practice, no emperor or king or anyone else may drive me away from here—I will run away from you without being driven!" In this connection he pointed to the universal church. "The custom in the whole of Christendom is to receive the holy sacrament from the priest's hands. . . . That is why one must be very careful not to institute any innovation contrary to the praiseworthy old tradition. . . . Do whatever you wish with the other externals, but leave God's own thing alone, and simply believe his words. So stop this abuse and arrangement; that is my sincere advice and urgent plea."

The sixth sermon also deals with the sacrament. Luther did not want anyone to be compelled to attend the Lord's Supper; he himself had experienced the fact that one is not always equally prepared. "Today I have the grace to do it, tomorrow I won't." He conceded to other Christians what he had himself experienced, and that is why he demanded freedom in the congregation.

Luther repeatedly reproached the congregation for lacking love. He elaborated on this in his seventh sermon and quoted Paul, 1 Cor. 13:1–3 (RSV): "If I speak in the tongues of men and of angels, but have not love, I am a noisy gong or a clanging cymbal. And if I have prophetic powers, and understand all mysteries and all knowledge, and if I have all faith, so as to remove mountains, but have not love, I am nothing. If I give away all I have, and if I deliver my body to be burned, but have not love, I gain nothing." Luther commented, "These are hard-hitting words; but you have not come this far yet." He addressed his congregation directly.

You here in Wittenberg have received great gifts of God, and many of them, including knowledge of scripture, which is a very great gift and blessing. Moreover, you have the pure, clear Gospel, but you do not want to come forth with love. You like it when God is good to you and shares his gifts with you. But you refuse to share anything with others: no one extends a hand to another, no one seriously cares for anyone else. Instead, all are concerned only with what is advantageous to themselves. . . . Since I have preached to you for so long and, in almost all my books, have preached nothing but faith and love, it is pitiful to feel no love at all in you.

He added a threat to this description of the situation. "I declare unto you that if among yourselves you do not show love for each other, God will send a great plague over you. For he does not want his word to be preached and revealed in vain; nor does he want his word dishonored or despised. You tempt God too much!" It was again Luther the officeholder who spoke warningly to his congregation; at the same time, he presupposed their responsibility and demanded action from them.

In his last Invocavit sermon Luther brought up a possible field of congregational activity: confession. He described the early church procedures: "If someone had sinned publicly, so that people knew about it, then that person was accused publicly before the crowd. If he recanted, they prayed to God for him and helped him to be reconciled. But if he did not recant and refused to heed the crowd or the congregation, then he was placed under the ban and expelled and excluded by the assembly." Luther quoted Jesus' words from Matt. 18:17, "If he refuses to listen even to the congregation, let him be to you as a heathen and a tax collector." Luther's interpretation followed. "If the congregation expelled him and accepted him back, then he was also expelled and accepted back by God." Luther turned to Matt. 18:18 for support—to the passage describing the conferring of power to bind and to loose on all the apostles. He regretted the fact that such public confession is no longer in normal use. "Whoever could reinstitute this confession would perform a valuable service. Even here, dear friends, you should have made an effort to reinstitute this confession and left other things alone. For no one would have been upset by these other things." This formulation made rather clear what Luther thought of the congregation: the congregation was active but had unfortunately chosen the wrong field of activity. They should not have tampered with the mass, the sacraments, or the images. Instead, they could have concerned themselves with confession. Luther painted what could happen with bold strokes but added with resignation: "This would be a Christian work for whoever could bring it about. But I do not trust myself to do it alone." We shall see that he made a similar judgment in 1526.

Luther thus tried to counteract a mistaken development from its inception: confession should not be made compulsory. That is what he accused the pope of having done, and then added, "Precisely because of this I refuse to confess, because the pope commanded it!" But confession in itself is helpful. "There are many doubtful and erroneous matters that people cannot deal with by themselves or even understand." Luther advised people who are troubled and seek consolation to "go and confess your sin to your brother in secret, and ask for absolution and a consoling word. If he gives you absolution and tells you your sins are forgiven, that you have a gracious God and merciful Father who will not count your sins against you, then believe this assurance and absolution cheerfully, and be sure that God himself is assuring you through your brother's mouth." This is the point at which Luther sought an active congregation: at the proclamation of God's grace.

This does not mean that Luther handed out a placebo to the congregation at the end. He did not simply invent this idea in 1522. It can be demonstrated that Luther placed great value on this point his whole life long: the congregation has full authority to forgive sins. That can be seen already in his "Response to the Dialogue of Silvester Prierias on the Power of the Pope" of 1518,[9] and in the "Resolution Concerning Thesis 13 on the Power of the Pope" of 1519.[10] We also encounter this idea in his "To the Christian Nobility of the German Nation Concerning

9. "Ad dialogum Silvestri Prieriatis de potestate papae responsio," *WA* 1:647–86.
10. "Resolutio Lutheriana super propositione XIII de potestate papae," *WA* 2:183–240.

the Reform of the Christian Estate" of 1520.[11] In 1530 Luther published a special treatise entitled "The Keys,"[12] and he made other relevant statements on this subject in 1537 and 1539.[13]

---

11. *WA* 6:412. *LW* 44:135.
12. *WA* 30²:435–507. *LW* 40:323–77.
13. In the "Smalcald Articles," 1537. See articles 7–9 on "the keys," "confession," and "excommunication," *BS*, pp. 452–57, *BC*, pp. 311–14; "On the Councils and the Church," 1539, *WA* 50:509–653; *LW* 41:143–66.

5

Luther's Encouragement of Congregations to Be Active, 1522–24

Luther was again involved with the problem of the office of the ministry and the congregation only a month after his Invocavit sermons. The city of Altenburg had a Catholic clergy under a provost, even though the majority of the population had already converted to Evangelical thinking. Now one of the clerical posts had become vacant. How should it be handled? The Altenburg city council wrote to Luther, and the Catholic provost turned to the Elector Frederick. Existing statutes favored the provost.

Luther took the matter in hand. He wrote to the Evangelical theologian Gabriel Zwilling to be ready to assume the position in Altenburg, and at the same time he wrote to the city council in Altenburg to encourage them to stand firm. The elector appointed a commission to resolve the conflict. Thereupon Luther, on his own authority, traveled to Altenburg to urge the Evangelical congregation, as represented by the city council, to act.

The post in question was tied to specific financial arrangements; yet Luther brushed that problem aside for the time being and stated, "But when it is a matter of doctrine and of the salvation of souls, no one is obliged to give way, to obey, to do or not to do whatever is contrary to correct doctrine."[1] He made the point that the Catholic provost and his priests did not proclaim the Gospel, that they even opposed it. That was why the

1. *WA Br* 2:507; the whole correspondence, 504–24.

city council should act, for Christ had warned, "Beware of false prophets!" Although the city council could drive this provost and his priests from Altenburg, Luther counseled patience. The council should, however, demand that the provost and his priests keep silent or preach the pure Gospel.

The Altenburg city council had some doubts: do laymen really have the authority to judge such things? Luther encouraged them: "Scripture gives . . . every Christian the power to judge teaching . . . to know and avoid the wolves. . . . Do not depend on the conclusions of other people, even if they be angels, but rather on the conscience of each, for each must have his own faith and must know the difference between correct and false teaching." This sounds like the beginning of the first Invocavit sermon, in which Luther reminded his Wittenburg congregation that they were responsible for their own salvation.

After making these basic observations, Luther dealt with the legal and financial details. He was of the opinion that a priest who opposes the Gospel loses his right to receive remuneration. "For they do not receive payment for murdering souls but rather for preaching the Gospel; when they do not do that, we shall not pay them." The provost had the legal right to make the first recommendation to fill the vacancy; but Luther explained that there can be no seal, law, custom, or authority against God!

The elector was not exactly enthusiastic about Luther's actions, especially since he had unpleasant memories of Luther's candidate, Gabriel Zwilling, as a troublemaker. Nevertheless, Luther was partially successful. The right to fill the preaching position was denied to the provost and transferred to the city council. The Danish Luther scholar Leif Grane stated with regard to the occurrence in Altenburg in 1522: "No docility at all is to be seen in Luther at this point. There are reasons for this, since it was not a matter here, as it had been in Wittenberg, of the structure of worship or of ecclesiastical traditions in general. Rather, it was a matter of what was to him all-important: the proclamation of the Gospel. He did not succeed in electing Zwilling . . . but the city council kept the right to fill the clergy position."[2]

Luther was consulted in connection with matters in another city that same year of 1522: Leisnig, around sixty-two miles south of Wittenberg. Here too the Reformation had taken hold among the population. Thus there was a congregation with Evangelical leanings, but the church administration was under the jurisdiction of a neighboring monastery. What should one do? A delegation from Leisnig approached Luther again in January 1523. He gave them a pamphlet with a long title, "That a Christian Assembly or Congregation Has the Right and Power to Judge All Teaching and to Call, Appoint, and Dismiss Teachers, Established and Proven by Scripture."[3] This pamphlet, in which Luther encouraged the small congregation to persist in their ways, is probably the clearest expression of his position.

Luther started with the viewpoint which to him is decisive:

> First of all it is necessary to know where and what the Christian congregation is, so that people do not engage in human affairs, as non-Christians have been used to doing since the beginning, in the name of the Christian congregation. One can certainly recognize the Christian congregation by the fact that that is where the pure Gospel is preached. For just as one can recognize the general and the army in the field by the sure symbol of the army's military banner, so does one recognize with certainty where Christ and his army are by the Gospel. We have God's sure promise of this in Isa. 55:10[-11], "My Word, says God, that goes forth from my mouth shall not return to me empty, but as the rain falls from heaven to earth, making it fruitful, so shall my Word accomplish everything for which I sent it."

Luther answered the small Leisnig congregation on the basis of that premise. "That is why we are sure that no matter where the Gospel is, there are Christians, however few there may be and however sinful and weak they may be." He thus gave the ques-

---

2. Leif Grane, "Thomas Müntzer und Martin Luther," in *Bauernkriegsstudien,* ed. Bernd Moeller, Schriften des Vereins für Reformationsgeschichte, no. 189 (Gütersloh, 1975), p. 81.
3. *WA* 11:408-16. *LW* 39:303-14.

tioning congregation a helpful answer: it is not a matter of the size of a congregation, not even of its accomplishments; it is a matter of God's promise.

Luther seriously questioned whether in his day the ecclesiastical authorities were fit or able to proclaim the Gospel. He therefore advised the congregation that one "should not care at all about human statutes, law, old tradition, custom, or habit . . . be it established by pope or emperor, prince or bishop, be it lasting for one or for a thousand years. For the human soul is an eternal thing above everything temporal, and therefore must be ruled and taken hold of only by the eternal Word. It is despicable to govern with human law and long-established custom before God, and so one must behave here according to scripture and God's Word."

The existing legal situation, which Luther had already attempted to push aside highhandedly in Altenburg, he now completely dismissed in Leisnig.

> Human words and teaching have established and ordained that judgment of teaching should be left to bishops, scholars, and councils. The whole world should regard their conclusions as law and articles of faith. . . . For one hears from them almost nothing but the boast that the authority and right to judge what is Christian or heretical rests with them, and that the common Christian should await their judgment and withhold his own. Look how this boast . . . shamelessly and foolishly rages against God's law and Word!

He drew on biblical evidence to show that a simple Christian can hear the voice of Christ and can therefore judge the teaching presented to him in a sermon. He took his first argument from John 10: Christ "takes both the right and the authority to judge teaching from the bishops, scholars, and councils, since in John 10[:3–5] he says, 'My sheep know my voice . . . my sheep will not follow strangers, but they will flee from them, for they do not know the voice of strangers.'" This argument probably made sense to the Leisnig congregation, for a herd of sheep is powerless and must depend on the help of the shepherd alone. Thus it will understand its shepherd's voice better than others who are not so dependent on that voice because they have control of their own means of power. Luther put it, "Bishops, pope, scholars, and everyone have power to teach, but the sheep should judge whether they are teaching Christ's voice or the voice of strangers. . . . That is why we let bishops and councils conclude and establish whatever they want; but if we have God's Word on our side it should be up to us, and not them, to decide whether it is right or wrong, and they should yield to us and obey our word." He gave the harsh explanation that "bishops, religious foundations, monasteries shamelessly take away the judgment of doctrine from the sheep and ascribe it to themselves through their own law and desecration." Thus the Christians were once again told that they might go their own way with a clear conscience.

Luther referred to other biblical passages as well. In Matt. 7:15 Jesus warns in the Sermon on the Mount, "Beware of false prophets." Luther interpreted, "You see, here Jesus does not give the power of judgment to the prophets and teachers but to the students and sheep. For how could one beware of false prophets if one could not consider, judge, and decide?" The third Bible passage is 1 Thess. 5:21: ". . . but test everything; hold fast what is good." Luther's interpretation was:

> See, he does not desire any tenet or teaching to be obeyed unless it is heard, tested, and recognized as good by the congregation that hears it. For this testing is not the concern of the teachers; rather, the teachers must announce beforehand that one should test. So here too judgment is withdrawn from the teachers and given to the students among the Christians, so that the situation is completely different among Christians from the way it is in the world. In the world, the rulers command what they wish and their subjects obey. But Christ says, "Among you this should not be so." Instead, among Christians, each is the judge of the other, and on the other hand, each is subject to the other, no matter how well the spiritual tyrants have succeeded in turning Christendom into a secular power.

Luther's reference to 1 Thessalonians was quite applicable to the situation in Leisnig: the congregation in Thessalonica had

become uncertain too. Some members had expected the imminent return of Christ, which did not occur; some of them had
even stopped working in the expectation of the end of the
world. It was to them that Paul had written the famous words
"Whoever does not work should not eat." The words "test everything; hold fast what is good" were meant to address this uncertainty in the congregation of the Thessalonians. Paul meant,
"Do your own thinking, make your own judgments, assume your
own responsibility." That is exactly what Luther wanted to say
to the Leisnig congregation in 1523, for they too were uncertain.
He summed up his thoughts: "All prophetic pronouncements
teaching us to avoid human teaching do nothing but take the
right and power to judge all teaching away from the fathers
and, on pain of losing their soul, place it on the listeners instead,
with the serious decree that they not only have the right and
power but are also duty bound to judge, on pain of incurring
the displeasure of divine majesty."

Luther's position is clear: consequences must be drawn from
the new knowledge of faith, for it is a matter of salvation of the
soul. Luther ended the first half with:

> Thus we conclude that if there is a Christian congregation that has
> the Gospel, they not only have the right and the power but also
> owe it to the salvation of their souls to do their duty—laid upon
> them by Christ in baptism—to avoid, to flee from, to depose, and
> to withdraw from the authorities, as long as the present bishops,
> abbots, monasteries, religious foundations, and their like act as
> they do, because it can be clearly seen that they teach and govern
> against God and his Word. So, for the time being, let this be es-
> tablished strongly enough and surely enough, so one can depend
> on it, that it is according to God's will and necessary for the soul's
> salvation to get rid of or to avoid such bishops, abbots, monasteries,
> and whatever belongs to this realm.

That is exactly what the Leisnig congregation had done.

The second part deals with the question of what more can
now be done. Luther outlined the problem: "Since a Christian
congregation neither can nor should exist without God's Word,
it follows clearly enough from the above that it must neverthe-

less have teachers and preachers who work with the Word." The Leisnig congregation had refused the Catholic pastor who had come from a neighboring monastery. Now they were required to become active. Luther said:

> We must follow scripture and call from among ourselves and elect those we find qualified, whom God has enlightened with intelligence, endowed with gifts, and anointed as priests, as Christ says in John 6[:45], "And they shall all be taught by God," and Ps. 45[:7], "Therefore God . . . has anointed you with the oil of gladness above your fellows." These fellows are the fellow Christians, the brothers of Christ who are anointed priests with him, as Peter also says in 1 Pet. 2[:9], "You are a royal priesthood, that you may proclaim the virtue of him who called you into his marvelous light."

It is obvious that Luther here repeated ideas he had expressed in 1520—only now, the doctrine of the general priesthood of all baptized is to be put into practice.

At this point the same doubts arose in Leisnig that had already come up in Altenburg. Luther said, "So you say, 'Yes, but how? If he is not called, he is not permitted to preach, as you yourself have taught!'" As a matter of fact, Luther had declared that not every Christian can simply preach whenever and wherever he may wish. He now dealt with the problem in detail: one cannot make doctrinaire decisions that must be adhered to in every case; much depends on the particular circumstances. He therefore wrote to Leisnig:

> Here you must imagine a Christian in two different places. First, if he is in a place where there are no Christians, he needs no other call than that he is a Christian, called and anointed internally by God. Here it is his duty to preach and teach the Gospel to the erring pagans and non-Christians, out of the duty of brotherly love, even though no human being has called him to do so. This is what St. Stephen did, Acts 6, who had not been commissioned to a preaching office but who preached anyway and did great wonders among the people. Philip the deacon, Stephen's companion, in Acts 8[:5] did the same thing, and he was not commissioned to a preaching office either; and so did Apollos in Acts 18. For in a case like this a Christian, out of brotherly love, sees the need of the poor lost souls and does not wait to see whether orders or a

letter will come from princes or bishops. Emergency breaks all laws and itself has no law. Thus love is duty bound to help wherever there is no one else who helps or should help.

One could interject here that Leisnig was not in such an extreme emergency. But Luther's point was clear: the Gospel must be proclaimed, and questions of order are of secondary importance. Moreover, he referred to three figures in Acts who preached without being commissioned to do so: Stephen, Philip, and Apollos. There were also some questions at the time about how Christians could continue to live under Muslim rule. So Luther did not present just pure theory to the Leisnig congregation. It was a way of making it clear to the Christians in Leisnig that they were still relatively well-off. They were a congregation, and they could act.

But how should the congregation proceed? Luther explained that a Christian should "not put himself forward, but rather wait to be commissioned and pulled forward . . . that he preach and teach in the stead of and at the request of the others." There might be a situation in which a Christian should open his mouth even without being commissioned: when he is convinced that false teaching is being proclaimed. But restraint is necessary even then. Luther reminded them of the congregation in Corinth, where Paul was forced to oppose many prevalent abuses. He referred to a passage we have already seen quoted many times: "If a revelation is made to another sitting by, let the first be silent" (1 Cor. 14:30 RSV). The application of this maxim can produce many consequences for the good order of a congregation! But Luther interpreted this Pauline verse unequivocally: "See what St. Paul does here: he tells the one who is teaching to be silent and to withdraw to the midst of the Christians, and the one who is listening to step up even if he is not commissioned, for need has no law." He did not want all the members to speak at once, as had occurred in Corinth. He was heading in a different direction: "So if Paul calls upon someone in the midst of the Christians to step up if it is necessary, even if he is uncommissioned, and commissions him through such a Word of God; and if he calls upon the other to withdraw, and dismisses him through the power of these words; how much more rightful it is that a whole congregation commission such a one to such an office, if necessary—as it was then, and is particularly so now." So the point is not that the Corinthian example be imitated in Leisnig in 1523. Rather, Luther encouraged the congregation to trust itself to do what individual Christians in Corinth trusted themselves to do. The Leisnig congregation "should have no doubt that the congregation which has the Gospel may and should select and commission someone from among themselves to teach the Word in their stead."

Of course Luther knew that the New Testament also contains examples of ministers being appointed by superiors. He wrote: "But you say, 'But St. Paul commanded Timothy and Titus to appoint priests [1 Tim. 4:13; Titus 1:5]; and we also read in Acts 14[:23] that Paul and Barnabas ordained priests in the congregations. That is why the congregation cannot call someone, nor can someone put himself forward to preach among Christians. Rather, the permission and command of bishops, abbots, or other prelates is necessary, for they represent the apostles.'" Luther answered that the bishops of the sixteenth century were not true bishops. But he added one important comment: officeholders were never appointed to congregations in the early church without the consent of the congregation in question. He wrote: "No bishop should appoint someone without that congregation's election, will, and call; instead, he should confirm the person chosen and called by the congregation. If he does not do this, the person should nevertheless be confirmed by virtue of the congregation's call." Luther turned to the Bible for documentation: "Neither Titus nor Timothy nor Paul ever appointed a priest without the congregation's election and call. This is clearly proven when he [Paul] says in Titus 1:[7] and 1 Tim. 3[:2] that a bishop or priest must be above reproach and [1 Tim. 3:10] that deacons should be tested first. Now Titus probably did not know who were above reproach; these reports must come from the congregation, who must name someone like that." Luther pointed to the first congregation in Jerusalem, in which, according to Acts 6[:1–6], the congregation chose the deacons and the apostles confirmed them. He added, "So then, if the apostles were not permitted on their own authority to place anyone into such an office, which is concerned only with the distribution of finite food, how could they have been so reckless as to appoint someone to the highest office—that of preaching—on their own authority and without the congregation's knowledge, will, or commission?"

Among the examples Luther cited from the history of the church was the circumstance that the pope too was elected by his own congregation. Today the pope is elected by cardinals from all over the world, and the Roman congregation has relatively little influence. But in previous centuries it was different, and that is why Luther could say that if the congregation in Rome could elect its bishop, the congregation in Leisnig could elect its pastor too.

Finally, Luther mentioned the fact that many ministers are appointed by secular authorities and that bishops and popes have had to reconcile themselves to it. Of course, Luther did express his concern that such appointments could mean a contempt for the preaching office. Accordingly he formulated the often-quoted words, "That is why he on whom the preaching office is imposed has the highest office in Christianity." Luther, at the end of the treatise, had come full circle back to his starting point: the proclamation of the Gospel is of the utmost importance, for which every single Christian and every congregation—no matter how small—is responsible. Soon afterward he gave the congregation a bit of concrete help by approving the "Ordinance of the Common Chest."[4] Magister John Gruner and Heinrich Kind were also a great help in Leisnig.

In addition there is a whole series of short reports from the years 1522–24 to show how often Luther supported other congregations or took positions on the topic "congregation." A letter dated 29 July 1522 is concerned with the election of an Evangelical minister by St. Michael's Church in Erfurt. Luther supported the position that the ruling prince ought not to op-

4. *WA* 12:11–30. *LW* 45:161–94.

pose the congregation's choice.[5] On 12 December 1522 Luther wrote to Count Schwarzburg-Leutenberg with the intention of achieving the Leutenberg parish church's independence from a monastery.[6] In May 1522 Luther was in Eilenburg to support the congregation there; he wrote to Spalatin on 5 May 1522 from Eilenburg, asking for his help as advisor to the elector to make the appointment of an Evangelical pastor to Eilenburg possible.[7] A treatise was sent to Prague dealing with the particular circumstances of the Bohemian church.[8] Luther mentioned the possibility of a father of the family assuming the function of priest. He could read the Gospel to his own family, he could baptize, he could govern himself and his family according to Christ's teaching. It is more than obvious that this argument is based on the universal priesthood. Such an arrangement would of course signify an emergency, and Luther is of the opinion that in such a case the administration of the Lord's Supper would have to be forgone. But it is not quite clear whether Luther designed this treatise on his own or whether he was adapting it in large measure to the pleas of his Bohemian guest.

In December 1523 Luther wrote letters to two widely separated places: the first, a "Letter of Consolation to the Christians in Augsburg,"[9] dealt with very particular troubles in that city; the second, to Margrave Albrecht of Prussia, Grand-Master of the Teutonic Order, "A Brief Instruction Concerning the Foundation on Which Christ Built His Church or Congregation,"[10] was more theoretical.

Luther took part in the Reformation in Magdeburg for many years. The congregations were eager to move ahead with the Reformation; but it was, after all, the city of Archbishop Albrecht of Hohenzollern, who had once sent out the indulgence preacher John Tetzel. Therefore the city council was compelled to exercise caution. Nicholas Amsdorf was to be sent to Magde-

---

5. To John Riedesel, 29 July 1522, *WA Br* 2:583.
6. *WA Br* 2:625–27.
7. To Spalatin, 5 May 1522, *WA Br* 2:515–17.
8. "Concerning the Ministry," 1523, *WA* 12:169–96. *LW* 40:4–44.
9. *WA* 12:221–27.
10. *WA Br* 3:209–14 (in Latin); 214–19 (in German).

burg from Wittenberg, but the elector wished to avoid any appearance of mixing in the affairs of Magdeburg.[11] Luther and Amsdorf then went to Magdeburg. In a letter dated 1 September 1524 Luther wrote that there were five Evangelical preachers active in the city, including his intimate friend Nicholas Amsdorf, and added, "Magdeburg is doing well and is growing in Christ."[12] In the same letter he reported that John Bugenhagen was to go to Hamburg. That plan was controversial, for Luther wanted to send another candidate to Hamburg. He wrote in general terms of the "Hamburg church" *(ecclesia Hamburgensis),* although there were in fact two congregations active there, the congregations of St. Nicholas and St. Peter.[13] Luther also supported the congregation in Kemberg in a letter dated 24 November 1524.[14]

11. For details, see Irmgard Hoess, *Georg Spalatin* (Weimar, 1956), pp. 256ff.

12. *WA Br* 3:337.

13. Franz Lau, "Der Bauernkrieg und das angebliche Ende der lutherischen Reformation als spontaner Volksbewegung," *Lutherjahrbuch* 26 (1959): 126. English version, "Did Popular Reformation Really Stop with the Peasants' Defeat?" trans. Kyle C. Sessions, in *Reformation and Authority: The Meaning of the Peasants' Revolt,* ed. Kyle C. Sessions (Lexington, Mass.: D. C. Heath & Co., 1968), pp. 94–101.

14. To Spalatin, 24 November 1524, *WA Br* 3:390–91.

6

Luther's Criticism of the Congregation in Orlamünde, 1524–25

LUTHER'S COLLEAGUE Karlstadt had left Wittenberg and moved to Orlamünde, about fifteen miles south of Jena. He had received about a hundred thirty guilders a year from his parish position in Wittenberg, but in Orlamünde the position was held by an assistant pastor, who had to make do with seventeen guilders.[1] Now Karlstadt wanted to take charge of this parish himself and relinquish his professorship in Wittenberg. Erich Hertzsch wrote:

> Karlstadt, who has the serious intention of beginning a new life, now moves to Orlamünde in order to function as pastor there. He can no longer tolerate his obligation as a member of the All Saints Chapter to take part in the worship services which he feels he must reject but for which he receives the large income of an archdeacon. He is no longer comfortable at the university. Many of his old friends suspect him, distrust him, avoid him, and indeed deride him. After all, he is pastor of Orlamünde. Why should he not turn this right into a duty that would fulfill his life?[2]

Karlstadt sharply rejected Luther's arguments in the 1522 In-

1. One sixteeth-century guilder was worth about $13.40 in 1950. See Ernest G. Schwiebert, *Luther and His Times* (St. Louis: Concordia Publishing House, 1950) p. 311.
2. Erich Hertzsch, "Luther und Karlstadt," in *Luther in Thüringen*, ed. R. Jauernigg (Berlin, 1952), p. 95. Hertzsch has demonstrated his ability as Karlstadt scholar through his *Karlstadt und seine Bedeutung für das Luthertum* (Gotha, 1932). See also Ronald J. Sider, ed., *Karlstadt's Battle With Luther* (Philadelphia: Fortress Press, 1978).

vocavit sermons. He had no desire to treat the weak with consideration; he wanted to enforce the law of God. In the spring of 1524 he wrote, "I ask whether I should leave the idols God has commanded me to remove until all the people agree to the removal; again, whether I am allowed to blaspheme God until the others stop blaspheming. . . . Should we teach God's commandments slowly? Should we wait for the crowd? Should one person look at the other and wait to see who will be first?" Karlstadt warned against speaking about brotherly love while leaving images alone until "the weak become strong." He demanded, "One should take away, the sooner the better, whatever God has forbidden, whatever leads to sinning against him, and whatever corrupts one's neighbor."[3]

A direct confrontation between Luther and Karlstadt took place in August 1524. Luther was to inspect the congregation of Orlamünde on one of his visitations. Along the way he preached in Jena against the "enthusiasts" *(Schwärmer)*. Karlstadt was in the audience and reproached Luther afterward. They met that evening in the Black Bear Inn, and Luther challenged Karlstadt to debate him in Wittenberg.[4]

Karlstadt responded, "I know how you have attached people to yourself." So the Wittenberg congregation was backing Luther, and Karlstadt no longer expected any sympathy from them.

Luther accused Karlstadt of preaching in Orlamünde without a proper commission. "For you certainly were not called. Or who asked you to preach?"

Karlstadt answered, "If we are talking about human calls, then I know very well that it is my due, because of the archdeaconate; but if we are talking about a divine call, then I also know I have something to report."

3. Karlstadt to Barthel Bach, in *Klassiker des Protestantismus*, ed. Reinhold Fast (Bremen, 1962), 4:251–69.
4. "What Dr. Andreas Bodenstein von Karlstadt Talked Over with Dr. Martin Luther at Jena" ("Was sich Dr. Andreas Bodenstein von Karlstadt mit Dr. Martino Luthero beredt zu Jena," *WA* 15:334–340. A different English translation available in Sider, *Karlstadt's Battle With Luther*, pp. 36–48.

Luther dug deeper: "Who asked you to preach in this parish?" Karlstadt answered, "Aren't these one and the same people who listen in All Saints Chapter and in the parish?"

Thus Karlstadt rested his argument on the fact that a congregation heard him as a preacher. Luther ignored that argument, and the conversation became quite heated. Luther gave Karlstadt a guilder so he could write against him. Karlstadt complained that anything he wrote against Luther would not be printed in Saxony.

It was after this preliminary bout that Luther arrived in Orlamünde. The report on the visitation stems from one of Karlstadt's friends, probably the preacher Reinhard, who had already accompanied Karlstadt to Denmark in 1521.[5] This report is critical of Luther but probably does not contain any falsifications. One can well imagine the event. Luther is portrayed as arrogant: he arrived late and refused to preach when asked to do so. He complained about a letter he had received from Orlamünde and is quoted as saying, "I consider you simple souls, and I cannot believe that you composed this letter yourselves. I will not hold the letter against you, and I give you the benefit of the doubt. But I suspect Karlstadt composed the letter and sent it under the seal of the city." This suspicion aroused the protest against Luther that the congregation certainly considered itself quite capable of composing a letter and that the city council protected its own seal.

The controversial letter was then reprinted. Luther objected to the passage "Our minister and pastor, Andreas Karlstadt, has . . ." and stated, "You call him your minister, but my lord Duke Frederick and the University of Wittenberg know nothing about it. Nor will it be conceded to him."

Whereupon a city official answered, "If Karlstadt is not our

---

5. "The Dealings Between Dr. Martin Luther and the Council and Parish of the City of Orlamünde" ("Die Handlung D. Martin Luthers mit dem Rat und Gemeinde der Stadt Orlamünde"), *WA* 15:341–47. See also Sider, *Andreas Bodenstein von Karlstadt*, Studies in Medieval and Reformation Theology, no. 11 (Leiden: E. J. Brill, 1974), chap. 5.

minister, then Paul taught falsely and your books must also be false. For we elected him, as our letter to the above-mentioned university proves."

According to the record, Luther in this case too ignored the fact that a congregation had elected a pastor. Instead he argued about whether or not Karlstadt should be present at the discussion. At this point Karlstadt voluntarily left the room, with the result that now Luther was indeed talking only to simple members of the congregation. The people who spoke up were the mayor, the secretary of the council, one member of the congregation, a cobbler, one councilman, and another member of the congregation. It was the cobbler who contradicted Luther on the issue of images, saying that images had been prohibited through Moses. He offered to bet Luther that the Books of Moses contain a prohibition against images. The record states:

> A councilman spoke. "Doctor, friendly brother, you will admit that Moses is an interpreter of the Ten Commandments?"
>
> Martin said, "Yes."
>
> Then the councilman continued, "It is written in the Ten Commandments, 'You shall not have idols' [Exod. 34:17], and soon afterwards, in Moses' interpretation, there follows, 'You shall remove the images and have none!'"
>
> Martin said, "Yes, that speaks about idolatrous images. Those to whom one prays are idolatrous. What harm does a crucifix on the wall do me if I do not pray to it?"
>
> A cobbler said, "I have often removed my hat in front of an image on the wall or along my way, and that is idolatry, an insult to God, and does great harm to a poor human being, and that is why one should not have images."
>
> Martin spoke. "Then you must also, because of abuses, kill all women and dump all wine."
>
> Another member of the congregation answered, "No, they are creatures of God, created for our succor, our abstention, and our need, which he has not ordered us to destroy. But we have been commanded to remove the images which were made by human hands."
>
> But Dr. Martin clung to the word "idolatrous images."
>
> The cobbler proceeded, "Indeed, I would concede this to you if all images had not been forbidden in Moses."
>
> Then Martin Luther said, "It does not say that in Scripture."

The cobbler said, "I bet you whatever you like, it does say it!" and they shook hands and bet.

The report continues:

> Then someone brought the Book of Moses, and the text was read to Martin which said: "Therefore take good heed to yourselves. Since you saw no form on the day that the Lord spoke to you at Horeb out of the midst of the fire, beware lest you act corruptly by making a graven image for yourselves . . . the likeness of male or female, the likeness of any beast . . . on the earth, . . . bird . . . in the air, . . . of anything that creeps on the ground, . . . of any fish that is in the water under the earth" [Deut. 4:15–18 RSV].

Luther picked up the passage and said that it was also written there that one should not pray to sun, moon, and stars (Deut. 4:19). Should one therefore remove sun, moon, and stars?

Then the cobbler answered, "Stars in heaven are not made by our hands, so we should not remove them either."

According to the report, Luther found himself rather hard pressed at this point. It must of course be admitted that a few members of the congregation in Orlamünde could certainly miss the target, and Luther was later able to laugh at them for referring to biblical passages that did not exist. But according to our report, it is true that by the end of this conversation Luther cut short the interview, which had been rather an uncomfortable one for him. He stood up and went out to his carriage. The report said, "When one of the city officials saw this, he said, 'Dear doctor, tell us about the articles on the sacrament and on baptism.' Then Luther turned around and said, 'I wrote enough about them; read my books.'" It is obvious that the members of the Orlamünde congregation were quite proficient and knew how to debate, even without their pastor Karlstadt. Luther had obviously underrated them very much when he did not even consider them capable of composing a letter.

Karlstadt was forced to leave Orlamünde a short time later. The decision came from the Saxon government authorities; whether or not Luther influenced that decision can no longer be determined with certainty. Karlstadt moved to Strasbourg, where he complained about Luther. On 24 October 1524 Luther was obliged to respond to queries from Strasbourg. In his "Letter to the Christians at Strassburg in Opposition to the Fanatic Spirit"[6] he also mentioned his journey to Orlamünde. "But when I arrived among his Christians in Orlamünde, at the request of the prince, I really found out what kind of seed he had sown there, so that I was glad not to have been driven out with stones and filth. For many of them gave me the blessing, 'So go, in the name of a thousand devils, may you break your neck before you even get out of town!' with which they adorned themselves . . ."

Shortly after his visit in Orlamünde, Luther set out to settle his controversy with Karlstadt in "Against the Heavenly Prophets in the Matter of Images and Sacraments," 1525.[7] He repeatedly mentioned "Brother Andreas" in mocking terms, as the one who wore a gray felt hat and who, as the "new layman," refused to assume any authority anymore over his congregation. But Luther did not speak about the congregation; he spoke about the mob. "For anyone who permits the mob to assault the images, without any authorities, must also permit anyone to go ahead and kill adulterers, murderers, rebels, and so on. For God commanded the people of Israel both to kill these people and to remove images."

As a matter of fact, any dealings with the Old Testament present a difficult theological problem, which lurked in the background here as well. But another circumstance was probably more important: it was the winter of 1524–25, the start of the Peasants' War, and the disturbances could be felt particularly in Thuringia. Consequently, to Luther this was not just a matter of images or of changes in the form of the Lord's Supper. Nor was it a matter of greater or lesser independence for congregations. He feared a general dissolution of all constituted order. He therefore said in the treatise mentioned above "that one can see very well that when God orders the congregation to do something, and names the people, he does not want it

6. *WA* 15:391–97; quotations, 395–96. *LW* 40:63–71; quotations, 69.
7. *WA* 18:62–125; quotations, 86–87, 94–98, 123–25. *LW* 40:75–223; quotations, 89–90, 103, 111, 113–15, 130, 142–43, 162, 222.

done by the mob [*Pöbel*] without the authorities [*Obrigkeit*], but by the authorities with the people, so that the dog does not learn to eat leather while on the leash—that is, use images to get accustomed to rebelling against the authorities as well." The analogy is more than clear: the congregation is to be compared to a dog which one must keep strictly on the leash! Luther even challenged the authorities directly "to exile the preachers who, instead of teaching quietly, attract the mob to themselves and, behind the back of the authorities, insolently and on their own assault images and destroy churches." The name mentioned in this context was that of Karlstadt, who was then driven out of Orlamünde.

Luther described Karlstadt as he saw him: Karlstadt "was appointed by the elector as an archdeacon to Wittenberg and given a stipend to preach, read, and debate the Word of God; that's where God sent him." Luther declared that at first Karlstadt "received more advancement from the elector than many others." The events of the turbulent 1521 Christmas celebration, as well as Luther's Invocavit sermons, were kept in the background; but Luther nevertheless spoke of "murderous prophets" who had made Karlstadt "wild and restless," so "that he wanted to teach something better and more unusual than what God teaches in the Bible." Luther described Karlstadt's move from Wittenberg to Orlamünde with bitter accusations: "Then, out of his own insolence, he moved to Orlamünde without the knowledge or consent of either the prince or the university, drove out the pastor who had legally been placed there by the prince and the university, and took over the parish on his own authority. What do you think of this little affair? Is this an example of quiet obedience to authority, or is it insolent rebellion among the mob?" But Luther also confronted the opposition's argument that Karlstadt had explained that he was serving a congregation which had wanted him: "He and all the Orlamünders claim they had elected him pastor and that he was therefore publicly commissioned. To this I answer, I don't care if they elected him afterwards. I am speaking of his first arrival. Let him present letters to prove that the people in Orlamünde sent for him in Wittenberg and that he did not go there on his own."

Thus Luther had no intention of disputing the Orlamünde congregation's loyalty to its pastor Karlstadt. Instead, he retreated to the events preceding Karlstadt's call in order to cast doubts on it.

One must also understand Luther, who saw in Karlstadt a colleague abandoning his post. In any case, one encounters many informative sources here for Luther's views on congregations at that time. "Dear one, if being called means that I, out of my duty and obedience, run to another city, and then place myself in so favorable a light and persuade people to elect me and drive others out—then I say that no principality is so great that I would be prince in it and drive the present princes out. How easily one can persuade a people!" It is an explosive passage, and it arouses many associations: "How easily one can persuade a people!"

Our contemporary ideals on the election of a pastor through the congregation—which can be supported so well by Luther's writings of 1523—are called into question by the treatise "Against the Heavenly Prophets in the Matter of Images and Sacraments."[8] But one really must know the background in order to see Luther's position of 1524–25 in context. He confronted the Orlamünde congregation's legal situation as he saw it. "Nor did the congregation at Orlamünde have a right to elect a pastor and pay him someone else's salary, because that was the affair of the prince and his laws." They should "not interfere in the right, property, and authority of their territorial ruler, elect a pastor behind his back, and pay a stipend (which is not theirs) to whomever they wish; much less should he accept it." One can feel the anger in Luther's next statements: "Now however they plot without the knowledge of the prince, elect pastors and appoint them as they themselves please. They appear to regard their natural liege lord and reigning prince as so much dirt, whose possessions and prerogatives they wantonly wrest from him and take into their own hands. Indeed both Karlstadt and the Orlamünders have deserved a good strong jolt, as an ex-

8. Ibid.

ample . . ."[9] But with all this, Luther attributed the major blame not to the congregation but to Karlstadt: "He hounded the poor people until they wrote such a proud and insolent letter to the university."

Let us take a quick look at the points of controversy. Karlstadt had prohibited the elevation of the eucharistic elements; Luther, on the other hand, wanted no law on this. He had reproached the pope for having made the elevation of the eucharistic elements a law, and now Karlstadt had fallen into the opposite error. "But because Dr. Karlstadt does not allow the freedom not to do it, and instead forces, with prohibition and teaching, that one not elevate them, he also attacks God in his office [*Amt*], replaces him, and makes a sin out of what neither could nor should be sin." We are reminded of Luther's 1522 Invocavit sermons, in which he had demanded freedom in the congregation and warned against new legalism.

The second point of controversy is similar: the use of the German language in worship. Luther favored several alternatives, but Karlstadt insisted on permitting only the German language.[10] The congregation is again the focus in this context. Luther here again—as so often before—appealed to the first congregation in Corinth, in which speaking in tongues was a problem. He compared the speaking in tongues at that time with the use of Latin in his own day. Just as speaking in tongues had not been prohibited, but was instead to be made fruitful, so should this happen with the use of Latin in Luther's day. He wrote, "Thus the custom has been maintained in all countries of reading the Gospel immediately preceding the sermon in Latin, which is what Paul called speaking in tongues in the congregation. But since the sermon follows immediately, and translates the tongues into German and interprets them, Paul neither prohibits nor rejects them. So why should I or someone else condemn it?" Luther was once more desirous of preserving free-

---

9. *LW* 40:114.

10. The Rostock reformer Joachim Slüter also wanted to permit only the Low German vernacular in worship services. See Gerhard Bosinski, *Das Schrifttum des Rostocker Reformators Joachim Slüter* (Berlin, 1971), pp. 262ff.

dom and variety in the congregation. "Not that I would wish to refuse to use nothing but German in the mass, but I refuse to allow anyone (without the Word of God and out of his own desire and insolence) to forbid the reading of the Gospel in Latin and make a sin where there is none." That one thing comes up here which was already decisive in Luther's letter to Leisnig: the Word of God. At that time, 1523, Luther had encouraged the congregation in Leisnig because it was necessary for the sake of the Word of God. Now, in 1524, he opposed the congregation in Orlamünde because in his opinion they were acting against the Word of God.

This is especially true in reference to the third item in controversy, the doctrine of the Lord's Supper. Luther reproached Karlstadt bitterly: "Now, this rebellious spirit's only concern is to excite the crazy mob and attract them. Anyone who lusts after strange new things should now really open his big mouth and say, 'My, what a first-rate man this Dr. Karlstadt is, who finds what is hidden from the whole world, yet wears a gray coat and felt hat and does not want to be called Doctor but Neighbor Andrew . . .'"

Luther's tract concludes with an urgent warning: "Finally, I want to warn all people, loyally and fraternally, to guard themselves against Dr. Karlstadt and his prophets, for two reasons. The first is that they run around and teach without a commission to do so. . . . The other is that these prophets avoid, flee from, and suppress the principal article of Christian teaching. For nowhere do they teach, as one should, how to rid oneself of sins and attain a good conscience and a peaceful, joyous heart before God. This is what really counts." Thus for Luther there was an intimate connection between false teaching and insufficient foundation for the office of the ministry.

The break with Karlstadt was a deep one. Yet it should be noted that two years later Luther stood up for Karlstadt before the elector,[11] after Karlstadt had written a letter describing his miserable situation.[12]

11. *WA Br* 4:133–34.
12. *WA Br* 4:131–32.

7

Luther's Statements on the Congregation After 1525

It would seem at first that Luther's unpleasant experiences with the congregation in Orlamünde led to a basic change in his viewpoint. This is particularly true for the spring of 1525, the time of the Peasants' War. The first point of the peasants' Twelve Articles had been a demand for free election of the pastor by the congregation. The connection with Luther is obvious. But Luther particularly wanted to disassociate himself from the peasants' movement. Therefore in his "Admonition to Peace: A Reply to the Twelve Articles of the Peasants in Swabia,"[1] he explained regarding the first article:

> A whole congregation should have the power to elect and dismiss a minister. This article is correct, if only it were also taken up in a Christian way—to say nothing of the chapters indicated in the margin, which do not support it. Now, if the possessions of a parish are derived from the authorities and not from the congregation, then the congregation may not give these same possessions to someone they themselves have elected, for that would be robbery and theft. Instead, if they desire a minister, they should humbly ask the authorities for him.

One can imagine the effect such a response must have had on the rebellious peasants.

Luther dealt with the immediate question of what should be done if the congregation wants a pastor the authorities do not want. He recommended to the congregation, "If the authorities

---

1. *WA* 18:291–334; quotations, 325. *LW* 46:5–43; quotations, 37–38.

refuse him, then let them [the congregation] elect their own, support him with their own possessions, and leave the possessions of the authorities alone and obtain them legally." Even this advice is impossible to implement in the situation the peasants were in at the time, but Luther went further: "But if the authorities refuse to tolerate the pastor elected and supported in this way, then let him flee to another city, and let those who wish flee with him, as Christ teaches. That is electing and having one's own minister in the Christian and evangelical way. Anyone doing it differently acts in an unchristian way as a robber and malefactor." We are appalled at this sort of proposition for regulating the relationship between the office of the ministry and the congregation, which is in any case completely unreasonable and impossible to carry out. Neither the minister nor the congregation can be helped by that method.

Let us remember how actively Luther had supported the freedom of pastoral elections in city congregations. He had contributed support with letters, recommendations, or visits to Altenburg, Eilenburg, Leutenberg, Leisnig, Bohemia, Prussia, Erfurt, Magdeburg, Hamburg, and Kemberg without ever losing sight of reality. Several times he pressed energetically for changes in the law. Now, in the spring of 1525, his advice to the peasants is completely different. One must conclude that Luther could not seriously conceive of the possibility of a rural congregation capable of functioning independently and also electing its own pastor. This conjecture is strengthened by the fact that later that same year, 1525, Luther reverted to the old line: on 27 September 1525 he wrote to Nicholas Hausmann, whom he could on occasion call "Bishop of Zwickau,"[2] to visit Schneeberg and other congregations when called.[3] On 28 October 1525 he wrote to Erfurt and encouraged that congregation to put its own polity into practice.[4] On 31 October 1525 he wrote to the Elector John asking him to aid Evangelical pastors in financial need, and at

2. For this title, see "An Order of Mass and Communion for the Church at Wittenberg," 1523, *WA* 12:205. *LW* 53:19. Letter of October 1525, *WA Br* 3:599.
3. *WA Br* 3:582.
4. To John Lang and the Other Erfurt Pastors (Brief an Johann Lang und die übrigen Erfurter Prediger), *WA Br* 3:591–92.

the same time he recommended visitations.[5] At the very beginning of 1526 he wrote a letter to Reutlingen to encourage this congregation too.[6]

In 1959 the Leipzig church historian Franz Lau demonstrated in great detail that the Reformation continued to move ahead in the cities, after the Peasants' War of 1525, without recognizable interruptions. Lau formulated his conclusion:

> Without exception, in the period between 1525 and 1532, the Reformation in the north German cities is pushed through by the townspeople, the guilds, and the common people in the parishes. In none of the listed cases is the nobility involved, and the initiative never comes from the city authorities. . . . The initiative comes from the citizens. In other words, the Reformation in the north German cities between 1525 and 1532 is a spontaneous reformation from below, just as it was in the beginning.[7]

A perusal of this essay leads one to yet one other conclusion: I found in it not a single statement by Luther; nor does Lau mention a single inquiry directed to Luther during these years. No doubt Lau was correct when he said that Luther's reputation had not suffered to any provable degree in the cities because of the Peasants' War, but it seems that not many questions were asked of Luther during this period. The decisive role in the formation of the new congregations was now unquestionably played by John Bugenhagen. He designed the church orders for the city of Braunschweig in 1528, for Hamburg in 1529, for Lübeck in 1531, for Pomerania in 1534, for the duchy Braunschweig-Wolfenbüttel in 1543, and for Hildesheim in 1544; and his influence was spread even further.[8] But we must also remember that Bugenhagen was a very close friend of Luther. No

---

5. *WA Br* 3:594–96. *LW* 49:130–37.

6. To Matthew Alber in Reutlingen, 4 January 1526, *WA Br* 4:7–8.

7. Franz Lau, "Der Bauernkrieg und das angebliche Ende der lutherischen Reformation als spontaner Volksbewegung," *Lutherjahrbuch* 26 (1959): 130–31. English version, "Did Popular Reformation Really Stop with the Peasants' Defeat?" trans. Kyle C. Sessions, in *Reformation and Authority: The Meaning of the Peasants' Revolt*, ed. Kyle C. Sessions (Lexington, Mass.: D. C. Heath & Co., 1968), pp. 94–101.

8. See Ernst Wolf, "Johannes Bugenhagen, Gemeinde und Amt," in *Peregrinatio: Studien zur reformatorischen Theologie und zum Kirchenproblem*, 2d. ed. (Munich, 1962), pp. 257–58.

doubt he also had a greater talent for organization than Luther, who would rather express himself on questions of liturgy.[9] Nevertheless the impression remains that Luther's relations to the congregation were no longer as intensive as in the years 1522–24.

Luther was faced with a new problem: should one aim for a small congregation of people who seriously strive to be Christians? He expressed himself on this point in the preface to "The German Mass and Order of Service," 1526.[10] These statements have often been interpreted in a variety of ways. The decisive sentences are:

> Those people who seriously strive to be Christians and to confess the Gospel with hand and mouth should register by name and perhaps assemble in some house to pray, to read, to baptize, to receive the sacrament, and to carry out other Christian functions. According to this order one could know, punish, improve, expel, or place under ban (according to the rule of Christ in Matt. 18[:15–17]) those who did not behave in a Christian way. Here one could also impose upon the Christians a common offering, which one could give willingly and distribute among the poor according to the example of St. Paul, 2 Cor. 9. There would be no need for much or for great singing. Here one could also have a nice short form of baptism and sacrament and direct everything to the Word, to prayer, and to love. Here one should have a good short catechism on faith, the Ten Commandments, and the Lord's Prayer. In short, if one had the people and persons who seriously yearned to be Christians, the order and forms could soon be established.

But Luther wrote this in the subjunctive mood. It is a case of possibility, of an ideal. The reality was quite different. Accordingly, Luther continued, "But I neither can nor desire to arrange or achieve such a congregation or assembly, for I do not yet have the people or persons to do it. Nor do I see many who press for it. But if the time ever comes when I must do it and am pressed to do it, when I cannot in good conscience refuse, then I will gladly do my share and do my best to help." But at

9. See Hans Liermann, "Luther ordnet seine Kirche," *Lutherjahrbuch* 31 (1964): 29–46, especially 37.
10. *WA* 19:72–113; quotations, 75. *LW* 53:53–90; quotations, 64.

that time, 1526, he in no way thought the time had come; on the contrary, he feared "it would turn into a mob. For we Germans are a wild, crude, raging people with whom not much can be done unless there is the direct need!"

At the end of 1526 Luther received the draft of a new church order which was to be instituted in Hesse. This "Homberg Church Order" provided for active participation on the part of the congregation. A small circle of active members was to get together and carry out specific tasks. Landgrave Philip of Hesse had sent the draft to Wittenberg to get an expert opinion on it, and Luther clearly advised against it. On 7 January 1527 he wrote that the time was not yet ripe, that one should not "institute in our territory such a heap of laws with such weighty words." Luther asked him to remember Moses, who had written down his laws only after they had already been commonly adopted. For the time being, one should rather concentrate on educating effective pastors.[11] Shortly thereafter the visitations began in Saxony, and the church was built up from above after all. The individual congregations had very little significance.

But this development does not mean that Luther had simply abandoned his old ideals. A few examples may demonstrate how he continued to pursue them. In 1526 he heard that Evangelical preachers whom the congregations found undesirable were about to be appointed in Gera and Arnstadt. Luther wrote to the Elector John on 14 April 1526 supporting the position that the congregation "should have the sole right."[12] In his fundamental treatise "Instructions for the Visitors of Parish Pastors in Electoral Saxony," 1528, Luther insisted that no member of a congregation may be forced against his will to receive the Lord's Supper in both kinds.[13] Luther published similar reservations twice more.[14]

Luther heard about troubles in the Nuremberg congregation:

11. *WA Br* 4:157–58.
12. *WA Br* 4:48–51.
13. *WA* 26:175–240, especially 214–15. *LW* 40:265–320, especially 290.
14. In two appendixes found among letters to the Elector John, 1528. *WA Br* 4:328–29, 330–31.

they were obliged to hold daily worship services, but sometimes not a single member attended. Luther therefore wrote to the Nuremberg city council secretary Lazarus Spengler on 15 August 1528, telling him that no clergyman should be expected to celebrate private mass, that is, a worship service without a congregation. One should hold worship services only as needed, only "if several communicants are present. In this way, none would be forced to the sacrament, and yet everyone would be satisfactorily served in an orderly manner."[15]

We see Luther in an unpleasant situation in 1531: he became embroiled in the conflicts of the Zwickau congregation. Superintendent Nicholas Hausmann, who had known for a long time that he was indebted to Luther, went to him with his troubles. The Zwickau congregation, represented by the Protestant city council, had dismissed a pastor whose behavior really had become clearly impossible. But the superintendent supported the pastor, and Luther allowed himself to be drawn into taking his side. Ruth Goetze has given a detailed account of the incident.[16] We have the correspondence between Wittenberg and Zwickau, which spanned several months.[17] Luther wrote a strong letter to the city council of Zwickau accusing them of behaving toward that pastor "exactly like a master toward his servant, even though he is not your servant and you are not the master of the church."[18] The Zwickau congregation should not have been allowed "to steal and rob such an office"! Luther pointed out the rights of the elector, but his greatest concern was for the rights of the authorized superintendent, without whom a congregation was not "permitted to appoint and dismiss preachers." The financial viewpoint is also mentioned: "The office of the ministry and the income are not yours." In Torgau, at a hearing before the elector in August, the decision was more in favor of the Zwickau congregation than Luther liked, but the congregation

---

15. *WA Br* 4:533–37; quotation, 535. *LW* 49:204–10; quotation, 206.

16. Ruth Goetze, *Wie Luther Kirchenzucht übte*, Theologische Arbeiten, no. 9 (Berlin, 1959), pp. 65–92. *Superintendent* was the designation corresponding in some ways to "bishop."

17. *WA Br* 6:46–107.

18. Ibid., 6:46.

had great difficulty afterward in filling the parish position, much to Luther's satisfaction.[19] He considered the members of the Zwickau congregation amputated limbs of Christ, and he even refused, as late as 1535, to lift the ban against his loyal follower Stephen Roth, city secretary in Zwickau.

Goetze criticized Luther's behavior:

> Luther imposed this most severe ecclesiastical penalty upon a man, among others, whose true faith and trustworthiness he had never until then doubted, solely on the basis of denunciations. Moreover, he in fact appropriated the authority and the power of a bishop without having either been given that rank or assumed that office. The regulation of church polity was still completely in the first conceptual stage of development, both for the Evangelical church as a whole and for individual congregations. . . . Since matters of external church polity can find no biblical justification, they do not carry the necessary weight to permit exclusion from a congregation because of a position taken toward them. As to the situation in Zwickau, when the city council attempted to retain its old right of patronage, it was not a matter of contempt for God; nor was it contempt for the spiritual office. It was instead a matter of the legal demarcation between the political and ecclesiastical communities.[20]

Finally, Luther also had to concern himself with events in Rostock. On 1 April 1531 a "raging mob" had stormed into the city hall to protest against the worship services. The Reformation in Rostock had already been effected in the 1520s through the preacher Joachim Slüter at St. Peter's Church. The other churches followed suit later and were reluctant to be as sweeping in their reforms. The Rostock city trustee John Oldendorp, a man with Reformation leanings, mentions "misunderstandings and schisms among the Evangelical preachers in Rostock." What was at stake was whether the whole worship service was to be conducted in German, as Slüter desired, or whether the use of Latin could still be permitted in a service. Another issue was

---

19. To Matthew Kratsch, 18 August 1531, *WA Br* 6:165.
20. Goetze, pp. 91–92. One can also judge Luther's opposition to the Zwickau city council from the aspect of its significance for Luther's position in the Age of Constantine. In this case his image appears much more modern.

private confession, which Slüter had abolished and which the other clergy wanted to retain. Oldendorp did not mention Slüter's name, but Gerhard Bosinski was able to prove the reference was probably to Slüter.[21] Slüter and Bugenhagen had a meeting in the summer of 1531. The conflict was settled, and Slüter was forced to make concessions. Oldendorp had asked for expert opinions from four theologians: Luther, Melanchthon, Bugenhagen, and Urbanus Rhegius. Luther and Melanchthon wrote jointly, the others individually. Luther and Melanchthon asserted that that radical preacher (therefore probably Slüter) was unknown in Wittenberg. One should

> seriously deal with him so that he stop all that quarreling, as was reported, and teach more peacefully those things that serve healing and fear of God. And even though we now think that he does not pay much attention to our advice, nevertheless please point out to him from me, Martin Luther, that I admonish him amicably as the one who has for a long time filled and tried [to fill] the preaching office by God's grace—just as Dr. John Pomeranus [Bugenhagen] has admonished him before—not to be so reckless in spiritual matters. For such recklessness is dangerous, as many examples of our time have shown. Let him also make sure not to cause trouble with his vain quarreling. But if he refuses to mend his ways after your dealings with him and admonition, our advice is to let him leave town amicably, and not to fear the following of the common people.[22]

This passage demonstrates how problematic it can be to speak about "congregation." There is no doubt that Luther supported the Rostock congregation, but it is the congregation as represented by the city council. St. Peter's congregation, under Slüter, which had already pledged itself to the Reformation much earlier, is on the other hand disparaged as a "satellite [*Anhang*] of the common people." Luther's motive is obvious: he had heard of disturbances, and these must be opposed—he would not tolerate a "mob."

21. Gerhard Bosinski, "Joachim Slüter und Martin Luther," in *Herbergen der Christenheit*, ed. Franz Lau (Berlin, 1970), pp. 67–128.
22. *WA Br* 6:225. Also reprinted in Bosinski, "Joachim Slüter und Martin Luther," pp. 102–3.

Once again in 1533 Luther took a position on our topic, the office of the ministry and the congregation, this time in greater detail. A pastor named Witzel, in Eisleben, had reverted to medieval Roman teaching. Luther dealt with this in "The Private Mass and the Consecration of Priests,"[23] in which Luther demonstrated that his conception of the relationship between the office of the ministry and the congregation had not basically altered since his theoretical exposition of it in 1520 and his practical application in Leisnig in 1523.

His starting point is again the Word of God: the church cannot introduce new things on its own. The sacrament, "according to Christ's intention, is commanded and instituted so that one should extend it or communicate it to other Christians as a communion and common food for the strength and consolation of their faith. Our private-mass celebrants do not do that; instead, they take it and keep it to themselves and do not share it with a single Christian." Luther pointed to baptism, which one cannot confer on oneself either:

> . . . for in baptism (even if it is an emergency baptism) there are always at least two persons present, the baptizer and the person to be baptized. Often there are many more persons present, and it is a ministry which of itself gives something to others just because they are members of the same community, not receiving something for itself and giving nothing to others, as is done in the mass. . . . Furthermore, why do you not also teach that one should or may baptize oneself? Why is that no baptism? Why is that no confirmation when a person confirms himself? Why is that no ordination when a person ordains himself? Why is that no absolution when a person absolves himself? Why is that no unction when a person anoints himself? . . . Why is that no marriage when a person wants to marry himself? . . . I have enumerated your seven sacraments. If it is true that no sacrament can be performed by an individual alone, how is it possible that by yourself you are able to effect this unique and most sublime sacrament?[24]

Luther pointed out that the institution of the Lord's Supper

23. *WA* 38:195–256; quotations, 200–201, 208, 217, 239–40, 248, 254. *LW* 38:141–214; quotations, 154, 159, 162, 172, 198–201, 204, 208–9, 212–13.
24. *LW* 38:154.

occurred in the circle of disciples. A community is necessary for the Lord's Supper.

> And it is not called the sacrament of parsons but the sacrament of the church; and a parson should be a servant of the church and not his own lord against the church. Now the church does not get its sacrament as it should in the private mass. Therefore the private-mass celebrant does not serve or administer it as he is duty bound to do, but instead he keeps it to himself and thus also robs the church of its sacrament.

He also pointed out the psychological effect of a community: it is a comfort to a weak Christian "when he sees, hears, and remembers how firmly and surely the others believe and do such things, and that the whole church neither doubts nor wavers."

The task of the minister is described once more.

> Our office is called and ought to be not one of producing [*machen*] or effecting conversion but solely one of offering and bestowing. A pastor or preacher does not produce the Gospel, nor does his preaching or office turn his word into Gospel. . . . Rather, he only offers and, through his preaching, gives the Gospel. For the Gospel, which is what our Lord Christ produced, is there first and must be there first. . . . Thus the only work remaining in the office of the ministry or preaching office is to give or offer the Gospel which Christ commanded to be preached. . . . Therefore the baptizer does not do a baptism; Christ did it first. The baptizer only offers and gives it. . . . Therefore, also, when the bread and wine become Christ's body and blood, it is not our doing, speaking, or work. . . but rather Christ's order, command, and institution. He himself commanded, as Paul says in 1 Cor. 11[:22ff.], that when we meet together and speak his words over the bread and wine, then it shall be his body and blood.

Luther thus continuously maintained his earlier position. The Corinthian congregation presented him with an essential criterion for 1533 as well. Again he found passages which reject the primacy of the officeholder in 1533 too: "For our faith and the sacrament must not depend on the person—be he pious or evil, consecrated or unconsecrated, commissioned or smuggled in, the devil or his mother—but rather on Christ, on his Word, on his office, on his command and order. If they are done right, then everything is all right."

Luther uses a very strange image for the lasting continuity of the church, the office of the ministry, and sacraments. "Let only those people be commissioned and appointed who can perform them, and they surely will be done. The horse is tamed and saddled. Even if you mount a naked boy on it who can ride, the horse will go as well as if the emperor or the pope were riding it." The concept is reformulated shortly afterwards.

> Then see to it that someone is placed into the office of the ministry, which is not his but Christ's office. And do not worry about whether or not he has been properly called, intruded himself, or bought it [the office] . . . be he Judas or St. Peter; it is not your concern. Just separate the office from the person, and the sacred from the abomination. Never mind, he is a pastor, and Christ has thus maintained his holy, beloved office of the ministry under the papacy, under the abomination.

The office of the ministry certainly appears to be more than something objective in formulations like these. The congregation is urged to accept any pastor with a certain passive readiness, insofar as he only passes along the objective gifts. But precisely this passing-along is his service. An office of the ministry without any usefulness for the congregation was rejected by Luther in 1533 as well as 1520. Luther wrote in 1533 as well that the pastor "is through baptism consecrated, anointed, and born to be a priest of Christ." The recipients of the Lord's Supper are "all true sacred fellow priests." Luther was happy with the Evangelical worship service: "Here one proclaims and preaches about Christ, here no avarice or idolatry can exist, here we are sure to have the opinion of Christ and of the church. Here we should not worry about whether the pastor speaks the words secretly, whether he is also changing, or whether he has faith. For we hear the words of institution plainly and speak them along fervently." Thus the significance of the congregation is clearly expressed. It is given even more emphatically in the following sentences: "If the pastor does not believe, or if he doubts, then we believe. If he stumbles over the words, or if he is confused and forgets whether he has said them, then we are there, listen, remain firm, and are sure they are said. That is why we cannot be deceived."

The congregation is thus given a very high value on account of the worship service. It can support a doubting pastor by its own faith; it can with faith receive words which a minister has spoken in confusion. Luther obviously included himself in the "we"; he desired to be a member of the congregation at this point too. Luther certainly put the highest value on the objectivity of the church, on the office of the ministry, and on the sacrament. But he also remembered the promises given to even the smallest congregation, "For where two or three are gathered in my name, there am I in the midst of them"! Luther drew upon this saying in Matt. 18:20 (RSV) in 1533 as well as in 1520.

He advanced one more biblical argument. He started from Jesus' command for mission, "Go therefore . . . to all nations . . . teaching them" (Matt. 28:19). Luther commented on this passage: "But what did he command them to do? Surely to preach the Gospel, to baptize, to offer the sacrament, to forgive sin. Now if the heathen are to keep this, then they must certainly have the power and right to preach, baptize, offer the sacrament, forgive sin. Indeed, they are commanded to do so. As St. Paul also writes to the Corinthians that he had received it from the Lord and given it to the Corinthians [1 Cor. 11:23] . . ." Accordingly, the congregation is the protector of the apostolic tradition, from which ministers emerge whenever required. Again the Corinthian congregation is the model! One cannot say that Luther, in his 1533 theological argumentation, retracted a single item of what he had written in his major Reformation treatises of 1520.

This impression can be documented from a lesser-known source. On 9 June 1535 Luther preached on Psalm 110. He attributed verses 3 and 4 ("Your sons will be born to you like the dew from the dawn. The Lord has sworn and will not regret it in eternity") to Christ, in accordance with ancient Christian tradition. But he also interpreted them in the sense of the universal priesthood of all baptized. At this point, the concepts Luther had proposed in 1520 recur. In 1535 too he compared the office of the ministry to the office of mayor, in the sense that it deals with an office which is carried out for a specific amount of time to serve a congregation. Luther also compared the ecclesiastical office to "all sorts of other offices and estates, such as father, mother, teacher, government, estate, and office. The office does not confer the essence and authority that everyone has; instead, that must be there first, from birth, and must make him fit to exercise the office." Once again this is followed by the assertion that baptism is the most important precondition for priestly service. There is also again, quite matter-of-factly, talk about the change of officeholders. Luther included himself and formulated it this way now: "When I no longer can or desire to preach, I will return to the common crowd; I shall be like you, and someone else will preach. Not everyone can hold the office . . ."[25]

Of course Luther's "Smalcald Articles" of 1537 are of great importance, since they were later accepted as part of the Lutheran Confessions. Part III of the "Smalcald Articles" deals with those matters over which Luther desired to confer with scholars on his own Evangelical side.

The section "The Gospel" contains directions for the kind of pastoral care that should occur in a brotherly conversation. Then comes the passage from Matt. 18:20, ". . . where two . . . are gathered . . . , " the same passage Luther had so often quoted. Just preceding it is the reference to the power of the keys, that is, the authority to forgive sins. Four sections later, the power of the keys is dealt with in greater detail. "The keys are an office and power of the church, given by Christ, to bind and to loose sins—not just the crude and well-known ones, but also the subtle, secret sins that God alone knows." In this 1537 writing, which was intended to stake out the Evangelical position in view of possible conciliar negotiations, Luther once again defended his view that the authority to forgive sins is not restricted to officeholders. Rather, every member of the congregation has the right to declare the forgiveness of sins.

The section "Ordination and Vocation" follows a little later. Luther was prepared to negotiate on this point, although he of

25. *WA* 41:204–10.

course disclosed his reservations. "If the bishops desire to be true bishops and take care of the church and the Gospel, then we should allow them to ordain and confirm our preachers, for the sake of love and of unity, not for the sake of emergency, provided they do it without pretense, humbug, and unchristian ostentation." Luther was of the opinion that the bishops of his day were not true bishops, but that the church nevertheless needed servants. Accordingly, he explained, "That is why, as the ancient examples of the church and the fathers teach us, we want to and should ordain zealous persons into such an office ourselves. And this they cannot forbid us or oppose."[26]

In conclusion, questions from the perspective of our topic should be put to Luther's "On the Councils and the Church" of 1539.[27] This treatise repeats many ideas we already know from earlier writings. Again it is stated, "The keys are an office and power of the church, given by Christ to bind and dissolve sin." Luther gave a more precise definition of the essence of the church, and it is clear that he was thinking of the individual congregation. The most important mark is the Word of God: "Now, wherever you hear and see such a Word preached, confessed, and followed, have no doubt that there must certainly be a true holy, catholic church there." Other marks are baptism and the Lord's Supper. But the universal priesthood also comes up again. It does not matter "whether you are a man or a woman, young or old," the decisive factor is baptism: ". . . then you are anointed highly and mightily enough, and garbed as a priest." Luther also spoke well-known words about the office of the ministry: "One must have bishops, pastors, or preachers . . . for the crowd itself cannot do such things for themselves; they must instead command someone, or have someone commanded, to do so." It is clear that Luther expressed ideas in 1539 which he had already voiced in 1520.

26. *WA* 50:192–254. *BS*, pp. 449–58. *BC*, pp. 310–14.
27. *WA* 50:509–653; quotations, 629, 631–32. *LW* 41:5–178; quotations, 150, 154–55.

8

The Congregation in Mecklenburg Lutheranism

It has often been said that the congregational principle has seldom gained recognition in Lutheranism. Thus Martin Schmidt wrote that it is easy

> to scold the Evangelical church, especially the church stamped by Luther, for not making use of these great possibilities. Without a doubt it can also be said that Luther, by concentrating the church on the Word and its proclamation—including the sacrament, which is the bodily form of this proclamation—had to bring the theologically educated pastor into the foreground of ecclesiastical activity, particularly since Lutheran polity relates everything extremely one-sidedly to the proclamation of the Word. Moreover, it is true that the laity's activity was always a serving one and thus quite naturally withdrew into invisibility.[1]

But ultimately Schmidt did want to stress some aftereffects of Luther on the Christian laity. He mentioned especially the Evangelical minority in Salzburg, who survived for centuries and who left their homeland in 1732 for the sake of their faith. Schmidt stated about this event, "Here a mature lay congregation, without the benefit of higher education, proved that it was capable of judging the basic truths of the Christian faith without guidance and supervision by the spiritual office." In addition to the Austrian, we shall have to remember the many Lutheran con-

---

1. Martin Schmidt, "Die Bedeutung Luthers für das christliche Laientum," *Theologische Literaturzeitung* 93 (1969): 7–8.

gregations in eastern and southeastern Europe who also survived for centuries as small minorities. These congregations could not expect the help of princes. The same is true for the Lutheran emigrants who formed new Lutheran congregations in America and Australia. The congregation also has great importance in Scandinavian Lutheranism, especially in Denmark.

One must of course admit that the picture was not as bright in the German principalities; the Lutheran territorial churches were often constricted and inflexible. But there are differences here too. A Pietistic movement, which strove for the ideal of an active congregation and thereby referred to Luther more than once, could grow even in Lutheranism's home territory. In the nineteenth century, Lutheran free (nonestablished, nonterritorial) churches were formed, in which the individual congregation attained great significance. The internal conflicts between Lutheran free churches in Europe and overseas are varied and sometimes hard to understand. Yet from the viewpoint of our topic, one must say that in the fragmented history of Lutheranism, there have been completely independent congregations who trusted themselves to make their own theological judgments.

But one should not paint too somber a picture of the traditional Lutheran territorial churches either. I would like to confine myself to one Evangelical-Lutheran territorial church which sometimes had the reputation of being particularly backward: the Evangelical-Lutheran territorial church of Mecklenburg. This territorial church was overwhelmingly rural, and the conditions for active participation of congregations were lacking in these areas. Gottfried Holtz gave a very detailed account of how dismal it was in the rural areas.[2]

The port city of Rostock, with its university, presented a different picture. Hans Leube, in his book *The Reform Ideas in the*

---

2. Gottfried Holtz, "The Mecklenburg Farmer and the Church" ("Der mecklenburgische Landarbeiter und die Kirche"), in *Herbergen der Christenheit,* ed. K. Blaschke (Berlin, 1975–76), 10:63: "The privileged estates had attained the separate reception of the Lord's Supper, which had been assured to them in 1755 in written form as a guaranteed right. And this occurred in the church of the 'universal priesthood'!"

German Lutheran Church in the Age of Orthodoxy,[3] said that the Rostock theologians deserved the reputation "of having been the leaders of the reform movement." But this was not a matter confined to the theological faculty, for the congregation also participated. This is documented for the year 1649, when the duke moved to dismiss the professor and preacher Joachim Lütkemann. The congregation in Rostock defended him strongly. Karl Schmaltz, in his *History of the Mecklenburg Church,* wrote, "The leaders of the congregation demanded support from the city council, because the congregation would not soon again get a preacher to equal this man's great gifts and enthusiastic Christian life style. Crowds of women besieged the mayors in their homes; more than two hundred of them appeared at city hall, weeping and moaning, and refused to give up until the council made one last attempt."[4]

We should not of course imagine an active, model congregation. But it is nevertheless impressive that the congregation was noticed at all at that time. The Rostock preacher Heinrich Müller, for example, lamented the fact that so few members of the congregation sang along at worship services. He therefore published in 1659 a hymnal entitled *Spiritual Soul Music,*[5] which was intended to serve the needs of the congregation.

Another witness is the fiery pastor Theophil Grossgebauer, who in 1661 wrote his *Watchman's Voice from Desolated Zion.* Grossgebauer too demanded a more active participation from the congregation. As justification, he pointed to the "royal priesthood" to which Luther had so often appealed. In the true sense of Luther, he demanded that the Christians in the congregation help each other toward salvation. "God wills that his newborn children and justified people should help each other along to eternal life and use the freedom of this childhood as those who are no longer held in bondage like slaves by the

---

3. Hans Leube, *Die Reformideen in der deutschen lutherischen Kirche zur Zeit der Orthodoxie* (Leipzig, 1924), p. 71.

4. Karl Schmaltz, *Kirchengeschichte Mecklenburgs* (Berlin, 1952), 3:17.

5. Heinrich Müller, *Geistliche Seelenmusik,* in Chr. Bunners, *Kirchenmusik und Seelenmusik* (Berlin, 1966), pp. 113–67.

guardians and trustees of the tribe of Levi." After this reference to Gal. 4:1–2, Grossgebauer attacked a popular form of expression. "We use the term 'spirituals' [*Geistliche*] for preachers, just as though other believers in Christ must be secular and worldly. And this is the cause of the madness—which has permeated the whole church like an evil yeast—that spiritual sacrifices, prayers, intercessions, teachings, exhortations, consolations, punishments, and warnings do not concern the so-called worldly at all. They say, 'The preachers have their commission to teach and preach.'"[6] Jesus' rule in Matt. 18:17, which Luther had used so often, was also picked up by Grossgebauer. "The advice to 'bring it before the congregation' cannot mean that the pastor brings it to the pulpit. Rather, it belongs in a congregational meeting." He also thought that church music restricted the independence of the congregation. There had been antiphonal singing earlier, but by 1660 music was being played by paid musicians. "It roars, resounds, rumbles, saws away, rings, and concertizes—but you never know what it is."[7]

In 1663 Johann Quistorp the Younger expressed himself more temperately than Grossgebauer. He entitled his work *Pious Desires (Pia Desideria)* twelve years before Phillip J. Spener did. In this treatise he requested the territorial prince to convene a synod. The congregations should be activated, and every congregation should set up a college of elders. The Lutheran Quistorp did not hesitate to appeal to arrangements in Reformed Switzerland for models.[8]

The extensive nineteenth-century discussion regarding Luther's concept of the universal priesthood also had participants in Mecklenburg. Theodor Kliefoth, for many years president of the Lutheran *Oberkirchenrat* (consistory) in Schwerin, in 1854 proposed a distinction according to which the office of the min-

---

6. Theophil Grossgebauer, *Wächterstimme aus dem verwüsteten Zion*, chap. 7, in the edition of Frankfurt and Leipzig, 1682; quoted in Eberhard Winkler, *Die Gemeinde und ihr Amt*, Aufsätze und Vorträge zur Theologie und Religionswissenschaft, no. 59 (Berlin, 1973), p. 13.
7. Schmaltz, 3:22.
8. Ibid., 3:19–20.

istry should be understood as an organ of the church, whereas the universal priesthood, as organ of the congregation, should be given subordinate value.[9] It no doubt reflected the situation of Mecklenburg at that time; but it certainly does not need elaborating that with this differentiation Kliefoth missed Luther's intentions completely. Luther, in case of doubt, had valued the word *congregation* more than the word *church*.

In Rostock, Kliefoth found himself opposed by the spirited professor of theology Michael Baumgarten, who was a member of the nineteenth-century modernist movement. The trend of that period is described by the Danish church historian A. P. Thyssen: "The first half of the nineteenth century is the era of revolutionary, nationalist, liberal, and ecclesiastical movements. These movements all represent a new self-confidence and a new feeling of responsibility within the nation and the church, insofar as private groups took on tasks which had heretofore been left to the rulers."[10]

Thyssen named Michael Baumgarten as a particularly great activist who had participated in the revolution of 1848 in Schleswig-Holstein and who had worked in Rostock since 1850. Baumgarten carried on some acrimonious quarrels with Theodor Kliefoth, which cost him his professorship and even landed him in prison occasionally. He appealed to Luther several times. Particularly informative to our topic is his tract "Luther's Church of the Future" ("Luthers Kirche der Zukunft"), 1883. This church of the future was to consist of active, independent congregations. The congregation was to be constituted of people who believe in Christ through free personal choice. The church should not be in the care of the state—not even by way of the detour over a Lutheran *Oberkirchenrat* or consistory appointed by the territorial ruler—but rather of the congregation, who

---

9. Theodor Kliefoth, *Liturgische Abhandlungen* (Schwerin and Rostock, 1854), 1:351ff.
10. A. P. Thyssen, "Kirchliche Erweckung und nationale Erhebung in Schleswig-Holstein 1817 bis 1850," *Wissenschaftliche Zeitschrift der Universität Rostock, gesellschafts- und sprachwissenschaftliche Reihe* 17, no. 4 (1968): 397.

should elect representatives to an independent church leadership agency *(Kirchenleitung)*. A Rostock dissertation entitled "The Theology of the Holy Spirit in the Writings of the Rostock Theologian Michael Baumgarten" contains the sentences: "Baumgarten certifies that Luther returned to the New Testament original image of the church when he started his church reform. But he had not succeeded in building up a church according to his ideals. The church had freed itself from the pope's authority but had then been subjected to another authority, that of the prince as supreme territorial bishop."[11] Baumgarten experienced a little of the liveliness of the congregation: when he was released from prison in 1862, he was met by five thousand people, students and citizens. They sang "A Mighty Fortress Is Our God," and Baumgarten thanked them in an address. But he could not really, at that time, realize his goal of building independent congregations.

An essentially different position was taken by August Wilhelm Dieckhoff, professor of theology in Rostock from 1860 to 1894. He dealt with our topic in his book *Luther's Teaching on Church Authority (Luthers Lehre von der kirchlichen Gewalt)*, 1865. It becomes clear that Lutherans cannot depend on Luther in every situation. Dieckhoff presented Luther's historical development: until 1520 Luther was a reformer like many others; he hoped for a general council, as many others had for the past hundred years. Only during the years between 1520 and 1523 did Luther go beyond this position; at that time he blurred the difference between the office of the ministry and the universal priesthood. Dieckhoff stated this with disapproval, but he did present the facts soberly. He wanted to excuse these regrettable occurrences in Luther by stating that these ambiguities were only temporary and that the later Luther once again insisted unequivocally on the primacy of the office of the ministry over the common priesthood. In a dissertation, "August Wilhelm Dieckhoff's Po-

---

11. G. Fohl, "Die Theologie des Geistes in den Schriften des Rostocker Theologen Michael Baumgarten" (Th.D. diss., University of Rostock, 1969), pp. 138–39. The prince as territorial bishop has the title "highest bishop" *(summepiskopat)*.

sition on the Church-Political and Theological Controversies of His Time," 1969, it is written:

> Dieckhoff attempts to clarify, if not resolve, Luther's tension between the office of the ministry and the universal priesthood on the one hand and spiritual and secular authority on the other, by way of an interpretation formed by his presupposition. He emphasizes one factor and criticizes the other, which means that Luther's understanding of the office of the ministry is strongly emphasized, but that of the general priesthood is dismissed as provisional. . . . Dieckhoff, on the basis of this work, was probably regarded as a basic theoretician by his like-minded friends. As a matter of fact, his research toward the intended goal was indeed important. His conclusion—that in Luther's later teaching, as early as after 1522, the universal priesthood moved into the background in favor of the office of the ministry—was instrumental in consolidating the understanding of the institutional church and therefore of the office of the ministry. Luther's temporary theory of universal priesthood was played down, and Luther's later view was emphasized. These alternative solutions remained in force until the twentieth century.[12]

The twentieth century brought great changes, particularly for Mecklenburg. Let me describe an episode which took place in a village in 1902, which Gottfried Holtz mentioned in his book *The Parish:* a village pastor quarreled with his sacristan. The pastor explained that he could not admit the sacristan to the Lord's Supper without an apology; so the sacristan went to Schwerin before Easter and received the Lord's Supper there. The event became known. This led to a trial, during which the sacristan was accused of having obtained the Lord's Supper by trickery, and he was fined thirty marks—a very large sum at the time. The explanation of the verdict was:

> This state has a regulation, Article 486, also recognized in the 1755 state constitutional inheritance contract, which states that every person must use the office of the father confessor (*Beichtvater*) in whose parish church he is registered; and he may not use another

12. S. Uhlig, "August Wilhelm Dieckhoffs Stellungnahme zu kirchenpolitischen und theologischen Streitfragen seiner Zeit unter dem Aspekt seiner reformationsgeschichtlichen Forschungen" (Th.D. diss., University of Rostock, 1969), pp. 61–62.

father confessor arbitrarily, even if he is involved in hostilities or a lawsuit with his own, unless he obtains dispensation from the bishop *(oberbischöflicher Dispensation)*. The enforcement of this regulation is entrusted first to the pastors, specifically to the penitent's lawful pastor, and to the alien pastor in whose church he desires to commune illegally.[13]

The revolution of 1918 brought far-reaching changes. The grand duke of Mecklenburg, until then the highest bishop of the territorial church, was forced to abdicate. A territorial bishop, Dr. Heinrich Behm,[14] was elected, and a territorial synod started work. Moreover, there were many initiatives from the congregations. The church constitution established that the church authority was to come from the congregation and was to be in the hands of its representatives, the territorial synod. The synod was to consist of one-third clergy and two-thirds laity elected by the congregations.[15]

The Church Conflict *(Kirchenkampf)* demonstrated that congregations could be surprisingly active. The retired bishop of the Evangelical-Lutheran territorial church of Mecklenburg, Dr. Niclot Beste, wrote a book in 1975, *The Church Conflict in Mecklenburg, 1933–1945*. A particularly telling example of congregational activity is recounted from this book:[16]

The Lutheran *Oberkirchenrat* (consistory) in Schwerin, the capital of Mecklenburg, had been thoroughly reorganized in 1933. The "German Christians" *(Deutsche Christen)* set the tone, and a new territorial bishop *(Landesbischof)*, known to be a Hitler supporter, had been installed. The legal basis for these changes was doubtful and was opposed by the "Confessing Church" *(Bekennende Kirche)*. An assistant pastor in the village of Massow who belonged to the Confessing Church was deposed. The congregation protested this action, and twenty-eight members drove

13. Gottfried Holtz, *Die Parochie* (Berlin, 1971), p. 25.
14. The first territorial bishop for Mecklenburg-Schwerin, Heinrich Behm, became prominent in 1912 with a significant work, *The Concept of the Universal Priesthood (Der Begriff des allgemeinen Priestertums)*. The synod members knew very well whom they were electing.
15. Quoted in Winkler, p. 28.
16. Niclot Beste, *Der Kirchenkampf in Mecklenburg 1933–1945* (Berlin, 1975), pp. 102–7. *Kirchenkampf* designates the conflict between church and state in Germany from 1933 to 1945. See Introduction, p. 11.

to Schwerin in a rented bus. A villager named Oltmann was appointed spokesman and later wrote a report which Beste quotes verbatim.

The twenty-eight members of the congregation were received in the office of the *Oberkirchenrat* by a pastor who asked them what they wanted. The answer: "We want our pastor back!" The pastor from the *Oberkirchenrat* brought up analogies: when a farmer sells a cow, it is a completed legal transaction. When a teacher disobeys his superiors, it too is a legal matter. Just the same held true for the assistant pastor, who had unfortunately disobeyed his ecclesiastical superiors. Oltmann responded, "Reverend, I'd like to point out that there is a basic difference between cow trading and teachers, on the one hand, and the action of the *Oberkirchenrat* on the other. Cow trading and the case of a disobedient teacher have a noncontroversial legal basis. The *Oberkirchenrat* and the whole church around *(Reichsbischof)* Ludwig Müller have no legality whatever."

The pastor in the *Oberkirchenrat* thought the assistant pastor in question had obviously worked on his congregation and coached them on what to say. At this point Oltmann responded, "Reverend, please be informed: I reject any such insinuation, for in the first place, I don't need in any case to have an assistant pastor much younger in years feed me his views; and in the second place, I have, out of deepest inner certainty, such a clear and unequivocal position on matters of faith that I don't need to avoid any theological disputes. And I am man enough to defend my biblically grounded position."

Meanwhile other members of the *Oberkirchenrat* had entered. The territorial bishop came too and sat down in an armchair, surrounded by his advisors, opposite the representatives of the Massow congregation. The report continues:

> In the name of the representatives of the congregation who had appeared today at the *Oberkirchenrat,* I requested the territorial bishop to revoke his decision with regard to the suspension of our minister, since the congregation supported him unanimously. Now several members of the congregation spoke up and reported that Assistant Pastor Baltzer took his ministry seriously and administered it loyally in every sense; that he was loved; and that

church attendance was greater than it had ever been with his predecessors.

At this point the territorial bishop interrupted to say, "It would now be the duty of the congregation to influence the assistant pastor to render the obedience to his superiors that he owed them." This point is significant for our topic: a congregation supports its pastor actively, and even the bishop demands that the congregation educate its minister. The relationship between the office of the ministry and the congregation had certainly altered radically since that event in 1902!

The debate in Schwerin in 1934 was becoming acrimonious. Oltmann reported:

> To a growing degree the situation was embellished by dramatic scenes on the part of the *Oberkirchenrat*. Above all President Schmidt, from Nedden, had to be calmed down repeatedly by his colleagues and from the bishop's armchair. When, despite his greatest efforts, he still failed to convince me regarding the incontestable legality of the national and territorial church's behavior, he screamed at me, shaking his little presidential fists in front of my nose, "My best friend, you are touching on my honor, you insult me," and so on. My response: "Mr. President, for your information, in the first place, I am not your best friend; secondly, I consider this tone and method of debate unworthy of a territorial church government. When negotiations are conducted in this place, the self-evident presupposition should be that brotherly love is the guiding principle of our discussions." After the usual efforts of smoothing matters over, the president also became very polite.

A theological discussion was begun: Oltmann accused the German Christians of appealing not only to the Bible but to other sources of revelation like national character and race. According to Oltmann's report, the territorial bishop responded,

> "As far as my arguments are concerned, it can in any case be said that the unaltered, pure Reformation teaching certainly acknowledges a revelation from God outside of Holy Scripture, for example in nature and in national character [*Volkstum*]."
>
> "Reverend bishop, I may assume that you also count Luther among the reformers. Would you please tell me in which of Luther's works, and in which passage, is God's revelation outside the Bible mentioned?"
>
> Embarrassment, awkward silences, heads put together, whisper-

ing. The territorial bishop mumbled something about dogmatics. Several clerical dignitaries rushed to the bookshelves. . . . I requested them to write down for me the exact passage in the Luther work in question, so that I could look it up at home. They didn't do it.

We must register the fact that the representatives of the responsible congregation appealed to Luther for substantiation! The conversation then touched on other matters: the meaning of the Ten Commandments, some specific pronouncements blamed on the German Christians.

Two hours later they were back at the starting point. The report states:

Then Oltmann asked, "Reverend Bishop, I now ask you officially: are you prepared to revoke your order regarding Assistant Pastor Baltzer?"

A raging storm broke out. I picked up my hat, turned to my companions, and told them we were leaving. Chairs were pushed back, coats were buttoned. I was already near the door when I felt myself held with the gentle hands of the *Oberkirchenrat*.

"Please, gentlemen, resume your seats, please? We cannot leave the matter under these particularly disagreeable circumstances. No, no, let us be calm and see what can be done."

Well, one could not, of course, revoke anything, but wouldn't there be some other possible courses?

We explained, "Assistant Pastor Baltzer is going to stay, with or without your permission. That's for sure."

Now if the *Oberkirchenrat* wanted to do something more, they could let the case of Massow rest. And surprise, surprise! This same member of the *Oberkirchenrat* who was so convinced he and his measures were one hundred per cent legal, and had felt it necessary to rant and rave in its defense—precisely this same man, at the end of his tether, declared that he would let the Massow case rest until a legal clarification of the church situation in Germany appeared, which would surely be soon . . . !

Thus the *Oberkirchenrat* gave in to the pressure of a congregation; the congregation had successfully defended its minister.

One of the participants, on leave-taking, announced that next time they would bring their wives and children. Oltmann concluded his report with an evaluation:

I cannot of course report on this two-hour-long session word for word, but I think I said the most important things. Even if it was quite clear to me beforehand that I could expect no surprises from this *Oberkirchenrat*, I must nevertheless admit that my most audacious expectations were exceeded by far. I would never have expected so much inner hollowness, such feelings of insulted honor, so much untruthfulness, contradiction, miserable helplessness, and immeasurable hatred from educated men. . . . It is shameful that a territorial church can put on such a pitiful performance before simple people who, given the narrow limitations of their perception, can be driven to the greatest misery of conscience or to indifference on account of this enormity. Let it be said once more: the Mecklenburg territorial church, in its *Oberkirchenrat*, whatever else it be, is not the church of Jesus Christ. 17 December 1934. [Signed] Oltmann!

The relationship between the office of the ministry and the congregation in the Evangelical-Lutheran territorial church of Mecklenburg had been shaped in a way no one could have expected beforehand.

If we look back to Luther from the perspective of the present, we can say two things: on the one hand, Luther had some points of view completely foreign to us. We consider his hopes for a Christian government only a bit of history, very far in the past and of no help to us today. On the other hand, though, we sympathize with his lifelong demand for a close connection between congregation and holders of ministerial office. We feel particularly close to the Luther who, between 1522 and 1524, accepted and supported an active role on the part of various congregations.

Bibliography

PERTINENT WORKS BY LUTHER

"Ninety-five Theses," 1517. *WA* 1:233–39. *LW* 31:19–33.

"Response to the Dialogue of Silvester Prierias on the Power of the Pope" ("Ad dialogum Silvestri Prieritatis de potestate papae responsio"), 1518. *WA* 1:647–86.

"Resolution Concerning Thesis 13 on the Power of the Pope" ("Resolutio Lutheriana super propositione sua XIII de potestate papae"), 1519. *WA* 2:180–240.

"Treatise on Good Works," 1520. *WA* 6:204–76. *LW* 44:17–114.

"On the Papacy in Rome, Against the Most Celebrated Romanist in Leipzig," 1520. *WA* 6:285–324. *LW* 39:51–104.

"To the Christian Nobility of the German Nation Concerning the Reform of the Christian Estate," 1520. *WA* 6:404–69. *LW* 44:117–217.

"The Babylonian Captivity of the Church," 1520. *WA* 6:497–573. *LW* 36:5–126.

"The Freedom of a Christian," 1520. *WA* 7:20–38. *LW* 31:329–377.

To Philip Melanchthon, 1 August 1521. *WA Br* 2:370–72. *LW* 48:277–82.

"The Misuse of the Mass," 1521. *WA* 8:482–563. *LW* 36:129–230.

To George Spalatin, 12. December 1521. *WA Br* 2:411–13. *LW* 48:353–55.

To John Lang, 18 December 1521. *WA Br* 2:413–14. *LW* 48:356–57.

To Nicholas von Amsdorf, 13 January 1522. *WA Br* 2:422–24. *LW* 48:360–64.

"Eight Sermons at Wittenberg," 1522. *WA* 10³:1–64.

To the Mayor and Council at Altenburg, 17 April 1522. *WA Br* 2:504–5.

To Gabriel Zwilling, 17 April 1522. *WA Br* 2:505–6.

To George Spalatin, 5 May 1522. *WA Br* 2:515–17.

Bibliography

To Elector Frederick, 8 May 1522. *WA Br* 2:519–22.

To the Mayor and Council at Altenburg, 8 May 1522. *WA Br* 2:522–23.

To Gabriel Zwilling, 8 May 1522. *WA Br* 2:523–24.

To John Riedesel, 29 July 1522. *WA Br* 2:583.

To John Henry of Schwarzburg-Leutenberg, 12 December 1522. *WA Br* 2:626–27.

"That a Christian Assembly or Congregation Has the Right and Power to Judge All Teaching and to Call, Appoint, and Dismiss Teachers, Established and Proven by Scripture," 1523. *WA* 11:408–16. *LW* 39:303–14.

"Ordinance of a Common Chest," 1523. *WA* 12:11–30. *LW* 45:161–94.

"Concerning the Order of Public Worship," 1523. *WA* 12:35–37. *LW* 53:9–14.

"Concerning the Ministry," 1523. *WA* 12:169–96. *LW* 40:4–44.

"Sermon on 1 Peter 2 (no date)," 1523. *WA* 12:301–41.

"A Brief Instruction Concerning the Foundation on which Christ Built His Church or Congregation" ("Eine kurze Unterrichtung, worauf Christus seine Kirche oder Gemeinde gebaut hat"), 1523. *WA Br* 3:209–14 (Latin), 214–19 (German).

"Letter of Consolation to the Christians in Augsburg" ("Trostbrief an die Christen zu Augsburg"), 11 December 1523. *WA* 12:221–27.

"What Dr. Andreas Bodenstein von Karlstadt Talked Over with Dr. Martin Luther at Jena" ("Was sich Dr. Andreas Bodenstein von Karlstadt mit Dr. Martino Luthero beredt zu Jena"), 1524. *WA* 15:332–40.

"The Dealings Between Dr. Martin Luther and the Council and Parish of the City of Orlamünde" ("Die Handlung D. Martin Luthers mit dem Rat und Gemeinde der Stadt Orlamünde"), 1524. *WA* 15:341–79.

To Henry of Zutphen, 1 September 1524. *WA Br* 3:336–42.

"Letter to the Christians at Strassburg in Opposition to the Fanatic Spirit," 1524. *WA* 15:380–97. *LW* 40:63–71.

To George Spalatin, 24 November 1524. *WA Br* 3:390–91.

"Against the Heavenly Prophets in the Matter of Images and Sacraments," 1525. *WA* 18:62–125. *LW* 40:75–223.

"Admonition to Peace: A Reply to the Twelve Articles of the Peasants in Swabia," 1525. *WA* 18:291–334. *LW* 46:5–43.

To Nicholas Hausmann, 27 September 1525. *WA Br* 3:582.

To John Lang and the Other Erfurt Pastors, 28 October 1525. *WA Br* 3:591–92.

To Elector John, 31 October 1525. *WA Br* 3:594–96. *LW* 49:130–37.

To the Council of Torgau, 31 October 1525. *WA Br* 3:596.

To Elector John, 30 November 1525. *WA Br* 3:628–29. *LW* 49:137–39.

To Matthew Alber in Reutlingen, 4 January 1526. *WA Br* 4:7–8.

To Elector John, 14 April 1526. *WA Br* 4:48–51.

"The German Mass and Order of Service," 1526. *WA* 19:72–113. *LW* 53:53–90.

"Advice on How a Firm Order Is to Be Taken Up in the Christian Congregation" ("Ein Ratschlag, wie in der christlichen Gemeinde eine beständige Ordnung solle vorgenommen werden"). *WA* 19:440–46.

To Elector John, 22 November 1526. *WA Br* 4:133–34.

To Landgrave Philip of Hesse, 7 January 1527. *WA Br* 4:157–58.

"Instruction for the Visitors of Parish Pastors in Electoral Saxony," 1528. *WA* 26:175–240. *LW* 40:265–320.

To Lazarus Spengler, 15 August 1528. *WA Br* 4:533–37.

To George Spalatin, December 1528. *WA Br* 4:623–24.

"The Keys," 1530. *WA* 30²:435–507. *LW* 40:323–77.

To Peter Hackenberg, 16 December 1530. *WA Br* 5:700–701.

To the Mayor and Council at Zwickau, 4 March 1531. *WA Br* 6:46–47.

To Nicholas Hausmann, 17 April 1531. *WA Br* 6:76–79.

To Nicholas Hausmann, 24 April 1531. *WA Br* 6:80–82.

To Stanislaus Hoffmann, 24 April 1531. *WA Br* 6:82–83.

To Conrad Cordatus, 23 May 1531. *WA Br* 6:106–7.

To Matthew Kratsch, 18 August 1531. *WA Br* 6:163–65.

To the Council of Rostock, 10 November 1531. *WA Br* 6:223–26.

To the Regents and Councilors of the Margraviate of Brandenburg-Ansbach and to the Council of the City of Nürnberg, 1 August 1532. *WA Br* 6:339–42. *LW* 50:61–67.

"The Private Mass and the Consecration of Priests," 1533. *WA* 38:195–256. *LW* 38:141–214.

"Sermon on Psalm 110," 9 June 1535. *WA* 41:204–10.

"The Smalcald Articles," 1537. *WA* 50:192–254. *BC,* pp. 287–318.

"On the Councils and the Church," 1539. *WA* 50:509–653. *LW* 41:5–178.

SECONDARY WORKS

Aarts, Jan. *Die Lehre Martin Luthers über das Amt der Kirche.* Schriften der Luther-Agricola Gesellschaft, no. A 15. Helsinki, 1972.

Bainton, Roland H. "Luther: Pastor, Consoler, Preacher." In *Encounters with Luther: Lectures, Discussions, and Sermons at the Martin Luther Colloquia of the Institute for Luther Studies, 1970–1974,* edited by Eric W. Gritsch, 1:3–16. Gettysburg, Pa., 1980.

Becker, Arthur H. "Luther as 'Seelsorger.'" In *Interpreting Luther's Legacy,* edited by Fred Meuser, pp. 136–50. Minneapolis: Augsburg Publishing House, 1969.

Bibliography

Beste, Niclot. *Der Kirchenkampf in Mecklenburg 1933–1945.* Berlin, 1975.

Bornkamm, Heinrich. "What is the Church?" In *Luther's World of Thought,* translated by Martin Bertram, pp. 134–55. St. Louis: Concordia Publishing House, 1958.

Bosinski, Gerhard. "Joachim Slüter und Martin Luther." In *Herbergen der Christenheit,* edited by Franz Lau, 7:67–128. Berlin, 1970.

————. *Das Schrifttum des Rostocker Reformators Joachim Slüter.* Berlin, 1971.

Brandmüller, Walter. *Das Konzil von Pavia-Siena 1423/24.* 2 vols. Vorreformatorische Forschungen, no. 16. Münster, 1968–74.

Bruce, G. M. "Luther and Church Government." *Lutheran Quarterly* 5 (1953): 370–78.

Brunotte, Wilhelm. *Das geistliche Amt bei Luther.* Berlin, 1959.

Bunners, Chr. *Kirchenmusik und Seelenmusik.* Berlin, 1966.

Dieckhoff, A. W. *Luthers Lehre von der kirchlichen Gewalt.* Berlin, 1865.

Dörries, Hermann. "Geschichte der vocatio zum kirchlichen Amt." In his *Wort und Stunde,* 3:347–86. 3 vols. Göttingen, 1970.

Eastwood, Cyril C. "Luther's Conception of the Church," *Scottish Journal of Theology* 11 (1958):22–36.

Ehler, Sidney Z., and Morrall, John B., eds. and trans. *Church and State Through the Centuries.* Westminster, Md.: Newman Press, 1954.

Fagerberg, Holsten. *Bekenntnis, Kirche und Amt in der deutschen konfessionellen Theologie des 19. Jahrhunderts.* Uppsala Universitets Årsskrift, no. 9. Uppsala, 1952.

Fischer, Robert H. "Another Look at Luther's Doctrine of the Ministry," *Lutheran Quarterly* 18 (1966): 260–71.

Fohl, G. "Die Theologie des Geistes in den Schriften des Rostocker Theologen Michael Baumgarten." Th. D. dissertation, University of Rostock, 1969.

Gerrish, Brian A. "Priesthood and Ministry in the Theology of Luther." *Church History* 34 (1965): 404–22.

Goetze, Ruth. *Wie Luther Kirchenzucht übte.* Theologische Arbeiten, no. 9. Berlin, 1959.

Grane, Leif. *Modus loquendi theologicus: Luthers Kampf um die Erneuerung der Theologie 1515–1518.* Acta theologica Danica, no. 12. Leiden, 1975.

————. "Thomas Müntzer und Martin Luther." In Bauernkriegsstudien, edited by Bernd Moeller, pp. 69–97. Schriften des Vereins für Reformationsgeschichte, no. 189. Gütersloh, 1975.

Green, Lowell C. "Change in Luther's Doctrine of the Ministry." *Lutheran Quarterly* 18 (1966): 173–83.

Gritsch, Eric W. "The Ministry in Luther's Theological Perspective." *Encounters with Luther: Lectures, Discussions, and Sermons at the Martin Luther Colloquia of the Institute for Luther Studies, 1970–1974,* edited by Eric W. Gritsch, 1:16–34. Gettysburg, Pa., 1980.

————, and Jenson, Robert W. *Lutheranism: The Theological Movement and Its Confessional Writings.* Philadelphia: Fortress Press, 1976. Chap. 5.

————. "Lutheran Teaching Authority: Past and Present." In *Lutherans and Catholics in Dialogue: Teaching Authority and Infallibility in the Church,* edited by Paul C. Empie, T. Austin Murphy, and Joseph A. Burgess, 6:138–48. Minneapolis: Augsburg Publishing House, 1979.

Gülzow, Henneke. *Cyprian und Novatian.* Beiträge zur historischen Theologie, no. 48. Tübingen, 1975.

Haendler, Gert. "Das neue Bild Kaiser Konstantins und der sogenannte Konstantinismus." In *Theologische Versuche,* 4:71–78. Berlin, 1972.

Harley, W. N. *Little Journeys with Martin Luther.* Columbus, Ohio, 1916.

Helmreich, Ernst C. *The German Churches Under Hitler: Background, Struggle, and Epilogue.* Detroit: Wayne State University Press, 1979.

Hertzsch, Erich. *Karlstadt und seine Bedeutung für das Luthertum.* Gotha, 1932.

————. "Luther und Karlstadt." In *Luther in Thüringen,* edited by R. Jauernigg, pp. 87–107. Berlin, 1952.

Hök, Gästa. "Luther's Doctrine of the Ministry." *Scottish Journal of Theology* 7 (1954): 16–40.

Holtz, Gottfried. *Die Parochie.* Berlin, 1971.

————. "Der mecklenburgische Landarbeiter und die Kirche." In *Herbergen der Christenheit,* edited by K. Blaschke, 10:49–76. Berlin, 1975–76.

Hoess, Irmgard. *Georg Spalatin.* Weimar, 1956.

Jensen, De Lamar. *Confrontation at Worms: Martin Luther and the Diet of Worms; with a Complete English Translation of the Edict of Worms.* Provo, Utah: Brigham Young University Press, 1973.

Joint Lutheran/Roman Catholic Study Commission. "Report on 'The Gospel and the Church.'" *Lutheran World* 19, no. 3 (1972), pp. 1–15.

Josefson, Ruben. "Das Amt der Kirche." In *Ein Buch von der Kirche,* pp. 386–401. Berlin, 1950. English version, "The Ministry as an Office in the Church." In *This Is the Church,* edited by Anders Nygren, translated by Carl C. Rasmussen, pp. 268–80. Philadelphia: Muhlenberg Press, 1952.

Junghans, Helmar. "Freiheit und Ordnung bei Luther während der Wittenberger Bewegung und der Visitationen." *Theologische Literaturzeitung* 97 (1972): 95–104.

Kliefoth, Theodor. *Liturgische Abhandlungen.* Schwerin and Rostock, 1854. Vol. 1.

Kraft, Heinz. "Die Anfänge des geistlichen Amtes." *Theologische Literaturzeitung* 104 (1975): 81–98.

Lau, Franz. "Der Bauernkrieg und das angebliche Ende der lutherischen Reformation als spontaner Volksbewegung." *Lutherjahrbuch* 26 (1959): 109–34. English version, "Did Popular Reformation Really

Bibliography

Stop with the Peasants' Defeat?" translated by Kyle C. Sessions. In *Reformation and Authority: The Meaning of the Peasants' Revolt*, edited by Kyle C. Sessions, pp. 94–101. Lexington, Mass.: D. C. Heath & Co., 1968.

————. "The Posting of Luther's Theses—Legend or Fact?" *Concordia Theological Monthly* 38, no. 11 (1967): 691–703.

Leder, G. "Studien zum 1. Clemensbrief." Th. D. dissertation, University of Greifswald, 1975.

Leube, Hans. *Die Reformideen in der deutschen lutherischen Kirche zur Zeit der Orthodoxie.* Leipzig, 1924.

Lieberg, Hellmut. *Amt und Ordination bei Luther und Melanchthon.* Forschungen zur Kirchen- und Dogmengeschichte, no. 11. Göttingen, 1962.

Liermann, Hans. "Luther ordnet seine Kirche." *Lutherjahrbuch* 31 (1964): 29–46.

Müller, Karl. *Kirche, Gemeinde und Obrigkeit nach Luther.* Tübingen, 1910.

Pauck, Wilhelm. "The Ministry in the Time of the Reformation." In *The Ministry in Historical Perspective*, edited by H. Richard Niebuhr and Daniel D. Williams, pp. 110–47. New York: Harper & Brothers, Publishers, 1956.

Pelikan, Jaroslav. "Continuity and Order in Luther's View of Church and Ministry." In *The Church, Mysticism, Sanctification and the Natural in Luther's Thought*, edited by Ivar Asheim, pp. 143–55. Lectures Presented to the Third International Congress on Luther Research, Järvenpää, Finland, 11–16 August 1966. Philadelphia: Fortress Press, 1967.

————. *Spirit Versus Structure: Luther and the Institutions of the Church.* New York: Harper & Row, Publishers, 1968.

Piepkorn, Arthur Carl. "The Sacred Ministry and Holy Ordination in the Symbolical Books of the Lutheran Church." *Concordia Theological Monthly* 40 (1969): 552–73.

Prenter, Regin. "Die göttliche Einsetzung des Predigtamtes und das allgemeine Priestertum bei Luther." *Theologische Literaturzeitung* 86, no. 5 (1961): 321–32.

Preus, James S. *Carlstadt's Ordinaciones and Luther's Liberty: A Study of the Wittenberg Movement, 1521–1522.* Cambridge, Mass.: Harvard University Press, 1974.

Reumann, John. "Ordained Minister and Layman in Lutheranism." In *Lutherans and Catholics in Dialogue: Eucharist and Ministry*, edited by Paul C. Empie and T. Austin Murphy, pp. 227–82. New York: U.S.A. National Committee of the Lutheran World Federation; Washington, D.C.: The Bishops' Committee for Ecumenical and Interreligious Affairs, 1970.

Ritter, Adolf-Martin, and Leich, G. *Wer ist die Kirche? Amt und Gemeinde im Neuen Testament, in der Kirchengeschichte und heute.* Göttingen, 1968.

Rogge, Joachim, ed. *1521–1971: Luther in Worms; Ein Quellenbuch.* Berlin, 1971.

Rohde, Joachim. *Urchristliche und frühkatholische Ämter.* Theologische Arbeiten, no. 33. Berlin, 1976.

Rupp, Gordon E. "Luther and the Doctrine of the Church." *Scottish Journal of Theology* (1956): 384–92.

Schille, Gottfried. *Anfänge der Kirche.* Munich, 1966.

———. *Die urchristliche Kollegialmission.* Stuttgart and Zurich, 1967.

Schmaltz, Karl. *Kirchengeschichte Mecklenburgs.* Berlin, 1952. Vol. 3.

Schmidt, Martin. "Die Bedeutung Luthers für das christliche Laientum." *Theologische Literaturzeitung* 93 (1969): 1–10.

Schott, Erdmann. "Amt und Charisma in reformatorischer Sicht." In *Reformation 1517–1967,* pp. 127–44. Wittenberger Vorträge. Berlin, 1968.

Schwede, Alfred Otto. *Der Widersacher: Ein Karlstadt-Roman.* 2d ed. Berlin, 1977.

Schweizer, Eduard. *Church Order in the New Testament.* Translated by Frank Clarke. Studies in Biblical Theology, no. 32. Naperville, Ill.: Alec R. Allenson, 1961.

Schwiebert, Ernest G. *Luther and His Times: The Reformation from a New Perspective.* St. Louis: Concordia Publishing House, 1950.

Selge, Kurt-Victor. "Der Weg zur Leipziger Disputation zwischen Luther und Eck im Jahr 1519." *Bleibendes im Wandel der Kirchengeschichte,* edited by Bernd Moeller and Gerhard Ruhbach [apparently a Festschrift for Hans von Campenhausen], pp. 169–210. Tübingen, 1973.

Sider, Ronald J. *Andreas Bodenstein von Karlstadt: The Development of His Thought, 1517–1525.* Studies in Medieval and Reformation Theology, no. 11 (Leiden: E. J. Brill, 1974).

———, ed. *Karlstadt's Battle with Luther: Documents in a Liberal-Radical Debate.* Philadelphia: Fortress Press, 1978.

Sommerlath, Ernst. *Amt und allgemeines Priestertum.* Schriften des theologischen Konvents Augsburgischen Bekenntnisses, no. 5. Berlin, 1953.

Spitz, Lewis W. "The Universal Priesthood of Believers with Luther's Comments." *Concordia Theological Monthly* 23 (1952): 1–15.

———. "Luther's Ecclesiology and His Concept of the Prince as 'Notbischof.'" *Church History* 22 (1953): 113–41.

Storck, H. "Das allgemeine Priestertum bei Luther." *Theologische Existenz heute,* n.s. 37. Munich, 1953.

Thyssen, A. P. "Kirchliche Erweckung und nationale Erhebung in Schleswig-Holstein 1817–1850." *Wissenschaftliche Zeitschrift der Uni-*

Bibliography

versität Rostock, gesellschafts- und sprachwissenschaftliche Reihe 17, no. 4 (1968): 397–404.

Uhlig, S. "August Wilhelm Dieckhoffs Stellungnahmen zu kirchenpolitischen und theologischen Streitfragen seiner Zeit unter dem Aspekt seiner reformationsgeschichtlichen Forschungen." Th. D. dissertation, University of Rostock, 1969.

von Campenhausen, Hans. "Die Bilderfrage in der Reformation." In his *Tradition und Leben,* pp. 361–407. Tübingen, 1960.

———. *Ecclesiastical Authority and Spiritual Power in the Church of the First Three Centuries.* Translated by J. A. Baker. Stanford University Press, Stanford, Calif., 1969.

Wentz, Frederick K. "The Development of Luther's View on Church Organization." *Lutheran Quarterly* 7 (1955): 217–32.

Williams, George H. "Congregationalist Luther and the Free Churches." *Lutheran Quarterly* 19 (1967): 283–95.

Winkler, Eberhard. *Die Gemeinde und ihr Amt.* Aufsätze und Vorträge zur Theologie und Religionswissenschaft, no. 59. Berlin, 1973.

Wolf, Ernst. *Peregrinatio: Studien zur reformatorischen Theologie und zum Kirchenproblem.* 2d ed. 2 vols. Munich, ca. 1962.

Zimmermann, Harald. *Papstabsetzungen des Mittelalters.* Vienna, 1968.